Praise for

Why We're Polarized

"Polarization is the story of American politics today. It affects almost every aspect of American political life and has been studied by scholars from many different angles, with dozens of good historical and experimental approaches. Wouldn't it be great if someone would digest all these studies, synthesize them and produce a readable book that makes sense of it all? Ezra Klein has done just that with his compelling new work, *Why We're Polarized*. . . . Powerful [and] intelligent."

—Fareed Zakaria, CNN

"*Why We're Polarized* delivers. . . . What Klein adds especially to [is] our understanding of how we got here—why Trump is more a vessel for our division than the cause, and why his departure will not provide any magical cure. . . . A thoughtful, clear and persuasive analysis."

—Norman Ornstein, *New York Times Book Review*

"Klein's careful book explains how different groups of Americans can see politics through such different lenses, examining how various psychological mechanisms allow committed partisans to rationalize almost anything their party does. . . . This book fully displays the attributes that have made Klein's journalism so successful."

—Dan Hopkins, *Washington Post*

"Eye-opening . . . Klein's brilliant diagnosis and prescription provide a path to understanding—and healing."

—*O, The Oprah Magazine*

"A fascinating book, rich in politics, history, psychology and more."
—David Leonhardt, *New York Times*

"Well worth reading."
—Andrew Sullivan, *New York* magazine

"Even at his most wonky, a deep strain of humanism runs through [Klein's] journalism and that infuses his new book, *Why We're Polarized.*"

—Krista Tippett, *On Being*

"In this thoughtful exploration of American politics, Ezra Klein challenges the conventional wisdom about why and how recently we've come apart, and suggests that the fantasy of some unified American middle is perhaps at odds with the ongoing fight for truly representational politics. *Why We're Polarized* makes the compelling case that the centuries-long battle to perfect our union means we were built to be split; Klein's provocative question is whether America's democratic systems and institutions can bear up under the weight of our divides."

—Rebecca Traister, *New York Times* bestselling author of *Good and Mad*

"Something has gone terribly wrong with American politics in the last decade or so, and Klein gives us the clearest and most comprehensive analysis I have seen. He shows how we entered the realm of political 'mega identity politics,' and how feedback loops between our tribal psychology and our rapidly evolving media ecosystem may be driving our democracy over a cliff. The book reviews so many studies that in lesser hands it would earn the label 'wonkish,' but Klein's writing is so good that it is a joy to read, even as you experience a range of negative emotions from what you are reading."

—Jonathan Haidt, Thomas Cooley Professor of Ethical Leadership, New York University Stern School of Business, author of *The Righteous Mind*, and coauthor of *The Coddling of the American Mind*

"A sharp explanation of how American politics has become so discordant . . . Deeply insightful . . . A clear, useful guide through the current chaotic political landscape."

—*Kirkus Reviews* (starred review)

"A timely, thought-provoking debut . . . This precise and persuasive guide helps to make sense of the current state of American politics. . . . Political junkies as well as general readers will learn from his analysis of the U.S. media landscape."

—*Publishers Weekly*

"Klein's accessible work is for anyone wondering how we got here; it shows how understanding history can help us plan for the future. . . . By combining political history with social commentary, this book will retain relevancy."

—*Library Journal*

"By weaving together a composite of group psychological theory and political history in the trademark, rigorously logical style of Vox's Explainer series, journalism, Klein traces the path of polarization from a time when the Republican and Democratic parties were virtually indistinguishable from each other to today."

—Emma Levy, *Seattle Times*

Why We're Polarized

Ezra Klein

AVID READER PRESS

New York   London   Toronto   Sydney   New Delhi

AVID READER PRESS
An Imprint of Simon & Schuster, Inc.
1230 Avenue of the Americas
New York, NY 10020

First Avid Reader Press trade paperback edition June 2021

AVID READER PRESS and colophon are
trademarks of Simon & Schuster, Inc.

For information about special discounts for bulk purchases,
please contact Simon & Schuster Special Sales at 1-866-506-1949
or business@simonandschuster.com.

The Simon & Schuster Speakers Bureau can bring authors to
your live event. For more information or to book an event,
contact the Simon & Schuster Speakers Bureau at 1-866-248-3049
or visit our website at www.simonspeakers.com.

Interior design by Kyle Kabel

Manufactured in the United States of America

1   3   5   7   9   10   8   6   4   2

Library of Congress Cataloging-in-Publication Data has been applied for.

ISBN 978-1-4767-0032-8
ISBN 978-1-4767-0036-6 (pbk)
ISBN 978-1-4767-0039-7 (ebook)

ILLUSTRATION CREDITS

p. 37: By Christina Animashaun. Source: analysis of American National
Election Studies data by Alan Abramowitz, Emory University.
p. 40: By Christina Animashaun. Source: Jonathan A. Rodden,
Why Cities Lose: The Deep Roots of the Urban-Rural Political Divide
(New York: Basic Books, 2019).
p. 205: By Christina Animashaun. Source: analysis of Supreme Court
Database by Lee Epstein, Washington University in St. Louis,
and Eric Posner, University of Chicago.
p. 215: By Christina Animashaun. Source: Frances E. Lee,
Insecure Majorities: Congress and the Perpetual Campaign
(London; Chicago: University of Chicago Press, 2016).

To Annie and Moshi

Contents

What Didn't Happen

" I 've spent part of nearly every day since November 8, 2016, wrestling with a single question," writes Hillary Clinton in *What Happened*. "Why did I lose?"[1]

What Happened is an unusual book. Published mere months after the 2016 presidential election, it is the defeated candidate's effort to understand how she fell short. At its core is the belief that something extraordinary and bizarre occurred in 2016—an outcome beyond the boundaries of the normal give-and-take of American politics, an aberration that must be explained.

If Mitt Romney had won in 2012, Barack Obama would not have released a book entitled *What the Hell?* So, too, if John Kerry had swept to victory in 2004; George W. Bush would not be joined by millions in puzzling over the breach. In American politics, loss is part of life. Thrumming through Clinton's book—and in the anguished flood of postelection commentary from liberals and never-Trumpers—is the belief that 2016 was not like 2012 or 2004. Reality had ruptured. We were owed answers.

To be fair, something strange had happened. Donald Trump won the election. There was a Maya Angelou quote that ricocheted across social media during the 2016 election: "When someone shows you who they are, believe them." Trump showed us who he was gleefully, constantly. He mocked John McCain for being captured in Vietnam and suggested Ted Cruz's father had helped assassinate JFK; he bragged about the size of his penis and mused that his whole life had been motivated by greed; he made no mystery of his bigotry or sexism; he called himself a genius while retweeting conspiracy theories in caps lock.

Even Trump's team didn't believe he was going to win. Plans were afoot for him to start a television channel in the aftermath of his loss. And then came election night. He won the electoral college even though 61 percent of voters, in Election Day exit polls, said he was unqualified to hold the presidency; even though most voters had a higher opinion of Clinton and believed Trump lacked the temperament for the office he sought.[2] The US presidency is a sacred trust, its occupant the wielder of unimaginable destructive power, and here, we had handed it to a human hurricane. And we had done so knowingly, purposefully.

It is this affront that motivates *What Happened*. Clinton is trying to explain how Trump's victory came to pass. She seeks exoneration, but the confusion is real. She is helped in this by the peculiar nature of Trump's triumph. He lost the popular vote by millions of ballots, and his electoral college margin rested on a sliver of the population. As Clinton writes, "if just 40,000 people across Wisconsin, Michigan, and Pennsylvania had changed their minds," she would have won.

With a margin that narrow—more than 136 million votes were cast in total—anything can explain the results. And that is where Clinton focuses her efforts, proving, convincingly, that everything from James Comey's letter to Russia's interference to deep-seated sexism could have, and probably did, account for the thin margin by which she lost.

But such analyses pose the easy question rather than the hard one. Rather than asking how Trump won, we should be asking how Trump was close enough to win. How did a candidate like Trump—a candidate who radiated contempt for the party he represented and unfitness for the job he sought—get within a few thousand votes of the presidency in the first place?

This was a question I posed in mid-2017 to Larry Bartels, a political scientist at Vanderbilt University. Over years of political reporting, I had come to value Bartels's unsentimental analysis of American politics. Speaking to him has the harrowing quality of feeding questions into a computer that doesn't care if you like the results. And as I poured out my theories of the election, he stared back with bemusement. After I had worn myself out, he replied in a way that has tormented me since: What if nothing unusual happened at all?

The premise of my questioning, Bartels calmly explained, was that the 2016 election was weird. And he was right, that was my premise. I had seen things happen in American politics that I would've rejected as laughable if they'd been on an episode of *House of Cards* and too dark to be funny if they'd been on *Veep*. And this wasn't a hysterical reaction unique to my anxious mind. Mine was a gentle version of the conventional wisdom. In the *New Yorker*, for instance, Adam Gopnik argued that Trump's victory offered support for the hypothesis that "we are living in a computer simulation and that something has recently gone haywire within it."[3]

But Bartels had been looking at the data and he disagreed. The 2016 election didn't look like a glitch, he said. It looked, for the most part, like every other election we've had recently. The simulation was, if anything, too stable, like we had unleashed tornadoes and meteors on our virtual city and only a few windows had shattered. It was the normalcy that was unnerving.

Take gender. Clinton was the first female candidate nominated by a major party for president. Trump was a male id in a suit, bragging about grabbing women by the pussy and offhandedly rating the sexual desirability of those who challenged him. This was, then, an election designed to split us more deeply by gender than any in recent history.

But turn to the exit polls. In 2004, the Republican candidate for president won 55 percent of men. In 2008, he won 48 percent of men. In 2012, 52 percent. And in 2016? Trump won 52 percent of men, precisely matching Romney's performance.

The story is similar among women. In 2004, the Republican won 48 percent of female voters. In 2008, he won 43 percent; in 2012, 44 percent. And in 2016? 41 percent. Lower, but only two percentage points beneath John McCain in 2008. No earthquake.

Let's look at it a different way. This was the white nationalism election, when the alt-right came into its own, when Trump promised to sweep in after the first black president in American history and put America back the way it was, to build a wall and make America great again. And yet, in 2004, the GOP candidate won 58 percent of white voters. In 2008, he won 55 percent of white voters. In 2012, he won 59 percent of white voters. Fast-forward to 2016: 57 percent.

Of course, there was no group Trump assailed more regularly than Hispanic immigrants. He launched his campaign by descending a golden escalator and proclaiming, "When Mexico sends its people, they're not sending their best. They're not sending you. . . . They're bringing drugs. They're bringing crime. They're rapists. And some, I assume, are good people." In 2004, the Republican candidate won 44 percent of Hispanic voters. In 2008, he won 31 percent. In 2012, 27 percent. And in 2016, 28 percent.

After the GOP's 2004 victory, the Republican Party's dominance was widely ascribed to Bush's deep, authentic bond with white, born-again Christians, of whom 78 percent pulled the lever for his reelection. In 2008, the GOP candidate won 74 percent of these voters. In 2012, it was back up to 78 percent. But Trump was different. He was a morally louche adulterer who flaunted his wealth, and when asked, on the campaign trail, if he ever turned to God for forgiveness, he said, "I am not sure I have." So how did he do among white, born-again voters? He won 80 percent.

Perhaps this is best viewed through the lens of partisanship. In 2016, Republicans nominated a thrice-married billionaire who had been a Democrat mere years before, who was dismissed in a *National Review* cover story as a threat to conservatism,[4] who had few ties to the Republican Party and viewed its previous standard-bearers with contempt, who spoke openly about his affection for Social Security, Medicare, and Planned Parenthood. In 2004, the Republican candidate won 93 percent of self-identified Republicans. In 2008, he won 90 percent. In 2012, he won 93 percent. In 2016, he won 88 percent. A drop, to be sure, but nothing calamitous.

The popular vote margin is also telling. In 2004, the Republican candidate won by 3 million votes. In 2008, the Democrat won by more than 9 million votes. In 2012, the Democrat won by almost 5 million votes. And in 2016, the Democrat again won by almost 3 million votes. The intervention of the electoral college overturned this margin, of course, but if you're just looking to the winds of popular support, 2016 isn't an obvious aberration.

Here, then, is Bartels's point: if you'd been given a printout of voter data from the past few elections and been asked to identify which campaign was the bizarre one, the one that would rock American politics and lead to book after book trying to explain the outcome, would you be able to do so? The results in 2016 mostly looked like 2012 and 2008 and 2004, even though the winning candidate is one of the most bizarre figures ever to crash into American politics.

What's surprising about the 2016 election results isn't what happened. It's what *didn't* happen. Trump didn't lose by 30 points or win by 20 points. Most people who voted chose the same party in 2016 that they'd chosen in 2012. That isn't to say there was nothing at all distinct or worthy of study. Crucially, white voters without college educations swung sharply toward Trump, and their overrepresentation in electorally key states won him the election.*5 But the campaign, by the numbers, was mostly a typical contest between a Republican and a Democrat.

The fact that voters ultimately treated Trump as if he were just another Republican speaks to the enormous weight party polarization now exerts on our politics—a weight so heavy that it can take an election as bizarre as 2016 and jam the result into the same grooves as Romney's contest with Obama or Bush's race against Kerry. We are so locked into our political identities that there is virtually no candidate, no information, no condition, that can force us to change our minds. We will justify almost anything or anyone so long as it helps our side, and the result is a politics devoid of guardrails, standards, persuasion, or accountability.

And yet, we have not changed so much, have we? We still coach Little League and care for our parents, we cry at romantic comedies and mow our lawns, we laugh at our eccentricities and apologize for harsh words, we want to be loved and wish for a better world. That is not to absolve us of responsibility for our politics, but to trace a lament oft heard when we step away from politics: Aren't we better than this?

---

* In an analysis published on Vox, political scientist and statistician Andrew Gelman and business and strategy professor Pierre-Antoine Kremp find that "per voter, whites have 16 percent more power than blacks once the Electoral College is taken into consideration, 28 percent more power than Latinos, and 57 percent more power than those who fall into the other category."

I think we are, or we can be. But toxic systems compromise good individuals with ease. They do so not by demanding we betray our values but by enlisting our values such that we betray each other. What is rational and even moral for us to do individually becomes destructive when done collectively.

How American politics became a toxic system, why we participate in it, and what it means for our future is the subject of this book.

Thinking in systems

Let me be clear from the beginning: This is not a book about people. This is a book about systems.

The story of American politics is typically told through the stories of individual political actors. We focus on their genius, their hubris, their decency, their deceit. We take you inside their feuds, their thoughts, the bons mots they deliver in private meetings and the agonies they quietly confide to friends. We locate the hinge moments of history in the decisions they make. And, in doing so, we suggest they could have made other decisions, or that other people, in their place, would have made different decisions. This assumption has the grace of truth, but not as much truth as we think, not as much truth as the breathless insider accounts of White House meetings and campaign machinations would have us believe.

As a journalist, I have studied American politics for the better part of twenty years. I have tried to understand it from the perspective of politicians, activists, political scientists, donors, voters, nonvoters, staffers, pundits—anyone who is affected by it or who is affecting it. In the course of that reporting, I have come across political actors who strike me as cynics, fools, and villains. They are the broken parts of American politics, and it is tempting to blame our problems on their low morals or poor judgment. Indeed, we do exactly that in election years, when our dissatisfaction with the way the system is working leads us to fire some of the people and hire other people, and then a few years later, we find the system still broken, and we do it again, and again, and again.

As I have watched one election's heroes turn into the next election's scoundrels, as I have listened to rational people give me thoughtful reasons for doing ridiculous things, I have lost faith in these stories. We collapse systemic problems into personalized narratives, and when we do, we cloud our understanding of American politics and confuse our theories of repair. We try to fix the system by changing the people who run it, only to find that they become part of the system, too. I knew Republicans who, though they voted for McCain, were hopeful about Obama—only to discover he was just another Democrat. I knew Democrats who were glad Trump was going to remake the Republican Party along populist lines, only to be bitterly disappointed when he signed on to almost everything the congressional GOP wanted.

Every few years, a new crop of politicians emerges promising to put country over party, to govern on behalf of the people rather than the powerful, to listen to the better angels of our nature rather than the howling of our factions. And then the clock ticks forward, the insurgents become the establishment, public disillusionment sets in, the electorate swings a bit to the other side, and we start again. This cycle is a tributary feeding into the country's political rage—it is maddening to keep trying to fix a problem that only seems to get worse.

My intention in this book is to zoom out from the individuals to better see interlocking systems that surround them. I will use specific politicians as examples, but only insofar as they are marionettes of broader forces. What I seek isn't a story but a blueprint, a map to the machine that shapes political decisions.

This is a mode of analysis common to other fields but often ignored in my own. In his book *Drift into Failure: From Hunting Broken Components to Understanding Complex Systems*, Sidney Dekker, founder of the Safety Science Innovation Lab at Australia's Griffith University, distinguishes between two different ways of diagnosing why a system is failing. The most traditional, and the most common, approach is we see a problem, hunt for the broken part, and try to replace it. Dekker studies accidents, so his examples are plane crashes and oil spills, where catastrophe is followed by an obsessive search for the nut that proved defective, the maintenance check that got missed, the wing flap that cracked in the cold. But much political analysis follows this model, too. American politics is broken, and the problem is money, political correctness, social media, political consultants, or Mitch McConnell. Fix the part, these analyses promise, and you fix the whole.

The reality, Dekker says, is that complex systems often fail the public even as they're succeeding by their own logic. If you discover the screw that failed or the maintenance shift that was missed, you might think you've found the broken part. But if you miss the way the stock market was rewarding the company for cutting costs on maintenance, you've missed the cause of the crisis, and failed to prevent its recurrence. Systems thinking, he writes, "is about understanding how accidents can happen when no parts are broken, or no parts are seen as broken."[6]

That may not sound like American politics to you. It is, at this point, cliché to call it broken. But that is our mistake. The American political system—which includes everyone from voters to journalists to the president—is full of rational actors making rational decisions given the incentives they face. We are a collection of functional parts whose efforts combine into a dysfunctional whole.

That the worst actors are so often draped in success doesn't prove the system is broken; it proves that they understand the ways in which it truly works. That is knowledge the rest of us need, if we are to change it. This quote from Dekker describes much of what I have seen and much of how I intend to approach this investigation:

> In stories of drift into failure, organizations fail precisely because they are doing well—on a narrow range of performance criteria, that is—the ones that they get rewarded on in their current political or economic or commercial configuration. In the drift into failure, accidents can happen without anything breaking, without anybody erring, without anybody violating the rules they consider relevant.

I am sensitive to these incentives because I live them. I am not outside the system looking in but inside the system looking out. I am a journalist, a pundit, and a cofounder of Vox, the explanatory news publication. I am a member of the political media, and I know that for all that we try to hide it, we are political actors, and the decisions we make are both cause and consequences of the broader forces that surround us. I am a voter, a news junkie, and a liberal. I am motivated in part by the radicalizing realization that I am often carrying out the biddings of a system I dislike, by the frustration that overcomes me when I realize I am acting more like American politics than like myself.

And I am not alone. I spend my days interviewing participants in the American political system, smart people doing their best, puzzling over the vast dysfunction that surrounds them and explaining away their own contributions to it. My background is in policy reporting, and over years of covering different issues, I have seen the same pattern play out again and again. Whatever the problem, it begins with meetings in which experts of all different perspectives sit together on panels and discuss the many ways it can be solved. At this point, there is always a large zone of agreement, a belief that a compromise can be reached that will leave everyone better off compared to the status quo. But as the process wears on, as the politicians focus their attention and the media focuses its coverage, agreement dissolves. What once struck participants as reasonable compromises become unreasonable demands. What was once a positive-sum negotiation becomes a zero-sum war. And everyone involved believes every decision they made along the way was reasonable. Usually, from their perspective, they are right.

As such, I have found that American politics is best understood by braiding two forms of knowledge that are often left separate: the direct, on-the-ground insights shared by politicians, activists, government officials, and other subjects of my reporting, and the more systemic analyses conducted by political scientists, sociologists, historians, and others with the time, methods, and expertise to study American politics at scale. On their own, political actors often ignore the incentives shaping their decisions and academic researchers miss the human motivations that drive political decision-making. Together, however, they shine bright light on how and why American politics works the way it does.

There is much awry in American politics, and I won't, in this book, attempt to catalog all of it. But I've come to believe the master story—the one that drives almost all divides and most fundamentally shapes the behavior of participants—is the logic of polarization. That logic, put simply, is this: to appeal to a more polarized public, political institutions and political actors behave in more polarized ways. As political institutions and actors become more polarized, they further polarize the public. This sets off a feedback cycle: to appeal to a yet more polarized public, institutions must polarize further; when faced with yet more polarized institutions, the public polarizes further, and so on.

Understanding that we exist in relationship with our political institutions, that they are changed by us and we are changed by them, is the key to this story. We don't just use politics for our own ends. Politics uses us for its own ends.

Rescuing "identity politics"

There are many different types of polarization possible, and I'll discuss some of them later in the book. But the locus of polarization I will focus on is political identity. And that requires saying a few words about a term that should be very useful in American politics but that has become almost useless: identity politics.

A core argument of this book is that everyone engaged in American politics is engaged in identity politics. This is not an insult, and it's not controversial: we form and fold identities constantly, naturally. Identity is present in politics in the way gravity, evolution, or cognition is present in politics; that is to say, it is omnipresent in politics, because it is omnipresent in us. There is no way to read the literature on how humans form and protect their personal and group identities—literature I will survey in this book—and believe any of us is immune. It runs so deep in our psyches, is activated so easily by even weak cues and distant threats, that it is impossible to speak seriously about how we engage with one another without discussing how our identities shape that engagement.

Unfortunately, the term "identity politics" has been weaponized. It is most often used by speakers to describe politics as practiced by members of historically marginalized groups. If you're black and you're worried about police brutality, that's identity politics. If you're a woman and you're worried about the male-female pay gap, that's identity politics. But if you're a rural gun owner decrying universal background checks as tyranny, or a billionaire CEO complaining that high tax rates demonize success, or a Christian insisting on Nativity scenes in public squares—well, that's just good, old-fashioned politics. With a quick sleight of hand, identity becomes something that only marginalized groups have.

The term "identity politics," in this usage, obscures rather than illuminates; it's used to diminish and discredit the concerns of weaker groups by making them look like self-interested, special pleading in order to clear the agenda for the concerns of stronger groups, which are framed as more rational, proper topics for political debate. But in wielding identity as a blade, we have lost it as a lens, blinding ourselves in a bid for political advantage. We are left searching in vain for what we refuse to allow ourselves to see.*[7]

All politics is influenced by identity. Those identities are most powerful when they are so pervasive as to be either invisible or

---

* In her book *How We Get Free*, Keeanga-Yamahtta Taylor traces the first usage of the term "identity politics" to the Combahee River Collective's 1977 statement of principles, which read:

This focusing upon our own oppression is embodied in the concept of identity politics. We believe that the most profound and potentially most radical politics come directly out of our own identity, as opposed to working to end somebody else's oppression. In the case of Black women this is a particularly repugnant, dangerous, threatening, and therefore revolutionary concept because it is obvious from looking at all the political movements that have preceded us that anyone is more worthy of liberation than ourselves. We reject pedestals, queenhood, and walking ten paces behind. To be recognized as human, levelly human, is enough.

As Barbara Smith, one of the founding members of the collective, tells Taylor, "What we were saying is that we have a right as people who are not just female, who are not solely Black, who are not just lesbians, who are not just working class, or workers—that we are people who embody all of these identities, and we have a right to build and define political theory and practice based upon that reality."

uncontroversial. "American" is an identity. So, too, is "Christian." When politicians, including the irreligious, end speeches with "God bless America," it is not because they are making an appeal to a higher power, but because they are making an appeal to our bedrock identities. If you don't believe me, ask yourself why there are so few open atheists or even agnostics in national politics.

This does not mean that politics is an equation solved by locating identity. Identity shapes our worldview, but it does not mechanistically decide it. And while we often speak of identity as a singular, it is always a dizzying plural—we have countless identities, some of them in active conflict with each other, others lying dormant until activated by threat or fortune. Much that happens in political campaigns is best understood as a struggle over which identities voters will inhabit come Election Day: Will they feel like workers exploited by their bosses, or heartlanders dismissed by coastal elites? Will they vote as patriotic tradition-alists offended by NFL players who kneel during the national anthem, or as parents worried about the climate their children will inhabit?

What we are often fighting over in American politics is group identity and status—fights that express themselves in debates over policy and power but cannot be truly reconciled by either. Health policy is positive-sum, but identity conflict is zero-sum.

Identity, of course, is nothing new. So how can it explain the changes in our politics? The answer is that our political identities are changing—and strengthening. The most powerful identities in modern politics are our political identities, which have come, in recent decades, to encompass and amplify a range of other central identities as well. Over the past fifty years, our partisan identities have merged with our racial, religious, geographic, ideological, and cultural identities. Those merged identities have attained a weight that is breaking our institutions and tearing at the bonds that hold this country together. This is the form of identity politics most prevalent in our country, and most in need of interrogation.

The first part of this book will tell the story of how and why American politics polarized around identity in the twentieth century and what that polarization did to the way we see the world and each other. The second half of the book is about the feedback loops between polarized political identities and polarized political institutions that are driving our political system toward crisis.

What I am trying to develop here isn't so much an answer for the problems of American politics as a framework for understanding them. If I've done my job well, this book will offer a model that helps make sense of an era in American politics that can seem senseless.

Let's get started.

Chapter 1

How Democrats Became Liberals and Republicans Became Conservatives

The first thing I need to do is convince you something has changed.

American politics offers the comforting illusion of stability. The Democratic and Republican Parties have dominated elections since 1864, grappling for power and popularity the whole time. Scour American history and you will find Democrats and Republicans slandering each other, undermining each other, plotting against each other, even physically assaulting each other.*[1] It is easy to cast a quick glance backward and assume our present is a rough match for our past, that the complaints we have about politics today mirror the complaints past generations had of the politics of their day. But the Democratic and Republican Parties of today are not like the Democratic and Republican Parties of yesteryear. We are living through something genuinely new.

---

* In her remarkable history of congressional violence, *The Field of Blood*, historian Joanne Freeman found that "between 1830 and 1860, there were more than *seventy* violent incidents between congressmen in the House and Senate chambers or on nearby streets and dueling grounds." And she assures me this is a substantial undercount.

1

Rewind to 1950. That was the year the American Political Science Association (APSA) Committee on Political Parties released a call to arms that sounds like satire to modern ears. Entitled *Towards a More Responsible Two-Party System*, the ninety-eight-page paper, coauthored by many of the country's most eminent political scientists and covered on the front page of the *New York Times*, pleads for a more polarized political system. It laments that the parties contain too much diversity of opinion and work together too easily, leaving voters confused about who to vote for and why. "Unless the parties identify themselves with programs, the public is unable to make an intelligent choice between them," warned the authors.[2]

It is difficult, watching the party-line votes and contempt for compromise that defines Congress today, to read sentences like "the parties have done little to build up the kind of unity within the congressional party that is now so widely desired" and hear the logic behind them. Summarized today, the report can sound like a call for fewer puppies and more skin fungus.

But as Colgate University political scientist Sam Rosenfeld argues in his book *The Polarizers: Postwar Architects of Our Partisan Era*, there were good reasons to worry about the muddle the parties had made of midcentury American politics. The activists and politicians who worked relentlessly, over years, to bring about the polarized political system we see today had good reasons for what they did. Appreciating the logic of the polarizers' argument, alongside the wreckage produced by their success, is a bracing antidote to both a golden view of the past and overly confident prescriptions for the future.*

To understand the political scientists' concerns, we need to understand the role political parties are supposed to play in a

---

* It would be reasonable to keep this warning in mind when you read the solutions found in the concluding chapter of this book.

democracy. Consider the issues that you, as a citizen, are routinely asked to render a judgment on. Should we go to war in Iraq, or Syria, or Iran, or North Korea? Does it make sense to organize our health-care system around private insurers brought to heel by regulations and an individual mandate? What is the proper term for a copyright—should it last for a decade, four decades, a hundred years, or until the sun burns out and dooms this fragile world? Should federal tax revenues equal 28 percent of GDP, 31 percent of GDP, or 39 percent of GDP over the next decade? What's the proper level of immigration each year, and how much of it should go to reuniting families and how much to filling economic needs? Would breaching the debt ceiling really damage America's creditworthiness forevermore? None of us can amass sufficient expertise on such a range of topics.

Political parties are shortcuts. The APSA report called them "indispensable instruments of government," because they "provide the electorate with a proper range of choice between alternatives of action." We may not know the precise right level for taxes, or whether it makes sense to create a no-fly zone over Syria, but we know whether we support the Democratic, Republican, Green, or Libertarian Party. The act of choosing a party is the act of choosing whom we trust to transform our values into precise policy judgments across the vast range of issues that confront the country. "For the great majority of Americans," the authors write, "the most valuable opportunity to influence the course of public affairs is the choice they are able to make between the parties in the principal elections."

The problem in 1950 was that the nation's two major political parties weren't honoring the intentions of their voters. A Minnesota Democrat pulling the lever for Hubert Humphrey, her party's liberal Senate candidate in 1954, was also voting for a Senate majority that would include Strom Thurmond, the South Carolina senator who was among the chamber's most conservative members. Rather than offering a choice, the parties were offering a mush.*

This was the problem as the members of APSA saw it. The state parties were organizing politics around lines the national parties were erasing. "The national and state party organizations are largely independent of one another, each operating within its own sphere, without appreciable common approach to problems of party policy and strategy," complained the authors. The US Congress included Democrats more conservative than many Republicans and Republicans as liberal as the most left-leaning Democrats. They were robbing voters of their most valuable opportunity to influence the course of public affairs.

Senator William Borah, an Idaho Republican, put it piquantly in 1923. "Any man who can carry a Republican primary is a Republican," he said. "He might believe in free trade, in unconditional membership in the League of Nations, in states' rights, and in every policy that the Democratic Party ever advocated; yet, if he carried his Republican primary, he would be a Republican."[3] Being a Republican did not mean being a conservative. It meant being a Republican. Party affiliation was a tautology for itself, not a rich signifier of principles and perspective.

In 1950, Thomas Dewey, the former governor of New York and the GOP's 1944 nominee for president, freely admitted that if the measure of a "real" political party was "a unified organization with a national viewpoint on major issues," neither the Republican nor Democratic Party qualified. Dewey thought this a great strength,

---

* It's important to note that not all political scientists agreed with this argument. J. Austin Ranney, for instance, published a prophetic dissent, arguing that "unified, disciplined and responsible parties are appropriate *only* to a government which seeks to locate *full* public power in the hands of popular majorities." America's political system, by contrast, was built to frustrate political majorities and required constant compromise. For that sort of system, Ranney said, polarized parties were "quite inappropriate." He was right.

since "no single religion or color or race or economic interest is confined to one or the other of our parties. Each party is to some extent a reflection of the other.... This is perhaps part of the secret of our enormous power, that a change from one party to the other has usually involved a continuity of action and policy of the nation as a whole on most fundamentals." He allowed that there were those who "rail at both parties, saying they represent nothing but a choice between Tweedledee and Tweedledum." If the critics had their way, he said, "they then would have everything very neatly arranged, indeed. The Democratic Party would be the liberal-to-radical party. The Republican Party would be the conservative-to-reactionary party."[4] (Narrator: They would have their way.)

In 1959, then vice president Richard Nixon—who would go on, as president, to create the Environmental Protection Agency, consider a basic minimum income, and propose a national health-care plan more ambitious than Obamacare—spoke with derision of those who sought to cleave the parties by their beliefs. "It would be a great tragedy if we had our two major political parties divide on what we would call a conservative-liberal line," he said. The strength of the American political system is "we have avoided generally violent swings in Administrations from one extreme to the other. And the reason we have avoided that is that in both parties there has been room for a broad spectrum of opinion."[5]

In this, if in little else, Nixon was joined by Robert F. Kennedy. The journalist Godfrey Hodgson recounts a conversation where Kennedy warned that "the country was already split vertically, between sections, races, and ethnic groups," so it would be "dangerous to split it horizontally, too, between liberals and conservatives."[6] Politics, in this telling, was meant to calm our divisions, not represent them.

In 1959, the Republican National Committee held an internal debate over whether the party should be driven by a distinct set of ideological values. At the inaugural meeting of the Committee on Program and Progress, which was tasked with designing the GOP agenda, the group invited the political scientist Robert Goldwin to make the case that "it is neither possible nor desirable for a major political party to be guided by principles." Our modern cleavages give Goldwin's concerns a force that they would not have carried in 1959. "With both parties including liberals and conservatives within their ranks," he said, "those differences which would otherwise be the main campaign issues are settled by compromise within each party." He warned that "our national unity would be weakened if the theoretical differences were sharpened."[7]

This is a profound enough point worth dwelling on for a moment. When a division exists inside a party, it gets addressed through suppression or compromise. Parties don't want to fight among themselves. But when a division exists between the parties, it gets addressed through conflict. Without the restraint of party unity, political disagreements escalate. An example here is health care: Democrats and Republicans spend billions of dollars in election ads emphasizing their disagreements on health care, because the debate motivates their supporters and, they hope, turns the public against their opponents. The upside of this is that important issues get aired and sometimes even resolved. The downside is that the divisions around them become deeper and angrier.

This debate exploded into the open during Barry Goldwater's 1964 presidential announcement speech. The address is now remembered for Goldwater's promise to offer "a choice, not an echo." Less well-known, but perhaps more telling, is the rationale for his candidacy that comes a few paragraphs earlier. Goldwater says, with some disgust, "I have not heard from any announced Republican candidate a declaration of conscience or of political position that could possibly offer to the American people a clear choice in the next presidential election." This was Goldwater's promise: if Republicans nominated him, the election would "not be an engagement of personalities. It will be an engagement of principles." Goldwater, of course, won the nomination and got destroyed by Lyndon Johnson.

Goldwater's convention was a harshly factional affair, with conservative Republicans doing their damnedest to expel the moderate wing of the party. In its aftermath, George Romney, then the governor of Michigan and a leading light of moderate Republicanism, wrote a twelve-page letter outlining his disagreements with Goldwater. "Dogmatic ideological parties tend to splinter the political and social fabric of a nation, lead to governmental crises and deadlocks, and stymie the compromises so often necessary to preserve freedom and achieve progress," he wrote, rather prophetically.[8] (Decades later, his son, who had carried on his father's legacy as the popular moderate governor of Massachusetts, would win the Republican nomination for the presidency by recasting himself as "severely conservative.")

Goldwater's electoral destruction entrenched the conventional wisdom of the age: ideologues lost elections. In his 1960 book *Parties and Politics in America*, Clinton Rossiter wrote, "There is and can be no real difference between the Democrats and the Republicans, because the unwritten laws of American politics demand that the parties overlap substantially in principle, policy, character, appeal, and purpose—or cease to be parties with any hope of winning a national election."[9] Better to be an echo than an also-ran.

The muddling of the parties carried well into the modern era. Stanford University political scientist Morris Fiorina notes that when Gerald Ford ran against Jimmy Carter, only 54 percent of the electorate believed the Republican Party was more conservative than the Democratic Party. Almost 30 percent said there was no ideological difference at all between the two parties.[10] Imagine, in a world where the ideological difference between the Democratic and Republican Parties was slim enough to confuse half the population, how much less force party identity must have carried.

Actually, we don't have to imagine. We can see it.

The power of negative partisanship

It used to be common for voters to split their tickets: perhaps you preferred Democrat Lyndon Johnson for president but Republican George Romney for governor. And if you were a ticket-splitter, and most of the people you knew were ticket-splitters, it was hard to identify too deeply with either party; after all, you occasionally voted for both.

In a striking analysis entitled "All Politics Is National," Emory University political scientists Alan Abramowitz and Steven Webster show how that behavior collapsed in the latter half of the twentieth century and virtually disappeared across the millennium's dividing line. Looking at districts with contested House races, they found that between 1972 and 1980, the correlation between the Democratic share of the House vote and the Democratic share of the presidential vote was .54. Between 1982 and 1990, that rose to .65. By 2018, it had reached .97![11] In forty years, support for the Democratic presidential candidate went from being a helpful, but far from reliable, predictor of support for a party's House candidate to being an almost perfect guide.

Ticket-splitting requires a baseline comfort with both political parties. Behind its demise is the evaporation of that comfort. Amid the battery of questions that surveyors ask Americans in every election lurks something called the "feeling thermometer." The thermometer asks people to rate their feelings toward the two political parties on a scale of 1 to 100 degrees, where 1 is cold and negative and 100 is warm and positive. Since the 1980s, Republicans' feelings toward the Democratic Party and Democrats' feelings toward the Republican Party have dropped off a cliff.

In 1980, voters gave the opposite party a 45 on the thermometer—not as high as the 72 they gave their own party, but a pretty decent number all the same. After 1980, though, the numbers began dropping. By 1992, the opposing party was down to 40; by 1998, it had fallen to 38; in 2016, it was down to 29. Meanwhile, partisans' views toward their own parties fell from 72 in 1980 to 65 in 2016.[12]

But it wasn't just partisans. In his important paper "Polarization and the Decline of the American Floating Voter," Michigan State University political scientist Corwin Smidt found that between 2000 and 2004, self-proclaimed independents were more stable in which party they supported than self-proclaimed strong partisans were from 1972 to 1976.[13] I want to say that again: today's independents vote more predictably for one party over the other than yesteryear's partisans. That's a remarkable fact.

Here's what's strange, though: over this same period, the electorate was shrugging off its party allegiances. In 1964, about 80 percent of voters said they were either Republicans or Democrats. By 2012, that had dropped to 63 percent—"the lowest percentage of party identifiers in the history of the American National Election Studies," notes Abramowitz and Webster—with the share of self-proclaimed independents rising sharply.

On first glance, these two trends contradict: How can the electorate become both more partisan in its voting behavior and more independent in its party membership? Shouldn't more consistent support for a party lead to a closer allegiance to that party?

The key idea here is "negative partisanship": partisan behavior driven not by positive feelings toward the party you support but negative feelings toward the party you oppose. If you've ever voted in an election feeling a bit bleh about the candidate you backed, but fearful of the troglodyte or socialist running against her, you've been a negative partisan. It turns out a lot of us have been negative partisans. A 2016 Pew poll found that self-described independents who tended to vote for one party or the other were driven more by negative motivations. Majorities of both Republican- and Democratic-leaning independents said a major reason for their lean was the other party's policies were bad for the country; by contrast, only a third of each group said they were driven by support for the policies of the party they were voting for.[14]

So here, then, is the last fifty years of American politics summarized: we became more consistent in the party we vote for not because we came to like our party more—indeed, we've come to like the parties we vote for *less*—but because we came to dislike the opposing party more. Even as hope and change sputter, fear and loathing proceed.

The question is *why* all this happened. What changed in American politics such that voters became so reliably partisan?

The rational partisan

"Partisan" is a pejorative in American life. The statement "Americans have become much more partisan since 1972" isn't neutral. It reads as an indictment. An insult. Partisanship is bad. It's unthinking, angry, even un-American.

Partisans are the ones George Washington warned us of in his farewell address. They:

put, in the place of the delegated will of the nation, the will of a party, often a small but artful and enterprising minority of the community; and, according to the alternate triumphs of different parties, to make the public administration the mirror of the ill-concerted and incongruous projects of faction, rather than the organ of consistent and wholesome plans digested by common counsels and modified by mutual interests.

Nasty stuff.

Washington's address prefigured much of what was to come in American politics. As the Princeton historian Sean Wilentz wrote in the *New Republic*, it was a "highly partisan appeal delivered as an attack on partisanship and on the low demagogues who fomented it."[15] Washington delivered the speech, cowritten by Alexander Hamilton, as America was splitting into a two-party system—the Federalists, led by John Adams and Hamilton, and the Democratic Republicans, led by Thomas Jefferson and James Madison. Washington was, in effect, a Federalist, and in warning against the development of factions, he was warning against those who had arisen to challenge his chosen successors. As Wilentz wrote, "Washington's address never explicitly mentioned Jefferson or his supporters, but its unvarnished attack on organized political opposition was plainly directed against them."

If Washington's intervention was partisan, his instincts were thoroughly American. This has been the balance Americans have struck ever since: a system defined by political parties whose existence we decry. We mistrust ideologues and partisans. We venerate centrists, moderates, independents. In a telling experiment, Samara Klara and Yanna Krupnikov cued subjects to think about political disagreements and then handed them photographs of strangers, some of whom were identified as independents and others of whom were said to be partisans. The independents were rated as more attractive, "even when, by objective standards, the partisans were actually more attractive." In another test of the theory, Klar and Krupnikov found that Americans are nearly 60 percent more likely to call themselves "independents" when they're told they need to make a good impression on a stranger.[16] Being independent isn't about whom you vote for. It's about your personal brand.

Our appreciation of independents reflects our denial of the substance of partisanship. We want to wish away the depths of our disagreements, and it is convenient to blame them instead on the maneuverings of misguided partisans. But partisans aren't bad people perverting the political system through irrationality and self-interest. They're normal people—you and me—reflecting the deep differences that define political systems the world over. And the more different the parties are, the more rational partisanship becomes.

What has happened to American politics in recent decades is that the parties have become visibly, undeniably more different, and the country has rationally become more partisan in response.

Since 1994, the Pew Research Center has conducted massive surveys of American political opinion, and the findings are stark.[17] In 1994, for instance, 39 percent of Democrats and 26 percent of Republicans said discrimination was the main reason many black people couldn't "get ahead" in society. By 2017, the number of Democrats who agreed with that statement had jumped to 64 percent, while the number of Republicans who agreed with it was just 14 percent.

Similarly, in 1994, 32 percent of Democrats and 30 percent of Republicans agreed that immigrants strengthened the country. By 2017, that had jumped to 84 percent of Democrats but only 42 percent of Republicans.

In 1994, 63 percent of Republicans and 44 percent of Democrats agreed that poor people had it easy because they could get government help without doing anything in return. By 2017, the number of Republicans who agreed with that statement had risen slightly, to 65 percent, but the number of Democrats who agreed with it had tumbled to 18 percent.

"The bottom line is this," concludes the report: "Across 10 measures that Pew Research Center has tracked on the same surveys since 1994, the average partisan gap has increased from 15 percentage points to 36 points."[18]

It's worth being clear about what this means: if you're a Democrat, the Republican Party of 2017 poses a much sharper threat to your vision of a good society than the Republican Party of 1994 did. It includes fewer people who agree with you, and it has united around an agenda much further away from yours. The same is true, of course, for Republicans peering at the modern Democratic Party.

This isn't just a quirky finding of the pollsters. It's visible in even the most cursory look at the parties' governing agendas— indeed, it's arguably been caused by the sharp divergence in the parties' agendas.*

Both Presidents Ronald Reagan and George H. W. Bush signed legislation raising taxes, for instance. That would be unthinkable in today's Republican Party, where almost every elected official has signed a pledge promising to never raise taxes under any

---

* This speaks to perhaps the biggest chicken-or-the-egg question in the polarization literature: Are political elites polarizing and the public is simply following along? Is the public polarizing and political elites are responding? My synthesis, which will become clearer over the course of the book, is that *everyone engaged in American politics* is subject to the broader forces of polarization. The more engaged you are, the more polarized you become. So yes, political elites are polarizing more and faster than the public at large, but as the public tunes in, it becomes more polarized, too. And since politicians are most responsive to the part of the public that is most polarized, we're all living in a hyper-polarized system and being faced with polarizing choices, whatever our personal level of polarization.

circumstances. Bush also signed the Americans with Disabilities Act into law and oversaw a cap-and-trade program to reduce the pollutants behind acid rain. Reagan, for his part, signed an immigration reform bill that today's Democrats venerate and today's Republicans denounce. "I believe in the idea of amnesty for those who have put down roots and who have lived here even though sometime back they may have entered illegally,"[19] Reagan said.

Yes, *Reagan* said that.

President Bill Clinton, meanwhile, launched his administration with a budget designed to reduce the deficit and an all-out effort to pass the North American Free Trade Agreement (NAFTA). He famously ran against the left wing of his own party, flying back to Arkansas to preside over the execution of a brain-damaged inmate and publicly denouncing the rapper Sister Souljah. He worked with congressional Republicans to slash welfare and balance the federal budget. During his second term, he proudly declared that "the era of big government is over."

Health care offers an even starker example. In 1965, a Democratic president created a massive, single-payer health-care system for the nation's elderly. But as liberal as Medicare was in both conception and execution, it received seventy Republican votes in the House as well as thirteen Republican votes in the Senate. Obamacare, by contrast, was modeled off Mitt Romney's reforms in Massachusetts and built atop many Republican ideas;* it relied on private insurers for the bulk of its coverage expansion and ended up sacrificing its public option. But as compromised as Obamacare was in design, and as desperate as the Obama administration was for bipartisan support—and believe me, I covered that fight, they would've traded almost anything for Republican

---

* Like the now-controversial individual mandate—more on that later.

backing—the legislation didn't receive a single Republican vote in either the House or the Senate.

It's easy to see how a liberal voter in 1965 might think Republicans were open to something like Medicare—*many Republicans really were open to something like Medicare.* Today, however, no voter would be confused as to which party supports the government doing more to guarantee health insurance. The choice between the two parties is much, much clearer.

Or take abortion. In 1982, Senator Joe Biden voted for a constitutional amendment that would let states overturn *Roe v. Wade.* He called it, at the time, "the single most difficult vote I've cast as a U.S. senator." Biden, a practicing Catholic, explained his decision in terms of his upbringing. "I'm probably a victim, or a product, however you want to phrase it, of my background." But as my Vox colleague Anna North has shown, he was also a product of his political moment.[20]

President Gerald Ford had opposed *Roe*, but his vice president, Nelson Rockefeller, had repealed abortion restrictions as governor of New York. The 1976 Republican platform called abortion "one of the most difficult and controversial [questions] of our time."[21] It went on to recognize the split inside the Republican Party, saying, "There are those in our Party who favor complete support for the Supreme Court decision which permits abortion on demand. There are others who share sincere convictions that the Supreme Court's decision must be changed by a constitutional amendment prohibiting all abortions." In Congress, Republicans and Democrats voted against abortion in similar numbers. In surveys, Democrats and Republicans were equally likely to say it should be legal in all circumstances as illegal in all cases.

Today, Biden says of the conservative effort to overturn *Roe*, "It's wrong. It's pernicious. And we have to stop it."[22] Similarly, modern Republican platforms mince no words on the issue. "We assert the sanctity of human life and affirm that the unborn child has a fundamental right to life which cannot be infringed," read the GOP's 2016 platform. Far from recognizing Republicans who support unfettered access to abortion, it assails Democrats for that position. "Democrats' almost limitless support for abortion, and their strident opposition to even the most basic restrictions on abortion, put them dramatically out of step with the American people," it says. Like on health care, it's easy to see how a pro-choice voter could have found a home in the Republican Party of the 1970s, just as it's easy to see how a pro-life voter could have found space among the Democrats. Today, however, there is no room for confusion. Democrats support *Roe*. Republicans oppose it. You can know almost nothing about politics and know that.

This helps explain a particularly striking finding of Smidt's. One of the questions the American National Election Survey asks is whether voters felt like they really understood the differences between the two parties. Looking at responses to that question over time, Smidt found that the voters were becoming much more aware of how the two parties differed. The change was so sharp, he wrote, that "independent and inattentive voters exhibit an awareness of candidate differences across more political issues than strong partisan or politically attentive Americans prior to 1980."[23]

To put that more simply, a voter who mostly ignores American politics today is clearer on the differences between the two parties than political junkies and partisan loyalists were in 1980. That's an incredible finding. But it's also an obvious one. Voters—even inattentive ones—are seeing differences between the parties more clearly because those differences are bigger. It's easier to tell apart a donkey and an elephant than a donkey and a mule.

As the parties' agendas have diverged, so, too, have the parties' views of each other. Earlier I mentioned the "feelings thermometer" results showing sharp drops in evaluations of the opposing party. That data, if anything, understates the change. Politics is driven by the most committed activists with the most intense opinions. And more telling than the drop in average assessments of the other party is the rise in panicked assessments of the other party. In 2014, Pew found that 37 percent of Republicans and 31 percent of Democrats viewed the other party as "a threat to the nation's well-being." By 2016, that was up to 45 percent of Republicans and 41 percent of Democrats.[24]

But that, too, makes perfect sense: if you're a Republican who believes the government spends too much on social programs, is too soft on unauthorized immigrants, and is too captured by radical environmentalists, the Democratic Party really has become scarier to you. If your concern with Democratic governance hasn't risen over the past few decades, you haven't been paying attention.

The question isn't why voters have become more reliably partisan as the parties have become more obviously different. Of course they did. It's why the parties have become so different.

That's a story, as so many are in American life, that revolves around race.

Chapter 2

The Dixiecrat Dilemma

On Wednesday, August 28, 1957, during the Senate's consideration of a watered-down civil rights bill, Strom Thurmond walked onto the Senate floor and kicked off the most famous filibuster in American history. He began by reading the election statutes of all forty-eight states. Then he read the Declaration of Independence, the Bill of Rights, George Washington's farewell address, and much else besides. He got one bathroom break, when Barry Goldwater took the floor on his behalf. He ate cold sirloin steak and pumpernickel bread his wife had packed him and sucked on throat lozenges. At times, his voice became too weak to hear. He finished twenty-four hours and eighteen minutes later by saying he intended to vote against the legislation. His annoyed and exhausted colleagues were not surprised.

Thurmond's filibuster was the longest in American history. It fills ninety-six pages in the *Congressional Record*. It was also one of the least effective. As Joseph Crespino recounts in *Strom Thurmond's America*, southern senators had spent months gutting the bill. They killed section 3, which permitted the attorney general to bring lawsuits against discrimination in public areas.

They kneecapped the voting-rights provisions by guaranteeing a jury trial in cases of voter obstruction; no southern jury would ever convict a white election official for stopping African Americans from voting. Thurmond himself celebrated the achievements. He said they'd pulled "the most venomous teeth from the so-called civil rights bill," and he praised Democratic senators Richard Russell and Lyndon Johnson, the leaders of the effort, for "a magnificent job." Then he decided to make their job harder.

The deal Russell and Johnson had cut was that if Republicans and moderate Democrats allowed them to weaken the legislation, they would persuade their fellow southerners to permit it to pass. In the clubby Senate of the 1950s, word was bond. Keeping your end of the deal was necessary to being able to make any future pacts. If southerners killed the bill, a Johnson staffer warned, the South could lose "not only the ability to have any impact on civil rights legislation but any influence it has in Congress at all." So the southern senators agreed: there would be no filibuster. *Time* magazine reported that Thurmond was "among the first to agree with the non-filibuster decision."[1]

But then the telegrams and the letters from outraged segregationists began. Thurmond asked Russell to reconsider an organized filibuster. Russell refused. So Thurmond filibustered on his own. He didn't imperil the bill, but he made his fellow southerners look bad. They were keeping quiet in order to sustain segregation. He went loud to further his career. He made it seem like he was the only senator with the courage to speak out and defend the South's racial hierarchy. "Oh God, the venomous hatred of his Southern colleagues," recalled an aide to Johnson. The courtly Russell condemned Thurmond's filibuster as an act of "personal political aggrandizement." The bill passed over Thurmond's objections.

The solitary, arguably counterproductive stand against the civil rights bill is Thurmond's most famous filibuster, but not his most consequential. That came in 1965, after President Johnson won reelection in a landslide and Democrats managed a remarkable two-thirds majority in the Senate. Democrats saw an opportunity to shore themselves up for decades by eliminating the Taft-Hartley provision that permits state right-to-work laws, which cripple organized labor's ability to unionize workplaces. If the bill passed, unions, freed from their most binding constraint, could organize more workers and muster more votes for Democrats.

It was supposed to be easy. With sixty-eight Democrats in the Senate, everything was supposed to be easy. But Thurmond led a group of southern Democrats and conservative Republicans in a business-backed filibuster of the legislation. That time, his filibuster lasted barely more than five hours. But then, it didn't have to be any longer. Unlike Thurmond's filibuster of the civil rights bill, this time he had allies—enough of them to kill legislation that otherwise would have passed. That filibuster drove a sharp nail deep into labor's coffin—and weakened the Democratic Party.

Thurmond typically received a zero on the Americans for Democratic Action scorecard, which is a rough measure of how liberal a senator is. He was Republican president Dwight Eisenhower's second most reliable ally in the Senate. He was one of Goldwater's closest confederates. Thurmond wasn't just a conservative on race. As his antilabor filibuster suggests, he was a conservative on everything. Crespino argues, convincingly, that Thurmond should be seen as a forefather of modern conservatism. "In 1948, when Goldwater was still a year away from running for the Phoenix City council and Reagan was still an actor, Thurmond was a presidential candidate denouncing federal meddling in private business, the growing socialist impulse in American politics, and the dangers of statism," he writes. But until a few months prior to that 1965 filibuster, Thurmond had been a Democrat. He was elected to the Senate as a Democrat in 1954, and he wouldn't switch to the Republican Party until 1964.

Thurmond's politics and path are America's twentieth-century political realignment in miniature. To understand what happened in American politics between 1950 and 2018, you need to understand what the southern Democratic Party was and what it became. As the famed political scientist V. O. Key Jr. observed, the South's Democratic Party was an institution unto itself. Within the South, "the Democratic party is no party at all but a multiplicity of factions struggling for office."[2] It had liberals and conservatives, machine politicians and reformers. In national politics, however, the South's Democratic Party was a united front, "the instrument for the conduct of the 'foreign relations' of the South with the rest of the nation."

That the South felt it needed something akin to a diplomatic strategy with the rest of America is little surprise. The Civil War was only one hundred years in the past at the time the Civil Rights Act passed, and during that interregnum, the white South had been trying to balance its top domestic priority—the enforcement of white supremacy, held in place by the dual weapons of law and violence—with its forced membership in the broader United States. The southern Democratic Party was the vehicle through which the white South negotiated that tension. Put simply, the southern Democratic Party was an authoritarian institution that ruled autocratically in the South and that protected its autonomy by entering into a governing coalition with the national Democratic Party. The Dixiecrats gave the national Democrats the votes they needed to control Congress, and the national Democrats let the Dixiecrats enforce segregation and one-party rule at home.

The Dixiecrat-Democrat pact is a powerful reminder that there are worse things than polarization, that what's now remembered as a golden age in American politics was purchased at a terrible cost. In his book *Paths Out of Dixie: The Democratization of Authoritarian Enclaves in America's Deep South*, Robert Mickey argues:

> In the 1890s leaders of the eleven states of the old Confederacy founded stable, one-party authoritarian enclaves under the "Democratic" banner. Having secured a conditional autonomy from the central state and the national party, these rulers curtailed electorates, harassed and repressed opposition parties, and created and regulated racially separate—and significantly unfree—civic spheres. State-sponsored violence enforced these elements in a system that ensured cheap agricultural labor and white supremacy.[3]

If it is strange to read about America in the language we often use to write about, say, post-Soviet republics, well, that's partly the point. "America is aspirational," says Carol Anderson, the author of *White Rage* and a professor of African American studies at Emory University. "That is part of what sets it apart. Marginalized people have used those aspirations to say, 'This is what you say you are, but this is what you do.' But what also happens is those aspirations get encoded as achievements. You get this longing for a mythical past."[4]

Demythologizing our past is necessary if we are to clearly understand our present. But an honest survey of America's past offends the story we tell ourselves—it offends our sense of America as a true democracy and the Democratic Party's sense of its own honorable history.

The reign of the Dixiecrats

During much of the twentieth century, the Democratic Party's rule in the South was hegemonic. At times, Democrats occupied a stunning 95 percent of all elected offices, and as is true with authoritarian rulers everywhere, they did so in part by suppressing free and fair elections. African American voters were legally barred from voting in many cases and, when that didn't work, beaten or even killed for trying to exercise the franchise. During his 1946 reelection campaign, Democratic senator Theodore Bilbo was chillingly blunt: "You and I know what's the best way to keep the nigger from voting. You do it the night before the election. I don't have to tell you any more than that. Red-blooded men know what I mean."[5] He won the race.

A group of fifty Mississippians argued that Bilbo shouldn't be seated because he'd used the threat of violence to keep African Americans from the polls. The Senate convened a committee of two Republicans and three Southern Democrats to hear testimony, but on a party-line vote, the Democrats affirmed Bilbo's election. "Any difficulties experienced by the Negro in his attempts to register and vote in the July 2 primary resulted from the traditional feeling between white and Negroes and their ideas of the laws in that state as regards participation by Negroes in the Democratic primaries," read the majority's opinion, "and it would have been the same irrespective of who the candidates might have been."[6]

The South's mixture of legal discrimination and racial terrorism worked. Within three years of the Civil War's end, "black voter registration ranged from 85 to 94 percent in the Deep South, and almost one million freedmen were voting throughout the region,"[7] records Mickey. Less than a century later, that fundamental freedom had been demolished. "By 1944, in the states of the old Confederacy, only 5 percent of age-eligible African Americans were registered to vote, which left millions of blacks politically voiceless," writes Anderson. The repression was fiercest where black political power was most feared. In 1953, in the so-called Black Belt—the region of Alabama where the black population exceeded the white population—"only 1.3 percent of eligible African Americans were registered. Two counties had no black voters whatsoever."[8]

There was violence here, and even attempted coups, as when members of Louisiana's White League stormed New Orleans in 1874, trying to eject Governor William Kellogg, a Republican, and install his unsuccessful Democratic challenger, John McEnery. The insurgents took control of the city, forcing President Ulysses S. Grant to send in federal troops to restore order. In a telling postscript, a monument was erected in New Orleans in 1891 memorializing the White League members who died trying to take over the city. It was finally pulled down in 2017.

"While some have driven by these monuments every day and either revered their beauty or failed to see them at all, many of our neighbors and fellow Americans see them very clearly," said New Orleans mayor Mitch Landrieu in a speech explaining his decision to remove the city's monuments to the Confederacy. "Many are painfully aware of the long shadows their presence casts, not only literally but figuratively. And they clearly receive the message that the Confederacy and the cult of the lost cause intended to deliver."

As the New Orleans coup suggests, the Democratic Party enforced one-party rule by crushing white Republicans, too. "Democrats controlled all election laws and election administration, and they took care to keep barriers to entry of potential opponents prohibitively high," writes Mickey. "Several states, by party rule or statute, barred previously disloyal candidates, or those who failed to pledge themselves to the values of the Democratic party, from running for office—even as independents."[9] And thus the southern Democratic Party succeeded in consolidating authoritarian control over the Deep South.

The question is why the rest of the country—a country that was, imperfectly but undeniably, operating under a liberal democratic system—permitted the South to make such a mockery of America's political values. Part of the answer lies in the path chosen in the aftermath of the Civil War, when President Andrew Johnson, a bitter white supremacist, abandoned the work of racial equality and restored the South to white control. In a fusillade against the reconstruction acts passed by Congress, Johnson warned they would allow black people to "rule the white race, make and administer State laws, elect Presidents and members of Congress, and shape to a greater or lesser extent the future destiny of the whole country. Would such a trust and power be safe in such hands?"[10]

The restoration of what was, in effect, the Confederate political hierarchy in the South set the country on a path that paired the power of white supremacy with the power of political transactionalism. Even when national Democrats weren't led by revanchist racists, the South was left to the warlords for the same reason territories are often left to warlords: it served the interests of those in power. National Democrats cared about passing the New Deal, about winning presidential elections, about building infrastructure projects. Given the choice between working with a southern Democratic Party that could provide them crucial votes or challenging a southern Democratic Party that could defect and doom the Democratic Party's national agenda, they chose accommodation.

Moreover, the Dixiecrats' total domination of the South gave them the numbers to dominate the national Democratic Party, too. "From 1896 to 1932, southerners made up two-thirds of the Democratic House caucus; from 1933 to 1953, their share never slipped below 40 percent," writes Mickey.[11] These figures, if anything, underestimate the South's political clout. In the US Congress of that era, seniority meant power. And because of the authoritarian structure southern Democrats operated at home, they were rarely exposed to anything even approaching electoral pressure, which let them amass more seniority, in greater numbers, than elected officials of any other region.

As Columbia University historian Ira Katznelson writes in *Fear Itself: The New Deal and the Origins of Our Time*, in 1933, "southerners chaired twenty-nine of the forty-seven committees in the House, including Appropriations, Banking and Currency, Judiciary, Foreign Affairs, Agriculture, Military Affairs, and Ways and Means." They also, crucially, dominated the Rules Committee, which controlled what legislation made it to the House floor and under what conditions. In the Senate, southerners helmed "thirteen of thirty-three committees, . . . including Agriculture, Appropriations, Banking and Currency, Commerce, Finance, and Military Affairs."[12]

The leverage this gave the region over Congress was near total. It's not just that most significant bills were at least partly under the jurisdiction of one of these committees. It's that every single senator had interests that ran through these committees. A northern liberal who didn't care all that much about race but cared deeply about health care needed to work with the chairman of the House Ways and Means Committee—and that was going to be hard to do if he'd infuriated the chairman of the House Ways and Means Committee by taking aim at civil rights, the single thing he, and all his southern colleagues, cared about above all others.

This power brought presidents to heel as surely as it did wayward congressmen. Faced with anti-lynching legislation in the late 1930s, President Franklin D. Roosevelt said that if he supported it, southern committee chairs would "block every bill I ask Congress to pass to keep America from collapsing."[13] Moreover, if you weren't acceptable to southern Democrats, you weren't going to be the Democrats' nominee for president in the first place: the party required a two-thirds supermajority of delegates to the national convention to approve a presidential ticket, which meant the South held an effective veto over a hostile nominee.

At the same time, the South's alliance with the Democratic Party was by no means purely cynical. They really were Democrats, their party loyalty locked in place by regional identity and interest. Abraham Lincoln was the first Republican president; the South's enmity toward the Republican Party was thus signed in blood. The Democratic Party supported redistribution from the rich to the poor—and the North was rich and the South was poor. "Around the turn of the twentieth century the southern Democrats represented the left wing of the Democratic Party," says Princeton University professor Howard Rosenthal. "They were basically populist. The questions of redistribution at that time were from a relatively well-off North to a poor South. Race was not on the table as an area of disagreement in Congress."

But then race became an area of disagreement. Democrats didn't just want to redistribute from rich northern whites to poor southern whites. They also wanted to redistribute from richer whites to poorer blacks. Furthermore, beginning in 1948, with President Harry Truman's military desegregation orders, the Democratic Party became a vehicle for civil rights, betraying its fundamental compact with the South. It's in this era that a

Republican—Barry Goldwater, running on a platform of "states' rights"—carried much of the old Confederacy in a presidential election for the first time.

The story of how the Democratic Party came to embrace civil rights is complex. It includes the idealism of politicians like Lyndon Johnson and Hubert Humphrey as well as the hard math of electoral coalitions that, particularly in the North, began to include nonwhite voters. It reflects the logical endpoint of economic progressivism, as attention to the poor demanded attention to what was keeping so many nonwhite Americans poor, and it reflected strategic decisions the Republican Party made along the way, particularly the conservative movement's successful effort to turn the GOP into an ideological vehicle defined by mistrust of the federal government, opposition to redistribution, and faith in state and local rule—attractive ideas for southerners looking to block national efforts to improve both the economic and political conditions of African Americans.

Still, at the moment of rupture, the parties remained blurred. It is remarkable, from our current vantage point where everything cuts red from blue, to see a debate that polarizes the country without splitting the parties. But that was the case with the 1964 Civil Rights Act. As Geoffrey Kabaservice shows in *Rule and Ruin*, his history of Republican moderation, "eighty percent of House Republicans supported the bill, as opposed to sixty percent of House Democrats."[14] In the Senate, the Judiciary Committee was helmed by Mississippi's James Eastland—a dead end for the bill. So rather than going through a normal committee process, the legislation was worked out between President Johnson and Everett Dirksen, the Illinois Republican who served as minority leader. Southern Democrats filibustered the bill, but Dirksen corralled twenty-seven of the thirty-three Republicans to break the filibuster. In the end, "as with the House vote, a greater proportion of Senate Republicans than Democrats voted for cloture and passage of the [Civil Rights Act]: more than four-fifths of the Republicans but only some two-thirds of the Democrats," wrote Kabaservice.

So why are the Democrats seen as the party that passed the Civil Rights Act? There, the answer is simple. Because they were the party that passed the Civil Rights Act. They held the majority in both chambers and the presidency. They chose to snap their alliance with the Dixiecrats to pursue justice. Bill Moyers, who served as special assistant to Johnson, recalls finding the president brooding in his bedroom the night he signed the Civil Rights Act. "I think we just delivered the South to the Republican Party for a long time to come," Moyers remembers Johnson saying.[15] Johnson, who as Senate majority leader had enforced the southern Democrats' blockage against racial equality, was right. The Democratic Party's hammerlock on the South took time to break, but that was the moment it began to weaken.

So why didn't Republicans become the party of civil rights? Largely, Kabaservice argues, because of Goldwater: "The credit— even the glory—that the Republican Party should have enjoyed for its support for the Civil Rights Act of 1964 was effectively negated when its presumptive presidential nominee voted against the measure." And sure enough, Goldwater's stance against civil rights paid dividends. His disastrous presidential campaign succeeded in only one region of the country: the old Confederacy, which realized that the language of small government conservatism could be weaponized against the federal government's efforts to right America's racial wrongs.

That, then, is the story of the long period of depolarization in American politics. The South was in the Democratic Party, but it didn't agree with the Democratic Party—particularly once liberalism's vision of redistribution and uplift expanded to include

African Americans. So southern Democrats had ideological reasons to compromise with Republicans but political reasons to compromise with national Democrats. Southern power kept the Democratic Party less liberal than it otherwise would've been, the Republican Party congressionally weaker than it otherwise would've been, and stopped the two parties from sorting themselves around the deepest political cleavage of the age.

Here, you can see the power and purpose of ticket-splitting in an era of mixed parties: southern Democrats could vote for a Republican for president and conservative Dixiecrat Democrats for Congress and governorships. It is not that American politics was not riven by sharp, even violent disagreement in this era; it's simply that these fights did not map cleanly onto party.

It couldn't last, and it didn't. The Democratic Party's embrace of civil rights, and the Republican Party's decision to unite behind a standard-bearer who opposed the bill, cleared the way for southern conservatives to join the Republican Party. And that set the stage for all that followed.

Polarization is not extremism, but it is sorting

Before we get to all that followed, I want to say a word about what polarization is and isn't. There's a long-running debate among political scientists about whether America is polarizing or just sorting. There's also a long-running public discourse in which "polarized" or "partisan" is used as a synonym for "extreme." For the sake of clarity, I want to address both.

Let's start with polarization versus sorting, using cannabis policy as an example. Imagine a hundred-person America, where forty people want cannabis outlawed, forty want it legalized, and twenty aren't sure. If the Democratic and Republican Parties find themselves with an equal number of members from each group, America is totally unsorted.

Now imagine that everyone who wants to legalize cannabis moves into the Democratic Party, everyone who wants to outlaw it joins the Republican Party, and the undecided voters are split evenly between the two parties. Now the parties are perfectly sorted but—and this is the crucial point—no one's opinion has actually changed. The country holds the same mix of beliefs about pot in both examples. It's just that in the second example, those beliefs are sorted by party.

So that's sorting. Now let's tweak the example again. Imagine the undecideds make up their minds. Now fifty Americans want to legalize cannabis and fifty want to outlaw it. That's polarization: the opinions themselves changed to cluster around two poles, with no one left in the middle.

The Georgetown University political scientist Hans Noel says that sorting is just a subcategory of polarization.[16] In practical terms, he writes, both of these "have the consequence of increasing the tension between the two ends of the spectrum," which is what polarization is meant to describe.

I agree with Noel and would take it a step further. The polarization versus sorting debate is better understood as describing issue-based polarization and identity-based polarization. Both cannabis examples show people clustering around poles. It's just that in one example, the poles that they're clustering around reflect their policy opinions, while in the other, the poles they're clustering around reflect their political identities.

Crucially, these forms of polarization reinforce each other. Issue-based polarization leads to political identity polarization: if there's more intense disagreement about cannabis policy, people will want their political representatives to fight for their beliefs, which will push the parties to polarize around the issue as well. You can argue that that's what happened in the civil rights example above, as intense polarization around the issue of civil rights drove party polarization around civil rights. The Goldwater campaign tried to seize political opportunity by providing a home to angry racial conservatives, which eventually led those racial conservatives to cluster in the Republican Party, and vice versa.

The reverse, of course, is also true: When people sort their disagreements by party, that can lead those disagreements to deepen. If people sort into two parties along the axis of their ideal marijuana policy, those two parties will offer increasingly clear positions on marijuana, and the undecided will be pushed to make a choice, thus further polarizing the country's beliefs about cannabis.

Polarization begets polarization. But it doesn't beget extremism. We often assume that voters and political systems that split the difference are less extreme than those that don't, but this idea proves incoherent upon a moment's inspection.

In 1965, most Senate Republicans joined with the Democratic Party to create Medicare, a single-payer health-care system for the elderly. In 2010, not a single congressional Republican voted for Obamacare, a health-care plan based on the system Republican governor Mitt Romney designed in Massachusetts. Under any definition, the 2010 system was more sorted and polarized than the 1965 system—opinions were better aligned by party, and fewer politicians found themselves in the middle.

But was the 2010 system more ideologically extreme? I'd argue, under our normal ideological definitions, it wasn't—Obamacare was a public-private system with Republican roots that paid for itself through a mixture of tax increases and spending cuts, while Medicare was a liberal government takeover of health care for the elderly that created an open-ended entitlement with no dedicated way to pay its full costs.

And that's assuming ideological extremism is an idea with internal logic in the first place, which I also doubt. What makes a national, government-run health-care system more "extreme" than a mixed system that leaves tens of millions of people uninsured? The former is treated as more radical within the confines of American politics, but it's the latter that's radical (and cruel) when judged by the standards of other developed nations.

Or, to go back to the main story of this chapter, in the era when Washington was least polarized, political consensus rested on a foundation of racial bigotry that most would find abhorrent today. The compromises Congress made to preserve the peace included voting down anti-lynching laws and agreeing to lock most African Americans out of Social Security. I would call that political system far more ideologically extreme than the one we have today, even as it was less polarized.

Political scientists agree that the mid-twentieth century was the low ebb of political polarization, particularly in Congress. But the mid-twentieth century was not an era in which the world outside Washington was either serene or moderate. This was the age of Joseph McCarthy, the Vietnam War, and the draft dodger. It was a time of political assassinations, of civil rights activists being beaten on bridges, of authoritarian rule in the South, of feminists marching in the streets and Native Americans occupying Alcatraz. The irony is that the American political system was most calm and least polarized when America itself seemed to be on the verge of cracking apart.

You'll often hear pundits talk about the "moderate majority." But as the political scientist David Broockman has shown, these so-called moderates tend to hold more "extreme" opinions than liberals or conservatives. The way it works is that a pollster will ask people for their position on a wide range of issues: marijuana legalization, the war in Iraq, universal health care, gay marriage, taxes, climate change, and so on. The answers will then be coded as to whether they're left or right. People who have a mix of answers on the left and the right average out to the middle—and they're labeled as moderate.

But they're not moderate. They're just internally unsorted. When you drill down into those individual answers you find a lot of opinions that are well out of the political mainstream. "A lot of people say we should have a universal health-care system run by the state like the British," Broockman told me. "A lot of people say we should deport all undocumented immigrants immediately with no due process. You'll often see really draconian measures towards gays and lesbians get 16 to 20 percent support. These people look like moderates but they're actually quite extreme."[17]

When polarization is driven by allegiance to political parties, it can be moderating. Political parties want to win elections, so they try to champion ideas that won't get their candidates crushed at the ballot box. People who aren't attached to one party or the other are free to hold much more unpopular opinions.

Extremism is a value judgment. To early twentieth-century Americans, our widespread acceptance of interracial and gay marriage would be extreme. To many of us, the ideological consensus that kept consenting adults of different races or the same gender from living happy, loving lives together seems vicious and ignorant. Today, vegans are dismissed as extremists. I hope that in the future, the suffering that we impose on animals through industrial-scale factory farming is considered the shocking position. When I say the political coalitions are becoming more sorted and more polarized, I mean only that: there is less ideological overlap, fewer of us are caught in the middle, and there is more tension between the poles. Nothing about those dynamics makes the opinions partisans hold in 2020 more extreme than those held by their forebears. Banal views held widely in that era would get you run out of polite society today, and rightly so.

That said, if the degree of extremism in our politics is often overstated, the stunning comprehensiveness with which we've sorted and polarized ourselves is often understated, as are its implications for our future.

One nation, sorted

The passage of the Civil Rights Act heralded the death of the Dixiecrats. The death of the Dixiecrats cleared the way for southern conservatives to join the Republican Party and northern liberals to join the Democratic Party. That let the parties sort themselves ideologically, such that there are no longer any House Democrats more conservative than any House Republicans or any House Republicans more liberal than any House Democrats. And with that essential clarity, the parties sorted around virtually everything else, too. This transformation has taken the two parties from being coalitions that looked alike, lived similar lives, and thought only somewhat differently to two warring camps that look different, live different lives in different places, and find themselves in ever-deeper disagreement.

In her book *Uncivil Agreement: How Politics Became Our Identity*, political scientist Lilliana Mason offers a stunning overview of the way the parties have changed in recent years. Back in 1952, she writes, the demographic differences between the parties were modest; with the exception of southerners (who, as we've seen, were Democratic) and Protestants (who leaned

Republican), no major demographic group saw "more than a
10 percentage point difference in the percentage of its members
represented within each party."[18] So the Democratic and Republican Parties looked reasonably similar in their representation of
African Americans and whites, of men and women, of married
and unmarried voters; even liberals were only slightly more
populous in the Democratic Party.

That is, to put it gently, no longer true. In the 1952 presidential election, the American National Election Survey found
that 6 percent of self-identified Democrats and 2 percent of
self-identified Republicans were nonwhite. In 2012, the same
survey found 43 percent of self-identified Democrats, but only
9 percent of self-identified Republicans, were nonwhite.[19] So not
only was the 2012 electorate far, far more racially diverse than
the 1952 electorate, but that diversity was concentrated in the
Democratic Party.

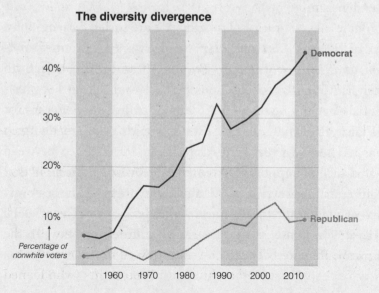

The diversity divergence

Percentage of
nonwhite voters

The religious divide is similarly stark. In 2014, Pew reported that the single largest religious group in the Republican coalition was evangelical Protestants. And the Democrats? Their single largest religious group was the religiously unaffiliated, the "nones."[20]

As demographics change, so do values. In 2002, 50 percent of Republicans and 52 percent of Democrats said it wasn't necessary to believe in God to be a moral person. By 2017, the number of Republicans agreeing with that statement had fallen slightly, to 47 percent, while the number of Democrats agreeing had shot up to 64 percent.[21] As Steven Levitsky and Daniel Ziblatt wrote in *How Democracies Die*, "the two parties are now divided over race and religion—two deeply polarizing issues that tend to generate greater intolerance and hostility than traditional policy issues such as taxes and government spending." I'd amend that slightly: the parties are dividing over fundamental *identities* that tend to generate intolerance and hostility, and the issue conflicts are just one expression of that division.

But it isn't just race and religion. We are sorted by geography, too. In his book *The Great Alignment: Race, Party Transformation, and the Rise of Donald Trump*, Abramowitz conducts an analysis I found shocking. Looking back over decades of presidential elections, he shows that for much of the twentieth century, the idea of red states and blue states wouldn't have made much sense. "There was very little relationship, for instance, between the pattern of support for George McGovern, a strong liberal from South Dakota, in 1972, and the pattern of support just four years later for Jimmy Carter, a moderate from Georgia," he writes.[22] The numbers here are stunning. From 1972 to 1984, the average difference between how a state voted in one presidential election and how it voted in the next was 7.7 percentage points. From 2000 to 2012, it was only 1.9 percentage points. We are fixed in political place.

The sorting continues far beneath the state level. In an analysis at FiveThirtyEight, Dave Wasserman looked at "landslide counties"—counties where the winning presidential candidate got at least 60 percent of the vote. In 1992, 39 percent of voters lived in landslide counties. By 2016, that had shot to 61 percent of voters. The numbers were even starker when Wasserman looked at counties where the winning candidate won by more than 50 points: the share of voters living in those "extreme landslide" counties more than quintupled, from 4 percent in 1992 to 21 percent in 2016. In less than twenty-five years, the percentage of voters who lived in a district where almost everyone thought like them politically went from 1 in 20 to 1 in 5.

You could imagine a world where this data said little about the kinds of places people lived—yes, we were more sorted politically, but those sorted spaces were randomly distributed across the country's geography. That's not the world we live in. Tucked inside these numbers is a growing urban-rural divide. There is no dense city in America that routinely votes Republican. There are few rural areas that vote Democratic. Marc Muro, the policy director at the Brookings Institution's Metropolitan Policy Program, calculates that the dividing line is at about nine hundred people per square mile: above that, areas trend Democratic; below it, they turn Republican.[23] Decades ago, when the parties were less sorted, the density of the place we lived did less to predict our partisanship. Today, as political scientist Jonathan Rodden shows in his book *Why Cities Lose*, the density of the place we live has become a powerful predictor of partisanship.

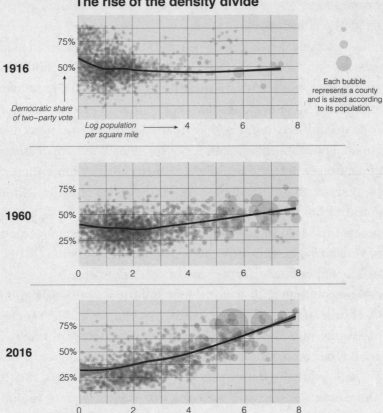

The rise of the density divide

1916

75%
50%

Democratic share
of two–party vote

Log population   ———→   4   6   8
per square mile

Each bubble
represents a county
and is sized according
to its population.

1960

75%
50%
25%

0   2   4   6   8

2016

75%
50%
25%

0   2   4   6   8

Call this the tale of two Clintons. As the political analyst Ron Brownstein wrote in *The Atlantic*, in both 1992 and 1996, Bill Clinton "carried nearly half of America's 3,100 counties. But since then, Democrats have retreated into the nation's urban centers."[24] In 2000, Al Gore won the popular vote with fewer than seven hundred counties. In 2012, Obama won the popular vote by much more than Gore, but carried only about six hundred counties. In 2016, Hillary Clinton won the popular vote with fewer than five hundred counties—more than one thousand counties fewer than her husband had won twenty-five years before.

What makes America's urban-rural divide particularly destabilizing is the economic divide it tracks. At a March 2018 conference in India, Hillary Clinton set off a political ruckus by saying, "I won the places that represent two-thirds of America's gross domestic product. So I won the places that are optimistic, diverse, dynamic, moving forward."[25] Putting aside the propriety of Clinton's comment, the data is solid. It comes from a Brookings report that found that "the less-than-500 counties that Hillary Clinton carried nationwide encompassed a massive 64 percent of America's economic activity as measured by total output in 2015."[26] As a comparison, the counties Gore won in 2000 accounted for 54 percent of total GDP.

The differences we can measure hide the differences we can't measure, or haven't thought to measure. In *The Big Sort: Why the Clustering of Like-Minded America Is Tearing Us Apart*, Bill Bishop writes eloquently of the dizzying array of factors that drive where we live:

> Between 4 and 5 percent of the population moves each year from one county to another—100 million Americans in the past decade. They are moving to take jobs, to be close to family, or to follow the sun. When they look for a place to live, they run through a checklist of amenities: Is there the right kind of church nearby? The right kind of coffee shop? How close is the neighborhood to the center of the city? What are the rents? Is the place safe? When people move, they also make choices about who their neighbors will be and who will share their new lives.[27]

All these choices and factors connect to our political dispositions and identities. After the 2018 election, for instance,

Wasserman calculated that House Democrats now represented 78 percent of all Whole Foods locations, but only 27 percent of Cracker Barrels. In theory, there is nothing about organic apples or all-day waffles that should predict our politics, but our affinities and preferences layer atop each other in complex ways.[28]

It's easy to overstate the direct role partisanship is playing in these decisions. While it's true that Democrats prefer to live among Democrats and Republicans like living among Republicans, research shows that the dominant considerations when people are choosing a place to move are housing prices, school quality, crime rates, and similar quality-of-life questions.[29] However, the big driver here isn't the small moves people make between communities, but the big decision they make—or that their parents, or their parents' parents, made—to live in an urban or rural area.

As the parties become more racially, religiously, ideologically, and geographically different, the signals that tell us if a place is our kind of place, if a community is our kind of community, heighten our political divisions. The more sorted we are in our differences, the more different we grow in our preferences. In 2017, Pew found that "most Republicans (65%) say they would rather live in a community where houses are larger and farther apart and where schools and shopping are not nearby. A majority of Democrats (61%) prefer smaller houses within walking distance of schools and shopping."[30] Thus, a preference that seems nonpolitical on its face—"I want a big house with a yard," or "I want to live in a diverse city with lots of new restaurants"—becomes yet another force pulling partisans away from each other.

There's a reason these divides are all stacking on top of one another. They don't merely track differences in our politics. They track differences in our psychologies.

The psychological roots of our politics

Let's start with the obvious. People are different. My older brother is a social animal, eager to make small talk, able to forge connections with strangers in seconds. I stand in the corner at cocktail parties, uncomfortable with people I don't already know well. My younger sister is a talented artist who designs jewelry and has been making psychedelic art since she was six. I have such bad penmanship that I started a course to improve my handwriting in my thirties, and if you ask me to sketch a person, I'll plop a small circle for a head over a fatter circle for a body, like a six-year-old who just learned to draw. As a result, my brother, who likes socializing more than I do, does more socializing. My sister, with her talent for art, makes more art.

Some of these differences are rooted in nurture, in experience. But others are evident from our earliest days. Psychologists speak of the Big Five personality traits: openness to experience, conscientiousness, extroversion-introversion, agreeableness, and neuroticism. Where we fall on these scales is measurable in childhood and shapes our lives thereafter. It affects where we live, what we like, who we love. And, increasingly, it shapes our politics.

In their book *Open versus Closed: Personality, Identity, and the Politics of Redistribution*, political psychologists Christopher Johnston, Christopher Federico, and Howard Lavine write that "Democrats and Republicans are now sharply distinguished by a set of basic psychological dispositions related to experiential *openness*—a general dimension of personality tapping tolerance for threat and uncertainty in one's environment."[31]

A similar argument, using slightly different data, can be found in political scientists Marc Hetherington and Jonathan Weiler's

Prius or Pickup? How the Answers to Four Simple Questions Explain America's Great Divide:

> Of the many factors that make up your worldview, one is more fundamental than any other in determining which side of the divide you gravitate toward: your perception of how dangerous the world is. Fear is perhaps our most primal instinct, after all, so it's only logical that people's level of fearfulness informs their outlook on life.[32]

Different studies categorize people in different ways, but the common thread is that openness to experience—and the basic optimism that drives it—is associated with liberalism, while conscientiousness, a preference for order and tradition that breeds a skepticism toward disruptive change, connects to conservatism. People high in openness are more likely to enjoy trying new foods, traveling to new places, living in diverse cities, keeping a messy desk. They're less sensitive to threatening photos and disgusting images, even when measuring subrational indicators like eye tracking and saliva chemicals. In *Predisposed: Liberals, Conservatives, and the Biology of Political Differences*, John Hibbing, Kevin Smith, and John Alford write:

> Numerous studies have linked these personality dimensions to differences in the mix of tastes and preferences that seem to reliably separate liberals and conservatives. People who score high on openness, for example, tend to like envelope-pushing music and abstract art. People who score high on conscientiousness are more likely to be organized, faithful, and loyal. One review of this large research literature finds these sorts of differences consistently cropping up across nearly 70 years of studies on personality research. The punch line, of course, is that this same

literature also reports a consistent relationship between these dimensions of personality and political temperament. Those open to new experiences are not just hanging Jackson Pollock prints in disorganized bedrooms while listening to techno-pop reinterpretations of Bach by experimental jazz bands. They are also more likely to identify themselves as liberals.[33]

This is why Whole Foods and Cracker Barrel locations track deep partisan divisions. Whole Foods is a grocer catering to those high in openness to experience. The aisles are thick with ethnic foods, unusual produce, and magazines touting Eastern spirituality. Cracker Barrel, by contrast, is aimed at those preferring tradition: it offers comforting, Southern favorites that are delicious without being surprising. These are large corporations with skilled teams that carefully choose the placements of new locations. Their choices map onto our politics not because they are trying to serve one side of the political divide but because our politics map onto our deeper preferences, and those deeper preferences drive much more than just our politics.

We like to think that we choose our politics by slowly, methodically developing a worldview, using that worldview to generate conclusions about ideal tax and health and foreign policy, and then selecting the political party that fits best. That's not how the political psychologists see it. They argue that our politics, much like our interest in travel and spicy food and being in crowds, emerges from our psychological makeup. "Certain ideas are attractive to some people and repulsive to others, and that means, essentially, that ideologies and psychologies are magnetically drawn to each other,"[34] says John Jost, a political psychologist at New York University.

When Obama paired the words "hope" and "change," he was expressing something fundamental to the liberal psychology:

change makes some fearful, but within the liberal temperament, it carries the hope of something better. The kinds of people most attracted to liberalism are the kinds of people who are excited by change, by difference, by diversity. Their politics are just one expression of that basic temperament—a temperament that might push them to live in polyglot cities, to hitchhike across Europe, to watch foreign-language films. By contrast, the job of the conservative, wrote *National Review* founder William F. Buckley, is to "[stand] athwart history, yelling Stop."[35] You can see how that might appeal to a person who mistrusts change, appreciates tradition, and seeks order. That kind of person might also prefer living in a small town nearer to family, going to a church deeply rooted in ritual, celebrating at restaurants they already know and love.

Depending on the type of person you are, you might read one of those descriptions as compliment and one as indictment. Don't think of it that way. Society needs lots of different kinds of people, with lots of different kinds of psychologies, to thrive. There are times when a mistrust of outsiders is necessary for a culture to repel a threat. There are times when enthusiasm about change is the only thing standing between a society and stagnation. Open isn't better than closed. Conscientious is a trait, not a compliment. Evolutionarily, the power is in the mix of outlooks, not in any one outlook—that's why this psychological diversity has survived.

What is changing is not our psychologies. What is changing is how closely our psychologies map onto our politics and onto a host of other life choices. As the differences between the parties clarify, the magnetic pull of their ideas and demographics becomes stronger to the psychologically aligned—as does their magnetic repulsion to the psychologically opposed.

In *Prius or Pickup?*, Hetherington and Weiler use a psychological scale they call "fluid" and "fixed." They write:

People with what we call a fixed worldview are more fearful of potential dangers, and are likely to prefer clear and unwavering rules to help them navigate all the threats. This mind-set leads them to support social structures in which hierarchy and order prevail, the better to ensure people don't stray too far from the straight and narrow. By contrast, people with what we call a fluid worldview are less likely to perceive the world as dangerous.

By extension, they will endorse social structures that allow individuals to find their own way in life. They are more inclined to believe that a society's well-being requires giving people greater latitude to question, to explore, and to discover their authentic selves.[36]

In the mid-twentieth century, this psychological dimension doesn't seem to have split American politics. It's notable, for instance, that opposition to the Vietnam War was evenly distributed across the two parties during the 1960s. As late as 1992, the fluid and the fixed were nearly identical in which party they chose. Now, though, these psychologies are the dividing line of American politics, at least among white voters (more on why the psychological sort is concentrated among whites, and what it means for politics, later). On the fluid side, 71 percent were Democrats and only 21 percent were Republicans. On the fixed side, 60 percent were Republicans and only 25 percent were Democrats. The results are even stronger if you look at ideology. According to Hetherington and Weiler, "Among the fixed, 84 percent of those who chose one of these two labels chose conservative. Among the fluid, 80 percent of those who chose one of them chose liberal."

Every dimension of our lives—ideology, religiosity, geography, and so on—carries a psychological signal. And those psychological signals strengthen as they align. What's been happening to

American life is we're taking the magnets and stacking them all on top of one another, so the pull-push force of that stack is multiplied—particularly for the people most engaged in politics.

In *Open versus Closed*, Johnston, Federico, and Lavine tested a variety of psychological tendencies against people's level of interest in politics. What they found, again and again, is psychology doesn't predict political opinions among people who don't pay much attention to politics, but it's a powerful predictor of political opinions among those who do. For the politically disengaged, "there is little dispositional sorting," but among the highly engaged, the effects are huge: different levels of openness to experience can account for as much as 35 percentage point swings in party identification, overwhelming almost all other factors.

These findings led the researchers to an interesting conclusion: "In forming an opinion, the question for the unengaged citizen is: what will this policy *do for* me? Among the engaged, however, reactions to economic issues are better understood as expressively motivated signals of identity. The question for the engaged citizen is: what does support for this policy position *say about* me?"[37]

Psychological sorting, in other words, is a powerful driver of identity politics. If you care enough about politics to connect it to your core psychological outlook, then politics becomes part of your psychological self-expression. And as the political coalitions split by psychology, membership in one or the other becomes a clearer signal, both to ourselves and to the world, about who we are and what we value. When we participate in politics to solve a problem, we're participating transactionally. But when we participate in politics to express who we are, that's a signal that politics has become an identity. And that's when our relationship to politics, and to each other, changes.

Chapter 3

Your Brain on Groups

I n 1970, Henri Tajfel published a paper with the anodyne title "Experiments in Intergroup Discrimination." It would prove among the most important in social psychology, and even today, it stands as one of the most unnerving windows into the subroutines of the human mind.

Tajfel began by recalling a Slovene friend of his detailing the stereotypes his countrymen had for Bosnian immigrants. Tajfel doesn't record what those stereotypes were, but they stuck with him. He thought he had heard them, or something like them, before. He decided to test his hunch. "Some time later I presented this description to a group of students at the University of Oxford and asked them to guess by whom it was used and to whom it referred," he writes. "The almost unanimous reply was that this was the characterization applied by native Englishmen to 'colored' immigrants: people coming primarily from the West Indies, India and Pakistan."[1]

From this, Tajfel took a lesson. Discrimination varies in its targets and intensity across cultures, but it is surprisingly similar in its rationalizations. Perhaps, he thought, the way we treat people we decide aren't like us isn't a product of our specific culture or experience but something deeper, something that reflects how humans think, organize, and bound their social worlds. "The most important principle of the subjective social order we construct for ourselves is the classification of groups as 'we' and 'they,'" he wrote, and once someone has become a "they," we are used to dismissing them, competing against them, discriminating against them—and, Tajfel hypothesized in a particularly chilling sentence, we will do that "even if there is no reason for it in terms of [our] own interests."

It is worth dwelling on the radical conception of human nature Tajfel was advancing. People had long nurtured their prejudices, but they believed those prejudices reflected reality—we disliked those we disliked because we had reason to dislike them. This is the whole point of racial and ethnic stereotypes: the greed, criminality, venality, or idiocy we ascribe to others justifies our hatred or fear of them. The post-Enlightenment view of humanity is that we are rational individuals whose actions may be inflamed by instinct but are ultimately governed by calculation. But what if it was the other way around? What if our loyalties and prejudices are governed by instinct and merely rationalized as calculation?

There is a reason Tajfel had these doubts. His life had taught him a cruel lesson in how thin the film of human civilization really was, how near to the surface our barbarism lurked, and how flimsy yet central group identity could be—how quickly it could shift from being meaningless to becoming the only thing that mattered.

Tajfel was a Polish Jew, born in 1919. He immigrated to France in the 1930s because Jews couldn't get a university education in Poland. With World War II ripping through Europe, he joined the French army in 1939 and was captured by the Germans in 1940. He spent the next five years in German prisoner-of-war camps.

"All through this period he lived under the false identity of being French," wrote his student and collaborator John Turner: "had it been discovered by the German authorities that he was a Polish rather than a French Jew he would have been killed."[2]

This became, Turner later recalled, the base layer of Tajfel's fixation on identity:

> The point he made was that no matter what his personal characteristics were or the quality of his personal relationships with the German guards, once his true identity had been discovered, it was that social category membership (of being Polish) which would have determined the reaction of the guards and his ultimate fate. His personal attributes and identity as a unique individual would have proved unimportant and irrelevant to their response.

Tajfel returned to France in May 1945. "Hardly anyone I knew in 1939—including my family—was left alive," he later recalled.[3] And why had his parents been murdered? Why was his brother killed? The answer, for them, was the same as the answer for 6 million other Jews: they were Jewish. It is not hard to understand why a man who endured this era, who survived only by slipping into an identity that was not his own, would find himself obsessing over the psychology of group identity.

Tajfel theorized that the instinct to view our own with favor and outsiders with hostility is so deeply learned that it operates independent of any reason to treat social relations as a competition. We do not need to hate or fear members of an out-group to turn on them. We do not need to have anything material to gain by turning on them. Once we have classified them as, well, "*them*," that is enough—we will find ourselves inclined to treat them skeptically, even hostilely, because that is what we are used to doing with anyone we see as a "them." It's an automatic response, like the gooseflesh that rises on your arm in reaction to the cold.

As a theory, it was elegant, if a bit grim. But it raised two predictions Tajfel realized he could test experimentally. The first was that we were so tuned to sort the world into "us" and "them" that we would do so based on the lightest of cues. The second was that once we had sorted the world into "us" and "them," we would act with favor toward our group and discriminate against the out-group—even in the absence of any reason to do so. Atop this theory, Tajfel conducted a series of famous experiments that would be farcical were the results not so chilling.

In the first, sixty-four boys between the ages of fourteen and fifteen were invited to Tajfel's laboratory. The children all came from the same school, so they came into the experiment knowing one another, already belonging to a community together. In the study's first portion, the boys were told the researchers wanted to test visual judgment. They were shown clusters of dots and asked to estimate how many they saw. They then sat and watched as the researchers busily pretended to score their work.

Then the researchers said they wanted to take advantage of the boys' presence to run another test, one that was in no way related to the first. To make life simpler, they were going to sort the boys into groups based on whether they had guessed high or low when judging dots in the previous study—in reality, this was fiction: the boys were split completely at random. The new task consisted of handing out a limited amount of real money to other boys in the study. The boys never gave themselves money; they were just allocating it to others. But they could see whether they were giving it to members of their group or the out-group.

It is worth pausing here to emphasize the absurdity of the situation. Sixty-four boys, all from the same school, were brought into a lab and sorted into groups based on a meaningless characteristic—how accurately they estimated dots on a screen—that wasn't even true. Then they were moved into a different study that had nothing to do with dots at all, where they were giving away money, none of which they would ever get. It was the lightest test of group identity possible. It was so light that Tajfel did not expect it to generate group behavior. "His idea was to establish a baseline of no intergroup behaviour and then to add variables cumulatively to see at what point intergroup discrimination occurred," wrote Turner.[4] In other words, this first experiment, with this silly categorization, was meant to be below the bar at which collective identity took hold, so Tajfel could then add stronger cues and pinpoint what it took to make people see themselves as part of a group.

Here, even Tajfel, despite his tragic past, was underestimating the power of group psychology. The results of this first test showed group identity taking hold and mutating into bias: "a large majority of the subjects, in all groups in both conditions, gave more money to members of their own group than to members of the other group."[5]

Importantly, this was not the optimal strategy for getting the most out of the experimenters, and it was not the strategy the boys chose when they weren't thinking in groups. When told they were choosing between two members of their own group, they tended to choose the fairest option. But when it was between a member of their meaningless group and the other meaningless group, they opted to make sure their co-over- or co-underestimator, whose name they didn't even know, got more, even if it meant everyone got less in total.

The results were so striking that Tajfel decided he needed to do a second study to make sure they held. Once again, he invited a bunch of boys into the lab. This time, the boys were shown paintings by Paul Klee and Wassily Kandinsky and asked to choose their favorite. The paintings were shown without signatures so that the boys could then be sorted, at random, into the Klee group or the Kandinsky group as the researchers moved to the next experiment. Once again, the boys were asked to hand out money, knowing nothing other than that they were often allocating between participants who agreed with their taste in art and participants who didn't, and even that thin reed of group identity was false.

But this time, the setup was designed to test whether making money for their group or screwing over the outsiders was more important for the assembled kids. In some scenarios, the boys would have to choose between maximizing the amount of money everyone received and maximizing how much more their group got, even if it meant their group got less in total. The latter proved the more popular option. Reflect on that for a second: they preferred to give their group less so long as it meant the gap between what they got and what the out-group got was bigger.

Some of the boys did not choose between an out-group and in-group member. Instead, they were asked to choose between two members of their group or between two members of the out-group. In those cases, there was no longer group competition to drive behavior. But here, too, the results were telling. The boys giving money to two members of their group gave more than when they were giving money to two members of the out-group. Even now, Tajfel's description of the boys' decision to punish out-group members even when there was no in-group member to give money to rings with astonishment. There was no scarcity driving their decisions. That they still chose to punish the out-group "represented, therefore, a clear case of gratuitous discrimination."[6]

In a 1971 paper reflecting on these results, Tajfel and his coauthors wrote that it was time to put to rest the idea that group conflict was primarily motivated by zero-sum collisions over resources or power. "Discriminatory intergroup behaviour cannot be fully understood if it is considered solely in terms of 'objective' conflict of interests," they concluded.[7] The boys in his studies often had nothing to gain—and sometimes even had something to lose—by punishing those they believed, based on flimsy and false categorizations, to be different from them. Far from their behavior showing a pure desire to maximize their group's gains, they often gave their group less to increase the difference between them and the out-group. Far from the money being the prime motivator, "it is the winning that seems more important to them," wrote Tajfel.

Again, these results were looking at boys who knew one another, who had no prior attachment to the meaningless groups they were randomly sorted into, who were allocating money that they knew they themselves would never get.

But before you comfort yourself by saying that this is just a few experiments with some random teenage boys, that no adult would act this way, it's worth looking at one sphere of human life in which this behavior plays out constantly around us.*

To hate like this is to be happy forever

It is time for me to admit something that I know will cost me the respect of some readers. I am not a sports fan. More than that, I don't understand sports fandom. I've tried! I have adopted teams, gone to games. When I was a kid, I obsessively collected baseball

---

* I should note that Tajfel's results have been replicated repeatedly, in all sorts of conditions, deploying all sorts of group identities, using adults as subjects. But permit me a smooth section transition.

cards, rattling off the stats of favored players. But I've never been able to develop allegiance. I grew up near Los Angeles, after the Rams had absconded to St. Louis,* so I knew these organizations had no loyalty to me; I liked following drafts and trades, and I saw that the players went where the money was rather than staying where their fans were.

But I am weird and broken. Sports remain ubiquitous, and they are ubiquitous because they respond to human beings' deep desire to sort "us" from "them," to see our group triumph over outsiders in combat and competition. Whether our team wins has no effect on our incomes, our futures, our children's education, or whether our job will move to China. But every week, millions, perhaps even billions, attach their happiness to the outcome of a game that they are not playing, whose material spoils they will not enjoy. They are not just watching for sportsmanship or prowess; they are watching, as Tajfel said, because it is the winning that is important.

The winning is so important that cities burn and people die in its aftermath. In 2015, FiveThirtyEight's Carl Bialik collected information on forty-nine recent North American sports riots. "The database tells a violent history of the aftermath of many sporting events: thousands of people arrested, hundreds injured, more than a dozen killed. The riots occurred in more than a dozen U.S. states and three Canadian provinces, in reaction to sporting events in all four major North American pro sports, plus college football, basketball and hockey."[8]

Again, this is all for contests in which the stakes are purely psychological and emotional, and yet the ecstasy of victory, and sometimes the pain of loss, so overwhelms our faculties that we destroy the very towns that form the basis of our affection for the teams we're supporting. This is how powerfully we attach to

---

* The team has since returned, which I'd say further proves my point.

groups. This is how little it takes for group identity to take over all our other faculties, for identitarian passions to push aside the tinny voice of our reasoning mind.

In 2006, Will Blythe published a book with a title I have never forgotten. It was called *To Hate Like This Is to Be Happy Forever*. How can you walk by a book with those words slashed across the cover? What could it be about?

When I picked it up, I was surprised to see that it was an exploration of the rivalry between the Duke and University of North Carolina basketball teams and the way that rivalry had given shape and meaning to the author's life in moments when little else did. "The living and dying through one's allegiance to either Duke or Carolina is no less real for being enacted through play and fandom," Blythe writes.[9]

I love that line. *The living and dying through one's allegiance.* If it sounds like hyperbole, consider the possibility that the emotional experience it describes is not just real, but rational. Human beings evolved to exist in groups. To be part of a group, and to see that group thrive, meant survival. To be exiled from a group, or to see your group crushed by its enemies, could mean death. Is it really so strange that we evolved to feel the life-and-death stakes of group belonging and status?

The emergent science of loneliness offers powerful insight here. We tend to dismiss the agony of social isolation or stigma as merely psychological. It isn't. To feel abandoned by community, to fear the opprobrium of others, triggers a physical assault on the body. You may have heard statistics like loneliness is worse for you than obesity or smoking. Medical professionals, like Vivek Murthy, the former surgeon general of the United States, say social isolation acts like a disease or an injury, crossing from psychological state to physical malady. The mechanism is evolutionary; our brains know we need our groups to survive. So when we feel cast out of our group, it triggers a massive stress response throughout the body:

> From a biological perspective, we evolved to be social creatures. Long ago, our ability to build relationships of trust and cooperation helped increase our chances of having a stable food supply and more consistent protection from predators. Over thousands of years, the value of social connection has become baked into our nervous system such that the absence of such a protective force creates a stress state in the body. Loneliness causes stress, and long-term or chronic stress leads to more frequent elevations of a key stress hormone, cortisol. It is also linked to higher levels of inflammation in the body. This in turn damages blood vessels and other tissues, increasing the risk of heart disease, diabetes, joint disease, depression, obesity, and premature death. Chronic stress can also hijack your brain's prefrontal cortex, which governs decision making, planning, emotional regulation, analysis, and abstract thinking.[10]

There's a particular finding in this research that's almost unbearably poignant. As Johann Hari describes in his book *Lost Connections,* "anywhere in the world where people describe being lonely, they will also—throughout their sleep—experience more of something called 'micro-awakenings.' These are small moments you won't recall when you wake up, but in which you rise a little from your slumber. All other social animals do the same thing when they're isolated too. The best theory is that you don't feel safe going to sleep when you're lonely, because early humans literally weren't safe if they were sleeping apart from the tribe."[11] That's how deep the experience of social anxiety runs: it literally wakes you up throughout the night, because your body knows it can't rest as deeply when it can't rely on others for protection.

Our brains reflect deep evolutionary time, while our lives, for better and for worse, are lived right now, in this moment. We are exquisitely tuned to understand and manage our role in the small, necessary groups that defined our world as hunter-gatherers, but we've not had long to adjust to the digitized, globalized, accelerated world we've built. The sensitivities that helped us thrive within the interplay of a few groups of a few hundred people can drive us mad when exposed to the scale, noise, and sophisticated manipulations of modern capitalism and politics. Our brains don't always know the difference between the life-and-death stakes that group fortunes once held and the milder consequences they typically carry today. In his book *Enlightenment 2.0: Restoring Sanity to Our Politics, Our Economy, and Our Lives*, University of Toronto philosopher Joseph Heath frames this nicely:

When it comes to large-scale cooperation, we humans have clearly exceeded our programming. We have become what biologists call an ultrasocial species, despite having a set of social instincts that are essentially tailored for managing life in a small-scale tribal society. It's crucial to recognize, however, that we have not accomplished this by reprogramming ourselves or overcoming our innate design limitations. We have accomplished this in large measure by tricking ourselves into feeling as though we are still living in small-scale tribal societies, even when we are not. Unfortunately, the trick works so well that we sometimes forget that we're using it, and so imagine that we can create large-scale systems of cooperation based on nothing more than our rational insight into the need for such institutions. This invariably leads to disappointment.[12]

I would amend that. It doesn't *invariably* lead to disappointment. Sometimes it leads to large-scale, wonderful advances in human cooperation, like the nation-state or religions. Sometimes it leads to hatred, violence, even genocide. And sometimes it just leads to everyone gathering on Sunday to watch two groups of people dressed in particular colors collide with each other on a lush green field.

I worry, writing this section, that some will read it and believe I am dismissing the power, or condescending to the experience, of sports rivalries. So let me say this clearly: my point is just the opposite. Sports are such a powerful force in human society precisely because they harness primal instincts that pulse through our psyche. The fact that teams can command such deep, violent loyalty based on nothing but being in the same town as fans— even as professional sports teams are transparently cynical in their loyalties, even as they demand stadium subsidies to locate and tax breaks to remain in the towns they profess to love, even as the players leave the moment another team offers a better deal—shows that we are no different from Tajfel's boys: a group does not have to be based on objectively important criteria for it to become an important part of our self-identity and for it to inspire loathing of those who stand outside its boundaries.

Another objection to this argument might be that sports are, well, sports. They are competition distilled to its purest form. They construct a world where for one side to win the other must lose. It's unfair to compare that with politics, isn't it?

Politics is a team sport

In 2015, Patrick R. Miller and Pamela Johnston Conover published a paper entitled "Red and Blue States of Mind." The paper looks at how Republicans and Democrats—as well as independents who lean toward one party or the other—act during elections. What motivates them? What do they feel? What drives them to participate? "The behavior of partisans resembles that of sports team members acting to preserve the status of their teams rather than thoughtful citizens participating in the political process for the broader good," the paper concludes.[13] Yikes.

The authors tested behavior in two stages. In the first, they looked at partisan action through the prism of feelings of anger toward, and rivalry with, the other party. Using mountains of survey data and pre- and postelection polling of the same groups, they tested the effect issue positions, ideology, age, education, political knowledge, church attendance, gender, partisan identity, race, and more had on a person's likelihood of feeling fury and competition in the midst of an election.

They found that while high-minded factors like policy ideas and ideology played some role in how partisans felt, the over-whelming driver was the strength of partisan identity. "Elections accentuate the team mentality of party identifiers, pushing them repeatedly to make 'us-them' comparisons between Democrats and Republicans that draw attention to what will be lost—status— if the election is not won," write Miller and Conover. "This results in both rivalry and anger."

The next question Miller and Conover considered was whether those feelings led to actions. So they ran a similar test, looking at how the same host of political forces, identities, and ideas drove a Republican or Democrat's likelihood of helping on a campaign or actually turning out to vote. Here, again, partisan identity dominated when compared to abstractions like issue positions or ideology. But then Miller and Conover did something inter-esting: they asked people to reflect on how much anger, rivalry, and incivility they felt toward the other side. Once they added those answers into their data, the effect of every other political factor plummeted.

How we feel matters much more than what we think, and in elections, the feelings that matter most are often our feelings about the other side. Negative partisanship rears its head again.

The big picture that emerges from this paper is that the people actually driving elections—the people knocking on doors, working for campaigns, and turning out to vote—are driven more by group rivalry than by tax policy. Miller and Conover are crisp on this point: "When partisans endure meetings, plant yard signs, write checks, and spend endless hours volunteering, what is likely foremost in their minds is that they are furious with the opposing party and want intensely to avoid losing to it—not a specific issue agenda. They are fired up team members on a mission to defeat the other team."

A 2016 Pew survey backed up these findings and their centrality to politics.[14] Among Republicans, moving from a "mostly unfavorable" view of the Democratic Party to a "very unfavorable" view increased the likelihood of regular voting by 12 points. By contrast, developing a deeper affection for the Republican Party increased regular voting among Republicans by only 6 points. Democrats didn't show the same effect—increases in negative and positive partisanship drove voting at similar rates.

But the data turned even starker as Pew moved up the ladder of engagement. When Republicans were asked whether they had contributed money to a candidate or group in the past few years, a very unfavorable view of Democrats raised the likelihood by 11 points, while a very favorable view of Republicans increased it by only 3. Among Democrats, a very unfavorable view of Republicans increased it by 8 points, while a very favorable view of their own party didn't increase it at all.

All of this points toward an important principle: the most-engaged experience politics differently than everyone else. In the previous chapter I mentioned the book *Open versus Closed*, which finds that the least-engaged voters tend to look at politics through the lens of material self-interest ("what will this policy do for me?") while the most-engaged look at politics through the lens of identity ("what does support for this policy position say about me?").

This helps illuminate a long-running debate, particularly on the left, about whether working class voters who pull the lever for Republicans are betraying their self-interest in voting for a party that will cut taxes on the rich and break the unions that protect the poor. What Johnston, Lavine, and Federico find is that as people become more involved and invested in politics, the "self-interest" they're looking to satisfy changes. It's a mistake to imagine our bank accounts are the only reasonable drivers of political action. As we become more political, we become more interested in politics as a means of self-expression and group identity. "It is not that citizens are unable to recognize their interests," they write, "rather, it is that material concerns are often irrelevant to the individual's goals when forming a policy opinion."[15]

Politicians, of course, are not equally responsive to all their constituents. They are most concerned about the most engaged: the people who will vote for them, volunteer for them, donate to them. And the way to make more of that kind of voter isn't just to focus on how great you are. It's to focus on how bad the other side is. Nothing brings a group together like a common enemy. Remove the fury and fear of a real opponent, and watch the enthusiasm drain from your supporters.

In 2017, Texas congressman Beto O'Rourke launched a long-shot Senate bid against Ted Cruz, one of the Democratic Party's bêtes noires. O'Rourke's candidacy was a sensation. He raised the most money ever recorded for a Senate race. He packed rafters, went viral. On Election Day, Beyoncé posted a photo on

Instagram, wearing a Beto hat. O'Rourke lost by three points, but the groundswell of support convinced him to run for president. He entered the Democratic 2020 primary with great fanfare and big fund-raising numbers, but he quickly plummeted in the polls. Strategic mistakes explain some of his struggles, but O'Rourke was the same candidate, and the same man, in 2019 as in 2018. The catalytic ingredient in his Senate campaign was liberal loathing of Cruz, the thrill that he might be defeated. When O'Rourke was running against other Democrats, his personal charisma failed to recapture the magic of his Senate race.

This is not to take away from the political power of inspiration. The most effective politicians thrill their supporters. But they do so in the context of the threat their opponents pose. And as politicians become less well-known and capable on the stump, they rely more and more heavily on activating fear of the other side.

The lesson is known by politicians the world over. You don't just need support. You need anger. That's why fund-raising emails often border on the apocalyptic (a few of the recent subject lines in the emails I've received from the Republican National Committee, in support of Trump's reelection campaign: "FAKE NEWS!" "AMERICANS MUST FIGHT BACK!" and my personal favorite, "FW: STOLEN?"—caps lock in the original, of course). It's why Trump is always fighting with the media. It's why presidential candidates find it hard to keep their supporters engaged when they win the White House—the terror of losing an election is more viscerally motivating than the compromises of daily governance.

What all this suggests is that one of the most important questions in American politics is how strong our group identities are—how much we feel we belong to one team and how much we fear losing to the other team.

But what if it's not just one team we belong to? What if it's many teams, and what if all those teams begin working together?

Identities politic

In 2004, Barack Obama gave that rarest of things: a speech that literally changed the course of American history. If John Kerry hadn't tapped Obama to keynote the Democratic National Convention, Obama wouldn't have become a national political superstar while still an Illinois state senator. If he hadn't become a national political superstar, he wouldn't have run for president in his first term as US senator. And if he hadn't run for president, well, you get the point.

That speech wasn't just a neat bit of rhetoric. It was an argument about the structure of polarization. "Even as we speak, there are those who are preparing to divide us," he said, "the spin masters and negative ad peddlers who embrace the politics of anything goes." Notice the rhetorical move Obama makes. We are not divided. We can only *be* divided. The polarizers are out there. We are their victims, our disagreements their product. He goes on to deny their dark arts, to argue that the country is not what they make us think it is. "There's not a liberal America and a conservative America—there's the United States of America," he says. "There's not a black America and white America and Latino America and Asian America; there's the United States of America." And as for "the pundits [who] like to slice-and-dice our country into Red States and Blue States"—that would be me, I fear—Obama had news for them: "We worship an awesome God in the Blue States, and we don't like federal agents poking around our libraries in the Red States."

Of every politician I have covered, of every politician I have met, Obama is the most thoughtful and reflective, the best at seeing American politics with historical perspective and analytical altitude. His position on this was considered. He didn't just dislike polarization; he doubted it. And why wouldn't he? If you were a skinny black kid with the middle name Hussein who shot from state senate to president of the United States in four years flat, wouldn't you? His life story was, itself, a rebuttal of polarization's coarse logic. This was the secret to his political success. He could speak to the best in America because he believed the best of America. He was like the friend who looked at you and saw the version of yourself you wanted to be.

But the paradox of Obama's political career is that he himself was a polarizing figure. In 2015, I interviewed him in the White House. By that point, he was the most polarizing president in the history of polling, breaking the record George W. Bush had set before him and that Bill Clinton had set before Bush (the crown now belongs to Trump, in case you were wondering). I believe Obama had sincerely tried to pursue a politics that he thought would foster compromise or at least understanding. But he had failed. So I asked him what advice he would give his successor about tamping down on polarization—a question that rings with dark irony today, given the way Trump pursues polarization as an explicit political strategy. Even so, I've struggled with Obama's answer in the years since.

"There are a couple of things that in my mind, at least, contribute to our politics being more polarized than people actually are," Obama said. "And I think most people just sense this in their daily lives. Everybody's got a family member or a really good friend from high school who is on the complete opposite side of the political spectrum. And yet, we still love them, right? Everybody goes to a soccer game, or watching their kids, coaching, and they see parents who they think are wonderful people, and then if they made a comment about politics, suddenly they'd go, 'I can't believe you think that!' "[16]

Obama's point here is that our political identities are not our only identities. And our other identities—Little League coach, PTA member, parent—are a lot less polarized than our political identities. Take me. I am an American, Jewish, Caucasian, male, Californian. My father is a Brazilian immigrant, so I care deeply about immigration, feel a familial attachment to Brazil, and find it relaxing to listen to English spoken in a Portuguese accent. I'm a husband, a father, and a dog owner, and you can activate any of those identities by criticizing my wife or my son or praising cats. I lived in Washington, DC, for fifteen years and tend to get defensive when others criticize it. I'm a journalist who is critical of my profession but protective of it when challenged. I'm a vegan, and because I think animal suffering is important and horribly ignored, I try to be at least somewhat strident about it.

Then there are the parts of my personality that seem like preferences but can act like identities when challenged. I grew up using Apple computers, and I remember spending endless time arguing their superiority to PCs, in ways that far outstripped the importance of the question.*[17] I dislike Manhattan, and that dislike comes out particularly strongly when people praise Manhattan as superior to places I've lived and love, which people in Manhattan do *all the damn time.* I'm an anxious person, and that's become,

---

* I am not alone in this, as the Verge's feature "Fanboys" reveals:

Anytime anybody in the universe says something negative about Microsoft, Brad Thorne loses it. He fires up Twitter: "You're fucking pathetic! . . . You have your head so far up your ass! . . . I can't wait until you eat your smug words!"

Thorne, a fortyish IT manager with a preppy wardrobe and shy grin, is actually a nice guy in person. He plays golf and enjoys spending time with his wife and step kids. He works as an IT director at a nonprofit charity organization in the South that's run by nuns. He is not religious—unless you count his relationship with Microsoft, of course.

"I'm a missionary," says Thorne. "For me, it's about being super passionate and super knowledgeable about their products, and not leaving that passion at the door when you leave work. You preach it all the time."

over time, part of how I understand myself, not just something I feel. I mention these not because they're as powerful as, say, fatherhood is for me, but because the line between what is and isn't an identity is fuzzier than we often think. If you don't believe me, spend some time watching television commercials and ask yourself whether they're advertising products or identities.

All of these are identities that can be called forth in me on a moment's notice. Some of them are strong identities that I could imagine driving me to violence if sufficiently threatened. Some of them are weak identities I could imagine being persuaded to abandon. Some situate me in a certain political camp. Others cross all boundaries. But they are all in me, simultaneously, and they interact in powerful and unpredictable ways.

Obama argued that polarized media, gerrymandering, and the flood of political money tended to balkanize us into our political identities. "So my advice to a future president," he said, "is increasingly try to bypass the traditional venues that create divisions and try to find new venues within this new media that are quirkier, less predictable."[18]

Obama was offering the right explanation for polarization from the wrong angle. He's right that it's all about which identities get activated, and he's right that our political identities are more polarized than our other identities. But he was too optimistic in believing that our nonpolitical identities could become our political identities, that they were somehow a truer reflection of our essential selves, and thus strong enough to overwhelm our partisan divisions. In practice, our political identities are polarizing our other identities, too.

In her book *Uncivil Agreement*, Lilliana Mason sums up the state of American politics—and perhaps American life—in a single, searing paragraph.

The American political parties are growing socially polarized. Religion and race, as well as class, geography, and culture, are dividing the parties in such a way that the effect of party identity is magnified. The competition is no longer between only Democrats and Republicans. A single vote can now indicate a person's partisan preference *as well as* his or her religion, race, ethnicity, gender, neighborhood, and favorite grocery store. This is no longer a single social identity. Partisanship can now be thought of as a mega-identity, with all the psychological and behavioral magnifications that implies.[19]

Up until now, I've largely talked about the polarization of American politics in terms of its objective demographic and ideological dimensions. The key point Mason is making, though, is that those traits also operate as identities, and in coming together, they fuse into a single sense of self. Living in a city, being a liberal, shopping at Trader Joe's, and dabbling in Zen meditation may not have much to do with one another in terms of public policy, but they reinforce a singular identity, and that identity is political, or at least easily politicized.

In 2004, the Club for Growth, a conservative interest group that advocates for lower taxes and deregulation, ran a famous ad against then presidential candidate Howard Dean. In the ad, an older white couple is stopped outside a shop with patriotic bunting and asked about Dean's plan to raise taxes.

"What do I think?" the man replies. "Well, I think Howard Dean should take his tax-hiking, government-expanding, latte-drinking, sushi-eating, Volvo-driving, *New York Times*-reading—" Then his wife cuts in: "Body-piercing, Hollywood-loving, left-wing freak show back to Vermont, where it belongs." And that, my friends, is pure, uncut mega-identity politics.[20]

You can see, in that riff, the way political identity transcends mere partisanship. You may be a democratic socialist living in Berkeley, California, who dismisses Democrats as spineless corporatists. But you know that ad is an attack on you, anyway. Once you begin looking for weaponization of seemingly nonpolitical identity markers, you find them everywhere. I began this book trying to persuade you that something in American politics has changed, that though we still use the terms "Democrat" and "Republican" and "liberal" and "conservative," our cleavages are different and deeper. This is what has changed. Our political identities have become political mega-identities. The merging of the identities means when you activate one you often activate all, and each time they're activated, they strengthen.

Obama used the example of Americans together at a soccer game. To shift it a bit, what about Americans together at a football game? That's one of those nice, depolarized identities. At least it was. But then some of the football players, led by 49ers quarterback Colin Kaepernick, began kneeling during the national anthem to protest police violence. Trump took up the case, tweeting that they should be fired. Democrats began defending them. Kaepernick was cut, and despite stats that should've gotten him a job on another team, no one would touch him (he later sued the NFL). In response, *GQ* made Kaepernick its citizen of the year.

There is nothing intrinsically liberal about football. But after Kaepernick's protest became a national flash point, the NFL polarized. Before the controversy, about 60 percent of both Clinton and Trump voters viewed the NFL favorably. Amid the controversy, the NFL's favorability among Clinton voters was unchanged, but its favorability among Trump voters plummeted to 30 percent and disapproval spiked to over 60 percent. Nike then made Kaepernick its new spokesman, even though he was no longer playing football professionally. In response, Trump supporters burned Nike gear, and Trump tweeted, "Just like the NFL, whose ratings have gone WAY DOWN, Nike is getting absolutely killed with anger and boycotts."[21]

Football fandom used to be an identity that cut across politics. Democrats liked the sport. Republicans liked the sport. Even I, sports hater that I am, played nose tackle in high school. But when the NFL came into contact with politics, it became part of politics. Rather than a shared loved of football pulling our political identities toward compromise, our political identities polarized our love of football. Intense supporters are catnip for brands, so Nike jumped into the fray, purposefully polarizing one of the biggest clothing brands in the world. And football fandom became, at least for a while, one more magnet in the political identity stack, attracting those on the Left and repelling those on the Right.

When we share identities with each other, they can act as a bridge. You're a '90s kid and I'm a '90s kid, so let's talk about how the '90s were the best decade for music. But when our identities separate us from each other, they can be a moat, widening the distance between us. In 2002, psychologists Marilynn Brewer and Sonia Roccas showed that people with a lot of crosscutting identities tended to be more tolerant of outsiders than people with highly aligned identities.[22] The insight here makes sense: the more your identities converge on a single point, the more your identities can be threatened simultaneously, and that makes conflict much more threatening.

Imagine two Democrats. One of them, Rick, is white, straight, and conservative. He attends an evangelical church, lives in a rural area, and belongs to a union. The other, Sarah, is black, gay, and liberal. She's skeptical of religion, lives in Los Angeles, and identifies as a feminist. Rick, looking at the candidacy of George

W. Bush, would find some of his identities under threat—Bush is a Republican and hostile to unions—but other identities would modulate his panic: like him, Bush is an evangelical Christian, a white man, a conservative, respectful of rural culture. John Kerry, meanwhile, is a pro-union Democrat, but he's also a liberal urbanite who evinced little understanding of rural America or the evangelical church. This is the kind of Democrat who would at least have considered voting for Bush.

Sarah, by contrast, would look at Bush and see all her identities under threat simultaneously: he's a Republican, an evangelical, a white man, a conservative. He shows little respect for urban life, for atheists, and he backed a constitutional amendment to ban gay marriages. This is the kind of Democrat who would fear Bush, who would see him as a genuine danger to her life, who would do almost anything to see him defeated. This is the kind of Democrat who would volunteer for Kerry's campaign, who would donate money, who would seek out harshly anti-Bush punditry and believe it easily.

Thus, though it seems that lots of different divisions would tear apart a society, it turns out that creating one bigger, deeper division—a mega-division—is more dangerous. Mason quotes the founder of American sociology Edward Alsworth Ross, writing in *The Principles of Sociology*, on this point:

> The chief oppositions which occur in society are between individuals, sexes, ages, races, nationalities, sections, classes, political parties and religious sects. Several such may be in full swing at the same time, but the more numerous they are the less menacing is any one. Every species of conflict interferes with every other species in society at the same time, save only when their lines of cleavage coincide; in which case they rein-force one another. . . . A society, therefore, which is riven by a

dozen oppositions along lines running in every direction, may actually be in less danger of being torn with violence or falling to pieces than one split along just one line.[23]

This isn't just theory. A 2012 study by Joshua Gubler and Joel Sawat Selway surveyed data from more than one hundred countries and found that civil war is "an average of nearly twelve times less probable in societies where ethnicity is cross-cut by socio-economic class, geographic region and religion."[24]

One way to read this data is it's just another way of describing policy disagreement. As our identities diverge, our worldview and agendas diverge, so all this is just a proportional response to deepening differences in self-interest. There's certainly some of that, but as Tajfel found long ago, and as sports fans show every weekend, much of our hostility is a pure expression of how we instinctively treat out-groups—it doesn't need policy differences to catalyze it.

Mason tested this directly. Using American National Election Studies survey data, she looked at what made people likely to rate the other party higher or lower on a "feelings thermometer" that went from 1 to 100, where 1 was the coldest you could feel toward the other party and 100 was the warmest. Cleverly, she cut the data to see self-identified Republicans whose policy views should've made them Democrats. They gave the Republican Party a rating of between 60 and 70 and the Democratic Party a rating between 30 and 50. As for Democrats with conservative policy positions, they rated the Democratic Party between 60 and 80 and gave the Republican Party between a 30 and 50.

Interestingly, it turns out that there's only a weak relationship between how much a person identifies as a conservative or liberal and how conservative or liberal their views actually are—to be exact, in both cases it's about a .25 correlation. One reason policy is not the driver of political disagreement is most people don't have very strong views about policy. It's the rare hobbyist who thinks often about cybersecurity and who should lead the Federal Reserve. But all of us are experts on our own identities.

Over and again, Mason finds that identity is far more powerful than issue positions in driving polarization. All else equal, if you compare people with the most moderate policy positions with those with the most crosscutting identities, the policy moderates will be more than twice as unfriendly to the other party as those whose crossed identities are restraining their partisanship. That is to say, feeling closer to the other side in identity does more to calm dislike than feeling closer to the other side on policy.

"This is the American identity crisis," Mason writes. "Not that we have partisan identities, we've always had those. The crisis emerges when partisan identities fall into alignment with other social identities, stoking our intolerance of each other to levels that are unsupported by our degrees of political disagreement."[25]

The stakes of politics, of course, are very real: fights over tax dollars, whether to go to war, whether to recognize same-sex marriages, whether to pass a universal health-care bill. But those are stakes that we have to do a lot of thinking and learning to connect to. They are stakes that exist in the more recently evolved parts of our brain, stakes we must work to feel. Viscerally and emotionally, the stakes of politics we have evolved to sense is whether our group is winning or losing, whether the out-group is gaining the power to threaten us or whether our allies are amassing the strength to ensure our safety and prosperity. As our many identities merge into single political mega-identities, those visceral, emotional stakes are rising—and with them, our willingness to do anything to make sure our side wins.

"Political identity is fair game for hatred"

Shanto Iyengar is director of Stanford University's Political Communication Laboratory, and he had noticed something odd. In
1960, Americans were asked whether they would be pleased, dis-
pleased, or unmoved if their son or daughter married a member
of the other political party. Respondents reacted with a shrug.
Only 5 percent of Republicans and 4 percent of Democrats said
they would be upset by the cross-party union. On the list of things
you might care about in a child's partner—are they kind, smart,
successful, supportive?—which political party they voted for just
didn't rate.

Fast-forward to 2008. The polling firm YouGov asked Republicans and Democrats the same question—and got very different
results. This time, 27 percent of Republicans and 20 percent of
Democrats said they would be upset if their son or daughter
married a member of the opposite party. In 2010, YouGov asked
the question again; this time, 49 percent of Republicans and 33
percent of Democrats professed concern at interparty marriage.

The numbers suggested to Iyengar that today's political differences were fundamentally different from yesterday's political
differences; the nature of American political partisanship, he
worried, was mutating into something more fundamental, and
more irreconcilable, than what it had been in the past.

If he was right, then party affiliation wasn't simply an expression of our disagreements; it was also becoming the cause of
them. If Democrats thought of other Democrats as their group
and of Republicans as a hostile out-group, and vice versa, then
the consequences would stretch far beyond politics—into things
like, say, marriage.

And the data was everywhere. Polls looking at the difference between how Republicans viewed Democrats and how Democrats viewed Republicans now showed that partisans were less accepting of each other than white people were of black people or than black people were of white people.

But there was no way partisanship—an identity we choose and sometimes change—could possibly have become a cleavage in American life as deep as race, right? That seemed crazy. So Iyengar decided to test it.

The experiment was simple. Working with Dartmouth College political scientist Sean Westwood, Iyengar asked about a thousand people to decide between the résumés of two high school seniors who were competing for a scholarship. The résumés could differ in three ways: first, the senior could have either a 3.5 or 4.0 GPA; second, the senior could have been the president of the Young Democrats or Young Republicans club; third, the senior could have a stereotypically African American name and have been president of the African American Student Association or could have a stereotypically Caucasian name. The point of the project was to see whether political hostility affected a nonpolitical task and to compare the effect with race.

I've read a lot of studies in the course of researching this book, but this one still surprises me. When the résumé included a political identity cue, about 80 percent of Democrats and Republicans awarded the scholarship to their copartisan. This held true whether or not the copartisan had the higher GPA—when the Republican student was more qualified, Democrats chose him only 30 percent of the time, and when the Democrat was more qualified, Republicans chose him only 15 percent of the time.

That is a profound finding: when awarding a college scholarship—a task that should be completely nonpolitical—Republicans and Democrats cared more about the political party of the student than the student's GPA. As Iyengar and Westwood wrote, "Partisanship simply trumped academic excellence."[26]

Remarkably, in this study, partisanship even trumped race. When the candidates were equally qualified, about 78 percent of African Americans chose the candidate of the same race, as did 42 percent of white Americans. When the candidate of the other race had a higher GPA, 45 percent of African Americans chose him, as did 71 percent of white Americans.

Iyengar's hypothesis is that partisan animosity is one of the few forms of discrimination that contemporary American society not only permits but actively encourages. "Political identity is fair game for hatred," he says. "Racial identity is not. Gender identity is not. You cannot express negative sentiments about social groups in this day and age. But political identities are not protected by these constraints. A Republican is someone who chooses to be Republican, so I can say whatever I want about them."[27]

You can see an example when you look at the media, Westwood observes. There are no major cable channels devoted to making people of other races look bad (though Tucker Carlson and Laura Ingraham get pretty close sometimes). But there are cable channels that are devoted to making members of the other party look bad. "The media has become tribal leaders," he says. "They're telling the tribe how to identify and behave, and we're following along."[28]

Westwood is quick to note that the comparison to racism doesn't mean that partisanship is somehow worse than racism, more pervasive, or more damaging. It's easier to see—and thus discriminate—against people based on their skin color than their partisanship, for instance. Moreover, political beliefs are a choice with moral implications while race is not. Judging someone on whether they support gay marriage, universal health care, or gun laws is far different from judging someone on the color of their skin.

Still, Iyengar and Westwood's research is a fundamental challenge to the way we like to believe American politics works. A world where we won't give an out-party high schooler with a better GPA a nonpolitical scholarship is not a world in which we're going to listen to politicians on the other side of emotional, controversial issues—even if they're making good arguments that are backed by the facts.

Iyengar and Westwood's research is confirmation of the way Tajfel thought people worked: here, again, we have people in a room, sorted by identities with no relationship to the task at hand, and using what power they have to reward the in-group and punish the out-group. "The old theory was political parties came into existence to represent deep social cleavages," Iyengar says. "But now party politics has taken on a life of its own—now it *is* the cleavage."[29]

A life of its own. It reminds me of something else Tajfel wrote, way back in 1970. Social scientists had created a distinction between "rational" and "irrational" forms of group conflict. As Tajfel described it, "the former is a means to an end: the conflict and the attitudes that go with it reflect a genuine competition between groups with divergent interests. The latter is an end in itself: it serves to release accumulated emotional tensions of various kinds." But, Tajfel went on to say, the distinction between the two kinds of hostility was less clear than his profession thought, because "they reinforce each other in a relentless spiral."[30]

This is, I think, the best way to understand the relationship between policy differences and identity conflict: they're mutually reinforcing, not opposed. Take immigration. Hispanics have become a more powerful and central part of the Democratic coalition. That's partly why Obama made the decision to protect law-abiding Dreamers from deportation. That decision, which angered many Republicans, is part of what opened space for

Trump to run an insurgent primary campaign heavy on anti-immigrant, pro-white rhetoric. In office, Trump has pushed a raft of anti-immigrant policies—including canceling Obama's protections for Dreamers—which has both offended Democrats on a moral level and pushed Hispanics yet more into the Democratic column, making them more powerful in the Democratic Party.

As a result, Democrats have increasingly united behind both pro-immigrant policies and pro-immigrant values—to the extent that most of the 2020 presidential candidates endorsed decriminalizing unauthorized border crossing and giving undocumented immigrants access to public health insurance, both unthinkable policies in the Democratic Party even a few years earlier. Behind the endorsement of these ideas is the Democrats' changing identity as a party that believes in diversity and welcomes immigrants, both documented and undocumented, as woven into the American narrative.

In 2019, I interviewed Julián Castro, the former secretary of housing and urban development, who was then running for president. "I see undocumented immigrants as being a part of the American story for generations, including this generation," Castro told me. "I see them as integral to building a strong future for the country. I always talk about the fact that, in many ways, we need undocumented immigrants, whether we want to admit it or not."[31]

What might have started as a limited question of immigration policy has become central to the conflict between the two parties. It's not just about what the coalitions want to do; it's about who they are, what they believe, who counts as their "we."

But identity doesn't just shape how we treat each other. It shapes how we understand the world.

Chapter 4

The Press Secretary
in Your Mind

The individual mandate made its political debut in a 1989 Heritage Foundation brief titled "Assuring Affordable Health Care for All Americans," as a counterpoint to the single-payer system and the employer mandate that were favored in Democratic circles. In the brief, Stuart Butler, the conservative think tank's health-care expert, argued, "Many states now require passengers in automobiles to wear seatbelts for their own protection. Many others require anybody driving a car to have liability insurance. But neither the federal government nor any state requires all households to protect themselves from the potentially catastrophic costs of a serious accident or illness. Under the Heritage plan, there would be such a requirement."[1]

In 1991, Milton Friedman, the legendary conservative economist, wrote a *Wall Street Journal* op-ed proposing "a requirement that every U.S. family unit have a major medical insurance policy."[2] Mark Pauly, an economist at the Wharton School, tried to persuade George H. W. Bush's administration to adopt an individual mandate because, he told me, "we were concerned about the specter of single payer insurance, which isn't market-oriented."[3]

The mandate made its first legislative appearance in 1993, in the Health Equity and Access Reform Today Act—the Senate Republicans' alternative to President Clinton's health reform bill—which was sponsored by John Chafee of Rhode Island and cosponsored by eighteen Republicans, including Bob Dole, who was then the Senate minority leader. "I was the one who came up with the idea to put it in the bill," Christine Ferguson, who directed Chafee's health policy team in the 1990s and would go on to lead Mitt Romney's Department of Public Health in Massachusetts, told me. "The Republicans had decided we'd need to put a bill together on our own. I was hearing all kinds of conversations on the Republican side about personal responsibility and how Republicans weren't nannies, and that really resonated with me. And so I said that if our concern was we want personal responsibility, why don't we say individuals have to take it up and the cost, if it's prohibitive, should have some kind of subsidy?"[4]

After the Clinton bill, which called for an employer mandate, failed, Democrats came to recognize the opportunity that the Chafee bill had presented. In *The System: The American Way of Politics at the Breaking Point*, Haynes Johnson and David Broder's history of the health-care wars of the nineties, Clinton concedes that it was the best chance he had of reaching a bipartisan compromise. "It should have been right then, or the day after they presented their bill, where I should have tried to have a direct understanding with Dole," he said.[5]

Ten years later, Senator Ron Wyden, an Oregon Democrat, began picking his way back through the history—he read *The System* four times—and he, too, came to focus on the Chafee bill. He began building a proposal around the individual mandate and tested it out on both Democrats and Republicans. "Between 2004 and 2008, I saw over eighty members of the Senate, and there were very few who objected," Wyden told me.[6] In December 2006, he unveiled the Healthy Americans Act. In May 2007, Bob Bennett, a Utah Republican who had been a sponsor of the Chafee bill, joined him.

Wyden-Bennett was eventually cosponsored by eleven Republicans and nine Democrats, receiving more bipartisan support than any universal health-care proposal in the history of the Senate. It even caught the eye of the Republican presidential aspirants. In a June 2009 interview on *Meet the Press*, Romney, who, as governor of Massachusetts, had signed a universal health-care bill with an individual mandate, said that Wyden-Bennett was a plan "that a number of Republicans think is a very good health-care plan—one that we support."[7]

Wyden's bill was part of a broader trend of Democrats endorsing the individual mandate in their own proposals. John Edwards and Hillary Clinton both built a mandate into their campaign health-care proposals. In 2008, Senator Ted Kennedy brought John McDonough, a liberal advocate of the Massachusetts plan, to Washington to help with health-care reform. That same year, Max Baucus, the chairman of the Senate Finance Committee, included an individual mandate in the first draft of his health-care bill. The main Democratic holdout was Senator Barack Obama. But by July 2009, President Obama had changed his mind. "I was opposed to this idea because my general attitude was the reason people don't have health insurance is not because they don't want it. It's because they can't afford it," he told CBS News. "I am now in favor of some sort of individual mandate."[8]

This process led, eventually, to the Patient Protection and Affordable Care Act—better known as Obamacare—which also included an individual mandate. The bill was designed to be a compromise proposal, and for a time, it looked like it was. In June 2009, Senator Chuck Grassley, then the top Republican on the powerful Senate Finance Committee, told Fox News, "I believe that there is a bipartisan consensus to have individual mandates."[9]

And then something went wrong. In December 2009, every single Senate Republican voted for a point of order calling the individual mandate "unconstitutional." Among them were Senators Bob Bennett, Lamar Alexander, Bob Corker, Mike Crapo, Lindsey Graham, Chuck Grassley, and Judd Gregg—all of whom were cosponsors of the Healthy Americans Act, which, again, *included an individual mandate*. There were no revolutions in constitutional law between January 2007 and December 2009. Nor did the individual mandate show itself to be fatally flawed in some particular way. Quite the opposite, in fact. It was being successfully implemented in Massachusetts as part of Romney's reforms.

But there had been a political change: Democrats had gone from opposing the mandate to supporting it. This shift—Democrats lining up behind the Republican-crafted mandate, and Republicans declaring it not just inappropriate policy but contrary to the wishes of the Founders—shocked Wyden. "I would characterize the Washington, D.C., relationship with the individual mandate as truly schizophrenic," he said.[10]

It was not an isolated case. In 2007, both Newt Gingrich and John McCain wanted a cap-and-trade program in order to reduce carbon emissions. A few years later, the entire party—including them—turned against the idea. In 2008, the Bush administration proposed, pushed, and signed the Economic Stimulus Act, a deficit-financed tax cut designed to boost the flagging economy. Under Obama, Republicans became staunch opponents of the idea that deficit-financed stimulus could help an economy, before re-embracing the idea under Trump. When Romney ran for president in 2012, he was mocked by Democrats for saying that Russia was America's foremost geopolitical threat; after Russia helped Trump win the 2016 presidential election, Democrats turned sharply against Russia, while Republicans came to view Vladimir Putin more favorably than they viewed Obama.[11]

There's an easy explanation for this: cynicism. Hypocrisy. Lying. And when we see it happening in others—particularly in an out-group—that's what we assume. But I've interviewed enough politicians, activists, and pundits who have changed their position alongside their party to know that it often feels sincere, at least to them. Hell, I've changed my mind and been accused of insincerity, or at least inconsistency. "Life comes at you fast!" read the gotcha tweets. But my mental processes always feel honest to me. After all, isn't changing our minds in response to new information and arguments what we're supposed to do? What separates political opportunism from intellectual growth?

Turns out the answer is: not much. We understand reasoning to be an individual act. This is, in many cases, wrong. "The central flaw in the concept of reason that animated the eighteenth-century Enlightenment is that it is entirely individualistic," writes philosopher Joseph Heath.[12] But decades of research has proven that "reason is both decentralized and dispersed across multiple individuals. It is not possible to be rational all by yourself; rationality is inherently a collective project."*

Put more simply: reasoning is something we often do in groups, in order to serve group ends. This is not a wrinkle of human irrationality, but rather a rational response to the complexity and danger of the world around us. Collectively, a group can know more and reason better than an individual, and thus human beings with the social and intellectual skills to pool knowledge had a survival advantage over those who didn't. We are their

---

* I find that people often react defensively to critiques of human reasoning faculties. This seems . . . unreasonable. As Heath argues in the book, the fact that we are not perfectly rational—the fact that our capacities for rationality seem to have evolved as a by-product of other capabilities, like language—underscores how precious the ability to reason is and how attentive we must be to its development. Mapping its boundaries so we can consciously remain within its jurisdiction is part of how we respect this gift, not a dismissal of it.

descendants. Once you understand that, the ease with which individuals, even informed individuals, flip their positions to fit the group's needs makes a lot more sense.

Reasoning in groups

In 1951, Solomon Asch, a professor at Swarthmore College, set out to study exactly how much of our reasoning we were willing to outsource to others. He showed subjects a card with a line and then asked them to match it to the line of corresponding length on another card. The test was easy. Under control conditions, fewer than 1 percent of the answers were wrong.[13]

The twist, however, was that the subjects weren't alone. There were also five to seven other participants who were actually working for Asch. And every so often, they would all give the same wrong answer. These were called the "critical trials." The results were remarkable: on critical trials, the participants gave the wrong answer 37 percent of the time. Given the choice between what their eyes were telling them and what the group was telling them, they went with the group. "I felt conspicuous, going out on a limb, and subjecting myself to criticism that my perceptions, faculties were not as acute as they might be," said one of the subjects in a post-experiment interview.

Asch's work, which showed the way a group can influence the opinions of an individual, has been the basis for a revolution in understanding not just how humans think, but how partisans think. Because what is a political party, after all, but a group?

In 2003, Geoffrey Cohen, then an assistant professor of psychology at Yale, gave students in an introductory psychology course a survey asking them, among many other questions, to rate how liberal or conservative they were and how strongly they felt about welfare. Then, later in the term, he asked the students who had rated themselves as the most ideological and the most passionate about welfare to come in and participate in a study testing their "memory of everyday current events." The participating students, who didn't know how or why they'd been chosen, were given two newspaper articles. The first was a dummy, which served no purpose other than to "reinforce the plausibility of the cover story." The second article described a proposed welfare policy.[14]

In one version of the article, the policy was extremely generous, offering:

> almost $800 per month to a family with one child, an extra $200 for every additional child, full medical insurance, $2,000 in food stamps, extra subsidies for housing and day care, a job training program, and 2 years of paid tuition at a community college. While it limited benefits to 8 years, it guaranteed a job after benefits ended, and it reinstated aid if the family had another child.

The other version of the article outlined a more spartan policy that "provided only $250 per month and $50 for each additional child. It offered only partial medical insurance, and imposed a lifetime limit of 1.5 years without the possibility of reinstating aid. In contrast to the generous policy, the stringent one provided no food stamps, housing, day care, job training, paid work, or college tuition."

The articles varied in another way, too: their group cues. In the "Democrats favor" variant, the article said that 95 percent of House Democrats favored the policy, while only 10 percent of

House Republicans did. It also included quotes from prominent Democrats saying that the law would "lighten the financial burden on the poor" and accusing Republicans of "victim blaming." In the "Republicans favor" version, the percentages were reversed, and there were quotes from prominent Republicans explaining that the program "provides sufficient coverage . . . without undermining a basic work ethic and sense of personal responsibility."

Participants were then asked to rate their favorability toward the program on a scale of one to seven. These were, remember, students with particularly intense ideologies and particularly strong feelings about welfare policy. But it didn't matter. "For both liberal and conservative participants, the effect of reference group information overrode that of policy content. If their party endorsed it, liberals supported even a harsh welfare program, and conservatives supported even a lavish one."

This kind of thinking is, according to psychologists, unsurprising. Each of us can have firsthand knowledge of just a small number of topics: our jobs, our studies, our personal experiences. But as citizens—and as elected officials—we are routinely asked to make judgments on issues as diverse and as complex as the Iranian nuclear program, the environmental impact of an international oil pipeline, and the likely outcomes of branding China a currency manipulator.

One of the roles that political parties play is helping us navigate these decisions. In theory, we join parties because they share our values and our goals—values and goals that may have been passed on to us by the most important groups in our lives, such as our families and our communities—and we trust that their policy judgments will match the ones we would come up with if we had unlimited time to study the issues. But parties, though based on a set of principles, aren't disinterested teachers in search of truth. They're organized groups looking to increase their power. Or, as the psychologists would put it, their reasoning may be motivated by something other than accuracy.

None of this, of course, describes you, dear reader. You're the kind of person who buys books like, well, this one. People who don't pay much attention to politics or know much about policy might use parties as shortcuts and be vulnerable to their deceptions. But knowledge is power, and you have the knowledge. The question is simply how to get everyone else that knowledge, too. Right?

This ladders up to a broader theory for fixing American politics. I can't tell you how many times I've been cornered by someone arguing that the answer to our problems is lifelong civic education or media literacy classes. This can take more extreme forms, too. In 2016, Georgetown University political theorist Jason Brennan released a book entitled *Against Democracy*, in which he argued for an "epistocracy," a system where the votes of the politically informed counted more than the votes of the politically naive.[15] "I call this the 'competence principle,'" he said in an interview with Vox. "The idea is that anyone or any deliberative body that exercises power over anyone else has an obligation to use that power in good faith, and has the obligation to use that power competently. If they're not going to use it in good faith, and they're not going to use it competently, that's a claim against them having any kind of authority or any kind of legitimacy."[16]

We might call this the "more information" hypothesis. In its less aggressive manifestation, it sits hopefully at the base of almost every speech, every op-ed, every article, and every panel discussion. It courses through the Constitution and the Federalist papers, through the philosophies of Thomas Dewey and the basic theory of high school government classes. It's the belief that many of our most bitter political battles, and most of our worst political thinking, are mere misunderstandings. The cause of these misunderstandings? Too little information—be it about climate change, taxes, Iraq, the budget deficit, or immigration. If only the citizenry were more informed, the thinking goes, then there wouldn't be all this fighting.

It's a seductive model. It suggests our fellow countrymen aren't wrong so much as they're misguided, ignorant, or—most appealingly—deceived by scoundrels from the other party. It holds that our debates are tractable and that the answers to our toughest problems aren't very controversial at all. The theory is particularly prevalent in Washington, where partisans devote enormous amounts of energy to persuading each other that there is a right answer to the difficult questions in American politics— and that they have it.

The only problem is it's wrong.

How politics makes smart people stupid

In April and May 2013, Yale Law professor Dan Kahan—working with coauthors Ellen Peters, Erica Cantrell Dawson, and Paul Slovic—set out to test a question that consistently puzzles scientists: Why isn't good data more effective in resolving political debates? For instance, why doesn't the overwhelming evidence that climate change is a real threat persuade more skeptics? The leading theory, Kahan and his coauthors wrote, is the "science comprehension thesis," which says the problem is that the public doesn't know enough about science to judge the debate.[17] It's a version of the "more information" hypothesis: a smarter, better-educated citizenry wouldn't have all these problems reading the science and accepting its clear conclusion on climate change.

But Kahan and his team had an alternative hypothesis. Perhaps people aren't held back by a lack of knowledge. After all, they don't typically doubt the findings of oceanographers or the existence of other galaxies. Perhaps there are some kinds of debates where people don't want to find the right answer so much as they want to win the argument. Perhaps humans reason for purposes other than finding the truth—purposes like increasing their standing in their community or ensuring they don't find themselves exiled by the leaders of their tribe. If this hypothesis proved true, then a smarter, better-educated citizenry wouldn't put an end to these disagreements. It would just mean the participants are better equipped to argue for their own side.

Kahan and his team came up with a clever way to test which theory was right. They took one thousand Americans, surveyed their political views, and then gave them a standard test used for assessing math skills. Then they presented them with a brainteaser. In its initial form, the brainteaser was a tricky math problem about how well a skin cream worked; it was designed to deceive you on first glance. If you didn't carefully run the numbers, or didn't have the statistical aptitude needed to run the numbers, you'd get it wrong. As expected, the better subjects were at math, the better they were at the brainteaser. This was true for both liberals and conservatives. Score one for the science comprehension thesis.

But Kahan and his coauthors also drafted a politicized version of the problem, which used the same numbers as the skin-cream question, but instead of being about skin creams, the narrative setup focused on a proposal to ban people from carrying concealed handguns in public. The question now compared crime data in the cities that banned handguns against crime data in the cities that didn't.

Presented with this problem a funny thing happened: how good subjects were at math stopped predicting how well they did on the test. Now it was ideology that drove the answers. Liberals were extremely good at solving the problem when doing so proved that gun-control legislation reduced crime. But when presented with the version of the problem that suggested gun control had failed, their math skills stopped mattering. They tended to get the problem wrong no matter how good they were at math. Conservatives exhibited the same pattern—just in reverse.

Being better at math didn't just fail to help partisans converge on the right answer. It actually drove them further apart. Among those with weak math skills, subjects were 25 percentage points likelier to get the answer right when it bolstered their ideology. But partisans with strong math skills were *45 percentage points* likelier to get the answer right when it fit their ideology. The smarter the person is, the dumber politics can make them.*[18]

I want to dwell on this for a minute, because it's an insane finding: being better at math made partisans *less likely* to solve the problem correctly when solving the problem correctly meant betraying their political instincts. People weren't reasoning to get the right answer; they were reasoning to get the answer that they wanted to be right.

The skin-cream experiment wasn't the first time Kahan had shown that partisanship has a way of short-circuiting intelligence. In another study, he tested people's scientific literacy alongside their ideology and then asked about the risks posed by climate

---

* This effect isn't limited to math, by the way. In their 1991 study "Everyday Reasoning and the Roots of Intelligence," David Perkins, Michael Farady, and Barbara Bushey brought students of different ages and intelligence levels into a lab and asked them their opinion on a complex social issue. Then they asked them to list all the arguments, on both sides of the issue, they could think of. IQ was the single largest predictor of how many arguments people listed, but it correlated only to how many *supporting* arguments they listed. "People invest their IQ in buttressing their own case rather than in exploring the entire issue more fully and evenhandedly," the researchers concluded.

change. If the problem was truly that people needed to know more about science to fully appreciate the dangers of a warming climate, then their concern should've risen alongside their knowledge. But here, too, the opposite was true: among people who were already skeptical of climate change, scientific literacy made them more skeptical of climate change.[19]

This will resonate with anyone who's ever read the work of a serious climate change denialist. It's filled with facts and figures, graphs and charts, studies and citations. Much of the data is wrong or irrelevant. But it feels convincing. It's a terrific performance of scientific inquiry. And climate-change skeptics who immerse themselves in researching counterarguments end up far more confident that global warming is a hoax than people who haven't spent much time studying the issue. This is true for all kinds of things, of course. Ever argued with a 9/11 truther? I have, and they are quite informed about the various melting points of steel. More information can help us find the right answers. But if our search is motivated by aims other than accuracy, more information can mislead us—or, more precisely, help us mislead ourselves. There's a difference between searching for the best evidence and searching for the best evidence that proves us right. And in the age of the internet, such evidence, and such experts, are never very far away.

In another experiment, Kahan and his coauthors gave out sample biographies of highly accomplished scientists alongside a summary of the results of their research. Then they asked whether the scientist was indeed an expert on the issue. It turned out that on highly politicized issues, people's actual definition of "expert" is "a credentialed person who agrees with me." For instance, when the researcher's results underscored the dangers of climate change, people who worry about climate change were 72 percentage points more likely to agree that the researcher was a bona fide expert. When the same researcher with the same credentials was attached to results that cast doubt on the dangers of global warming, people who tended to dismiss climate change were 54 percentage points more likely to see the researcher as an expert.[20]

What's striking here is that the effects are strongest among the voters who pay the closest attention to the issues. In a 2006 paper, "It Feels Like We're Thinking," the political scientists Christopher Achen and Larry Bartels looked at an American National Election Study, a poll supported by the National Science Foundation, from 1996. One of the questions asked whether "the size of the yearly budget deficit increased, decreased, or stayed about the same during Clinton's time as President." The correct answer is that it decreased dramatically. Here, again, more information led to more self-deception. Achen and Bartels categorized the respondents according to how politically informed they were. Among the least-informed respondents, Democrats and Republicans picked the wrong answer in roughly equal numbers. But among better-informed voters the story was different. Republicans who were in the fiftieth percentile gave the right answer more often than those in the ninety-fifth percentile.[21]

Bartels found a similar effect in a 1988 survey, in which "a majority of respondents who described themselves as strong Democrats said that inflation had 'gotten worse' over the eight years of the Reagan administration; in fact, it had fallen from 13.5 percent in 1980 to 4.1 percent in 1988."[22] If you were a lightly informed Republican in the Clinton years or Democrat in the Reagan years, you knew you didn't like the president, and you knew the economy was pretty good. But if you were deep in the partisan literature of the Reagan era, you knew people *thought* the economy was good, but were they paying attention to the budget deficit? Did they realize the tax cuts were going straight to the rich? So, too, in the Clinton era. Elite Republicans could tell you quite a lot about the trade deficit with China or the credit bubble keeping the economy aloft.

At any given moment there are a lot of facts out there and a lot of smart people offering them to you in different configurations. "Even among unusually well-informed and politically engaged people, the political preferences and judgments that look and feel like the bases of partisanship and voting behavior are, in reality, often *consequences* of party and group loyalties," write Achen and Bartels in their book *Democracy for Realists: Why Elections Do Not Produce Responsive Government.* "In fact, the more information the voter has, often the better able she is to bolster her identities with rational-sounding reasons."[23]

Kahan is quick to note that, most of the time, people are perfectly capable of being convinced by the best evidence. There's a lot of disagreement about climate change and gun control, for instance, but almost none over whether antibiotics work, or whether the H_1N_1 flu is a problem, or whether heavy drinking impairs people's ability to drive. Rather, our reasoning becomes rationalizing when we're dealing with questions where the answers could threaten our group—or at least our social standing in our group. And in those cases, Kahan says, we're being perfectly rational when we fool ourselves.

Imagine what would happen to, say, Sean Hannity if he decided tomorrow that climate change was the central threat facing the planet. Initially, his viewers would think he was joking. But soon, they'd begin calling in furiously. Some would organize a boycott of his program. Dozens, perhaps hundreds of professional climate skeptics would begin angrily refuting Hannity's new crusade. Many of Hannity's friends in the conservative media world would back away from him, and some would seek advantage by denouncing him. Politicians he respects would be furious at his betrayal of the cause. He would lose friendships, viewers, and money. He could ultimately lose his job. And along the way he would cause himself immense personal pain as he systematically alienated his closest political and professional allies. The world would have to update its understanding of who Sean Hannity is and what he believes, and so, too, would Sean Hannity. Changing your identity is a psychologically and socially brutal process.

Kahan doesn't find it strange that we react to threatening information by mobilizing our intellectual artillery to destroy it. He thinks it's strange that we would expect rational people to do anything else. "Nothing any ordinary member of the public personally believes about the existence, causes, or likely consequences of global warming will affect the risk that climate change poses to her, or to anyone or anything she cares about," Kahan writes. "However, if she forms the wrong position on climate change relative to the one [held by] people with whom she has a close affinity—and on whose high regard and support she depends on in myriad ways in her daily life—she could suffer extremely unpleasant consequences, from shunning to the loss of employment." The reality, he concludes, is that "the cost to her of making a mistake on the science is zero," but "the cost of being out of synch with her peers potentially catastrophic," making it "individually rational" to put group dynamics first when thinking about issues like climate change.[24]

Kahan calls this theory "identity-protective cognition": "As a way of avoiding dissonance and estrangement from valued groups, individuals subconsciously resist factual information that threatens their defining values." Elsewhere, he puts it even more pithily: "What we believe about the facts," he writes, "tells us who we are." And the most important psychological imperative most of us have in a given day is protecting our idea of who we are and our relationships with the people we trust and love.

Anyone who has ever found themselves in an angry argument with their political or social circle will know how threatening it feels. For a lot of people, being "right" just isn't worth picking a bitter fight with the people they care about. That's particularly true in a place like Washington, where social circles and professional lives are often organized around people's politics, and the boundaries of what those tribes believe are getting sharper. In an interview I did with David Brooks in 2019, the genially conservative *New York Times* columnist reflected on the social agony criticizing Trump had caused him. "I had been part of the conservative movement my whole life," he told me. "The *Weekly Standard*. The *Wall Street Journal*. *National Review*. *Washington Times*. Suddenly, I wasn't the kind of conservative all the other conservatives were, and so my social circles drifted away." Brooks was living alone at the time, and the consequences, for his life, were painful. "My weekends were just howling silences," he says.[25]

You can think of Washington as a machine for making identity-protective cognition easier. Each party has its allied think tanks, go-to experts, favored magazines, friendly blogs, sympathetic pundits, determined activists, and ideological moneymen. Both the professionals and the committed volunteers who make up the party machinery are members of social circles, Twitter worlds, Facebook groups, workplaces, and many other ecosystems that would make life very unpleasant for them if they strayed too far from the faith. And these institutions end up employing a lot of very smart, very sincere people whose formidable intelligence makes certain that they typically stay in line. To do anything else would upend their day-to-day lives. What's worse is that it never feels cynical, it never reads as rationalization. It always, always feels like our honest search for the truth has led us to the answer that confirms our priors. The problem, of course, is that these people are also affecting, and in some cases controlling, the levers of government.

The mandate's day in court

On March 23, 2010, the day that President Obama signed the Affordable Care Act into law, fourteen state attorneys general filed suit against the law's requirement that most Americans purchase health insurance, on the ground that it was unconstitutional.

At the time, it was hard to find a law professor in the country who took them seriously. "The argument about constitutionality is, if not frivolous, close to it," Sanford Levinson, a University of Texas Law School professor, told McClatchy. Erwin Chemerinsky, then the dean of the law school at the University of California at Irvine, told the *Times*, "There is no case law, post 1937, that would support an individual's right not to buy health care if the government wants to mandate it." Orin Kerr, then a George Washington University professor who had clerked for Justice Anthony Kennedy, said, "There is a less than one-per-cent chance that the courts will invalidate the individual mandate."[26]

These expert assessments were wrong. Republican-appointed judges repeatedly ruled against the mandate, even as judges appointed by Democrats repeatedly ruled in its favor. By the time the case was before the Supreme Court, Kerr told me the chances that the Court would overturn the mandate was about fifty-fifty.

In the end, the mandate survived on a split-the-difference decision. Chief Justice John Roberts gave Republicans some comfort by accepting their argument that the mandate was not justified under the federal government's power to regulate interstate commerce—a ruling that expanded the kinds of cases they could bring to the Court in the future by narrowing one of the federal government's broadest powers—but he decided the penalty was a tax, and the government's taxation power was broad, so he joined with Kennedy and the Court's liberals to uphold it.*

This preserved the policy, but it convinced no one of the mandate's constitutionality. Roberts was George W. Bush's choice to lead the court. He was a former Reagan staffer. But the conservative movement didn't take those credentials as reason to listen to him, to revise their views and see the mandate as cleanly constitutional. It took them as reason to feel betrayed by him. "Why are Republicans so awful at picking Supreme Court justices?" lamented Marc Thiessen, a former Bush speechwriter, in the *Washington Post*. "Democrats have been virtually flawless in appointing reliable liberals to the court. Yet Republicans, more often than not, appoint justices who vote with the other side on critical decisions."[27]

What the Obamacare case did convince many of was the waning legitimacy of the Supreme Court. The near success of what seemed like a ridiculous argument to liberals persuaded them of the judiciary's increasing politicization. Conservatives, meanwhile, suspected Kennedy and Roberts of motivated reasoning on behalf of the Court itself—they knew it would've been institutionally

---

* I should note that this fight is ongoing. Republicans subsequently took Congress, failed to repeal Obamacare, but changed the law so the mandate's penalty was zero dollars. Then, a group of Republican attorneys general launched the *Texas v. Azar* case, which argues that the mandate can't be a tax if it doesn't raise any money, which makes the mandate unconstitutional, and if the mandate is unconstitutional, the Supreme Court should declare the entire law unconstitutional. Texas Judge Reed O'Connor, a former Senate GOP aide, ruled in their favor, though the case is now being appealed. "If you were ever tempted to think that right-wing judges weren't activist—that they were only 'enforcing the Constitution' or 'reading the statute'—this will persuade you to knock it off," wrote law professor Nicholas Bagley.

disastrous for the Court to overturn Obamacare, so they found an excuse to back down. And while I obviously find one of those arguments more persuasive than the other, I can't tell you that's not just my motivated reasoning in action.

Jonathan Haidt, a professor of psychology at New York University's business school, sees the role that individual reason plays in political arguments as akin to the job of the White House press secretary. In his book *The Righteous Mind: Why Good People Are Divided by Politics and Religion*, he writes,

> No matter how bad the policy, the secretary will find some way to praise or defend it. . . . Sometimes you'll hear an awkward pause as the secretary searches for the right words, but what you'll never hear is: "Hey, that's a great point! Maybe we should rethink this policy." Press secretaries can't say that because they have no power to make or revise policy. They're told what the policy is, and their job is to find evidence and arguments that will justify the policy to the public.[28]

For that reason, Haidt told me, "once group loyalties are engaged, you can't change people's minds by utterly refuting their arguments. Thinking is mostly just rationalization, mostly just a search for supporting evidence."[29] Psychologists have a term for this: "motivated reasoning." Just as a press secretary is motivated to defend his or her boss's positions, so, too, is our mind motivated to defend our group's positions or the conclusion we need to reach for other reasons.

To spend much time with this research is to stare into a kind of intellectual abyss. If the work of gathering evidence and reasoning through thorny, polarizing political questions is actually the process by which we trick ourselves into finding the answers we want, then what's the right way to search for answers? How can we know the answers we come up with, no matter how well intentioned, aren't just more motivated cognition? How can we know the experts we're relying on haven't subtly biased their answers, too? How can I know that this book isn't a form of identity protection? Kahan's research tells us we can't trust our own reason. How do we reason our way out of that?

I first wrote about motivated reasoning and Obamacare's individual mandate in 2012. In response to that piece, the psychologist Paul Bloom wrote an article in the *Atlantic* that didn't quarrel with anything in my argument but included this gotcha: "notice that Klein doesn't reach for a social-psychology journal when articulating why he and his Democratic allies are so confident that Obamacare is constitutional."[30]

Bloom's right, of course. But the implications are more radical than he seemed prepared to admit. The question isn't whether I fall victim to motivated reasoning, too, or whether I'm less psychically guarded when faced with information that accords with my values and worldview. Of course I am. The question is what it means that all of us are doing this, to greater or lesser degrees, all the time.

There are mysteries in life that have testable, knowable answers. Do antibiotics clear strep throat? Does iodine make river water safe to drink? Magnets—how do they work? But there are plenty that don't. Constitutional interpretation is one of them. The Founding Fathers themselves differed on what the Constitution meant and permitted, not to mention how such questions should be decided. Thomas Jefferson, for instance, believed every branch of government should be permitted to interpret the Constitution for itself. He lost that fight, and the Supreme Court was given ultimate authority over constitutional arbitration.

But the Supreme Court itself is just nine robed judges—and, increasingly, nine robed judges who are chosen not just for their brilliance but for their ideological reliability (more on that later).

The Court isn't meant to be political, but the cases it faces are often political, and the process by which a judge is nominated and confirmed is thoroughly politicized. The edifice of constitutional interpretation—and the legitimacy we give it—is that there is a right answer to a question like "Is the individual mandate constitutional?" But perhaps there isn't. And even if there is one answer, there's no particular reason to believe a handful of extremely adept debaters, all of whom distinguished themselves for the job by persuading politicians of their ideological reliability, would find it, or that the rest of us would care if they did.

You can see what I mean when I say that taking this literature too seriously can feel like staring into the abyss. My whole career—and much of politics more generally—is based on the idea that gathering good information helps us understand hard policy issues and that putting the two together can change minds and lead to a better world. But once our political identities and interests push themselves in front of our cognition, that model of reasoning falls to pieces.

Kahan's work suggests that cognition exists on a spectrum, ranging from issues where the truth matters and our identities don't to issues where our identities dominate and the truth fades in importance. One implication of an era where our political identities are becoming more sorted and more powerful is that it will bring with it a rise in identity-protective cognition, and that's particularly true if the relevant identity groups are able to construct sophisticated architectures of information that we can use to power our reasoning.

But it's also worth focusing on the word "protective." As Kahan's term suggests, our reasoning is most vulnerable when our identities are most threatened. And for many, this is an era of profound threat.

Chapter 5

Demographic Threat

I n 2008, Barack Obama held up change as a beacon, attaching to it another word that channeled everything his young and diverse coalition saw in his rise and their newfound political power: "hope." An America that would elect a black man president was an America in which a future was being written that would read thrillingly different from our past.

In 2016, Donald Trump wielded that same sense of change as a threat; he was the revanchist voice of those who yearned to make America the way it was before, to make it great *again*. That was the impulse that connected the wall to keep Mexicans out, the ban to keep Muslims away, the birtherism meant to prove Obama couldn't possibly be a legitimate president. An America that would elect Trump president was an America in which a future was being written that could read thrillingly similar to our past.

This is the core cleavage of our politics, and it reflects a defining trend of our era: America is changing, and fast. According to the Census Bureau, 2013 marked the first year that a majority of

US infants under the age of one were nonwhite.[1] The announcement, made during the second term of the nation's first African
American president, was not a surprise. Demographers had
been predicting such a tipping point for years, and they foresaw
more to come.

The government predicts that in 2030, immigration will
overtake new births as the dominant driver of population
growth. About fifteen years after that, America will phase into
majority-minority status—for the first time in the nation's history, non-Hispanic whites will no longer make up a majority of
the population.[2]

That cross will come in part because America's black, Hispanic, Asian, and mixed-race populations are expected to grow—
indeed, the Hispanic and Asian populations are expected to
roughly double by 2060 and the mixed-race population to triple.
Meanwhile, the non-Hispanic white population is, uniquely,
expected to fall, dipping from 199 million in 2020 to 179 million
in 2060. The Census Bureau minces no words here: "The only
group projected to shrink is the non-Hispanic White population."[3]

This isn't just a statement about the future; it's a description
of the present. The economist Jed Kolko notes that the most
common age for white Americans is fifty-eight, for Asians it's
twenty-nine, for African Americans it's twenty-seven, and for
Hispanics it's eleven.[4] A report out of the University of Wisconsin–
Madison's Applied Population Lab found that white births are
now outnumbered by white deaths in twenty-six states, up from
seventeen in 2014 and four in 2004.[5]

Meanwhile, America's foreign-born population is projected
to rise from 14 percent of the population today to 17 percent in
2060, more than 2 percentage points above the record set in

1890. The rise has been staggering in its speed: as recently as the 1970s, America's foreign-born population was under 5 percent.

The country's gender dynamics are also in flux. Hillary Clinton was not just the first female presidential candidate to win the popular vote but the first to be nominated by a major political party. Women now make up 56 percent of college students[6] and are 8 percentage points more likely than men to have earned a bachelor's degree by age twenty-nine.[7]

In 2018, for the first time, Americans claiming "no religion" edged out Catholics and evangelicals to be the most popular response to the General Social Survey's question on religion.[8] Different ways of grouping religious sects will give you different perspectives on the decline of organized religion in America. The GSS, for instance, lists mainline Protestants and evangelical Protestants separately. But in *The End of White Christian America*, Robert Jones, the CEO and founder of the Public Religion Research Institute, projects the religiously unaffiliated will edge out all Protestants in 2051—"a thought that would have been unimaginable just a few decades ago," he writes.[9]

These demographic categories interact in important ways. Jones, for instance, argues that the dominant culture in America has been white *and* Christian. Power, no less than oppression, is intersectional. Viewed through that lens, however, the tipping point has already happened. When Obama took office, 54 percent of the country was white and Christian. By the 2016 election, that had fallen to 43 percent. To put it even more starkly, about seven out of every ten seniors are white and Christian, compared with fewer than three in ten young adults—a trend being driven not just by demographic change but by fewer young people identifying as Christian. "These changes are big enough to feel, they're fast enough to feel," says Jones.[10]

Demographers can and do disagree over whether these projections will hold in the future. Perhaps Hispanic whites will begin identifying simply as whites in the coming years, much as the Irish became white in the twentieth century. Race is a construct, and we reconstruct its categories continuously. But that's only to say that it's often our *perception* of race and power that matters. And our perception of demographic change outpaces even the reality: in 2013, the Center for American Progress, PolicyLink, Latino Decisions, and the Rockefeller Foundation surveyed Americans and found that the median participant believed the country was 49 percent nonwhite; the correct answer was 37 percent.

I spent months talking with politicians, social psychologists, and political scientists about what happens in moments like this one, moments when a majority feels its dominance beginning to fail. The answer, attested to in mountains of studies and visible everywhere in our politics, is this: change of this magnitude acts on us psychologically, not just electorally. It is the crucial context uniting the core political conflicts of this era: Obama's and Trump's presidencies, the rise of reactionary new social movements and thinkers, the wars over political correctness on campuses and representation in Hollywood, the power of #MeToo and Black Lives Matter, the fights over immigration. There is nothing that makes us identify with our groups so strongly as the feeling that the power we took for granted may soon be lost or the injustices we've long borne may soon be rectified.

"An identity is questioned only when it is menaced," wrote James Baldwin, "as when the mighty begin to fall, or when the wretched begin to rise, or when the stranger enters the gates, never, thereafter, to be a stranger: the stranger's presence making *you* the stranger, less to the stranger than to yourself."[11]

Demographic change, and the fears and hopes it evokes, is one of the tectonic forces shaping this era in American life. But to understand what it is doing to us as a country, we need to begin by understanding what it does to us as individuals.

Change makes us conservative

In 2014, psychologists Maureen Craig and Jennifer Richeson analyzed the responses of 369 white self-identified political independents who had completed one of two surveys.[12] Participants were randomly assigned to receive a survey that asked them whether they knew that California had become a majority-minority state—which is to say, a state where whites no longer made up more than 50 percent of the population—or a survey devoid of threatening demographic information.

This was a gentle test of an unnerving theory: that the barest exposure to the concept that whites were losing their numerical majority in America would not just make whites feel afraid but sharply change their political behavior. The theory proved correct. Among participants who lived in the western United States, those who read that whites had ceded majority status were more than 13 points likelier to subsequently say they favored the Republican Party.

In a follow-up study, Craig and Richeson handed some white subjects newspaper articles about geographic mobility, while others read a piece explaining that "ethnic/racial minorities will comprise a majority of the U.S. populace by 2042." The group that read the racially tinged release shifted toward more conservative views not just on directly related policy questions—like immigration levels, affirmative actions, and paths to citizenship—but on health-care reform and defense spending.*[13]

Perhaps the most striking experiment in this space was conducted by Harvard social scientist Ryan Enos. He attempted something rare in social science: an actual test of what seeing more diversity in our everyday surroundings does to our political opinions. His explanation of both the experiment and its results is worth reading:

> I sent Spanish speakers to randomly selected train stations in towns around Boston to simply catch the train and ride like any other passenger. I focused on stations in white suburbs. The intent was to create the impression, by subtle manipulation, that the Latino population in these segregated towns was increasing.
>
> Before and after sending these Spanish speakers to the train platforms, I surveyed passengers on the platforms about their attitudes about immigration. After being exposed to the Spanish speakers on their metro lines for just three days, attitudes on these questions moved sharply rightward: The mostly liberal Democratic passengers had come to endorse immigration policies—including deportation of children of undocumented immigrants—similar to those endorsed by Trump in his campaign.[14]

So here, then, is what we know: even gentle, incidental exposure to reminders that America is diversifying—and particularly

* It's worth noting that these dynamics cut in the other direction, too: a 2016 study by Alexander Kuo, Neil Malhotra, and Cecilia Hyunjung Mo split a sample of Asian American college students into two groups. One group was subjected to a staged microaggression during the study—their US citizenship was doubted by the researcher managing the experiment. The incident sparked a sharp shift toward support of the Democratic Party.

to the idea that America is becoming a majority-minority nation—pushes whites toward more conservative policy opinions and more support of the Republican Party.

What happens when the exposure isn't so subtle?

The post-racial myth

When Obama was elected in 2008, there was much talk of America moving into a post-racial moment. But as UC Irvine political scientist Michael Tesler shows in his powerful book *Post-Racial or Most-Racial?*, the mere existence of Obama's presidency further racialized American politics, splitting the two parties not just by racial composition but by racial attitudes. What Tesler proves is that in the Obama era, attitudes on race began shaping attitudes on virtually all political questions. The black-white divide in support for Obamacare was 20 percentage points larger than the black-white divide over Bill Clinton's similarly controversial health-care proposal, for instance.

But it wasn't just health care. Party identification became significantly more divided by race. Perceptions of the economy became significantly more divided by race. Even perceptions of the president's dogs became more divided by race: shown pictures of the Obamas' dog Bo, more racially resentful Americans liked the dog better when told it was a picture of Ted Kennedy's dog Splash.

"There's no doubt that there's some folks who just really dislike me because they don't like the idea of a black President," Obama told *The New Yorker's* David Remnick. "Now, the flip side of it is there are some black folks and maybe some white folks who really like me and give me the benefit of the doubt precisely because I'm a black President."

You might assume, seeing all this, that the reason for the racialization of American politics under Obama's presidency was that Obama, being African American, discussed racial issues and put forward race-conscious policies more often than past presidents. You'd be wrong. "According to content analyses conducted by political and communication scientists, Barack Obama actually discussed race less in his first term than any other Democratic president since Franklin Roosevelt," writes Tesler.[15]

Obama's presidency didn't force race to the front of American politics through rhetoric or action. Rather, Obama himself was a symbol of a browning America, of white America's loss of control, of the fact that the country was changing and new groups were gaining power. That perception carried the force of fact. In his 2012 reelection campaign, Obama won merely 39 percent of the white vote—a smaller share than Michael Dukakis had commanded in 1988. A few decades ago, the multiracial Obama coalition couldn't elect a president; by 2012, it could.

The changes that led to Obama's presidency are everywhere in our culture. We live in an America where television programs, commercials, and movies are trying to represent a browner country; where the film *Black Panther* is a celebrated cultural event and #OscarsSoWhite is a nationally known hashtag; where NFL players kneel during the national anthem to protest police brutality and pressing 1 for English is commonplace. There's a reason why, when the Russians wanted to sow division in the American election, they focused their social media trolling on America's racial divisions.[16]

White voters who feel they are losing a historical hold on power are reacting to something real. For the bulk of American history, you couldn't win the presidency without winning a majority—

usually an overwhelming majority—of the white vote. Though this changed before Obama—Bill Clinton won slightly less of the white vote than his Republican challengers—the election of an African American president leading a young, multiracial coalition made the transition stark and threatening.

But this demographic transition is ongoing, not settled, and that makes the current moment particularly unstable. As Yale Law professor Amy Chua writes in *Political Tribes*:

> For two hundred years, whites in America represented an undisputed politically, economically, and culturally dominant majority. When a political tribe is so overwhelmingly dominant, it can persecute with impunity, but it can also be more generous. It can afford to be more universalist, more enlightened, more inclusive, like the WASP elites of the 1960s who opened up the Ivy League colleges to more Jews, blacks, and other minorities—in part because it seemed like the right thing to do.
>
> Today, no group in America feels comfortably dominant. Every group feels attacked, pitted against other groups not just for jobs and spoils but for the right to define the nation's identity. In these conditions, democracy devolves into zero-sum group competition—pure political tribalism.[17]

Exacerbating this instability is an imbalance in who holds power where. A useful rule of thumb is that political power runs a decade behind demographics, with older, whiter, more Christian voters turning out at higher rates. "The ballot box acts like a time machine," Robert Jones told me, "taking us back 10 years in race and religion. We reached the tipping point of white Christians being a minority of the population during Obama, but our calculations are it'll be 2024 before we see that at the ballot box." America's political geography—through the structure of the

Senate, the drawing of House districts, and the composition of the electoral college—further amplifies the power of whiter, more rural, more Christian voters, giving that coalition more political power than sheer demographics would predict.

But cultural power runs a decade or more ahead of demography, with brands and television networks chasing younger, more urban, more diverse consumers. That's why it's become a veritable Super Bowl tradition to wade through controversy over some venerable brand's surprisingly woke ads.

In 2019, for instance, Gillette released a pre–Super Bowl ad showing boys roughhousing, men touching women inappropriately in corporate boardrooms, and an infinite chorus of barbecuing dads excusing the behavior with "boys will be boys." In a twist on Gillette's tagline, the commercial asked, "Is this the best a man can get?"

The backlash was swift. "Men are saying, we feel marginalized, criticized and accused rather than feeling inspired[,] empowered and encouraged," a branding executive told the *Wall Street Journal*. "We are taking a realistic look at what's happening today, and aiming to inspire change by acknowledging that the old saying 'Boys Will Be Boys' is not an excuse," responded Pankaj Bhalla, Gillette's brand director for North America.[18]

For Gillette, this wasn't truly a controversy. It was a business decision. Brands want to be where the culture is going, not where it's been. But most people live in the culture rather than profiting from it, and they experience the changing mores reflected in ads and movie casts as a shift in power that either excites or unnerves them. The result is that the Left feels a cultural and demographic power that it can only occasionally translate into political power, and the Right wields political power but feels increasingly dismissed and offended culturally.

This is the crucial context for Trump's rise, and it's why Tesler has little patience for those who treat Trump as an invader in the

Republican Party. In a field of Republicans who were trying to change the party to appeal to a rising Hispanic electorate, Trump was alone in speaking to Republican voters who didn't want the party to remake itself, who wanted to be told that a wall could be built and things could go back to the way they were.

"Trump met the party where it was rather than trying to change it," Tesler says. "He was hunting where the ducks were."[19]

White identity under threat

One way of looking at Trump is as a disruptive force that crashed, like a once-in-a-generation comet, into American politics. But the other way of looking at Trump—the correct way—is as a master marketer who astutely read the market. Conservative politics was becoming more racialized in response to Obama and the changes he represented. During this period, Trump was testing the waters by championing birther conspiracy theories. The water was warm.*[20]

It's worth taking a moment to consider the kinds of rhetoric that conservatives had been hearing, the rhetoric that created the context for Trump. In 2009, Rush Limbaugh went on the air to tell his listeners:

---

* There's an interesting debate about whether Trump became a culture warrior out of calculation or authentic fury. After Romney lost in 2012, Trump criticized him for telling undocumented immigrants to "self-deport" and argued for a gentler GOP. "The Democrats didn't have a policy for dealing with illegal immigrants, but what they did have going for them is they weren't mean-spirited about it," he told Newsmax. "They didn't know what the policy was, but what they were is they were kind."

How do you get promoted in a Barack Obama administration? By hating white people, or even saying you do, or that they're not good, or whatever. Make white people the new oppressed minority, and they are going along with it, because they're shutting up. They're moving to the back of the bus. They're saying I can't use that drinking fountain, okay. I can't use that restroom, okay. That's the modern day Republican Party, the equivalent of the Old South, the new oppressed minority.[21]

In 2012, on the evening of the election, Bill O'Reilly, then the top-rated cable news anchor in the country, sat down to tell his viewers what this all meant:

Because it's a changing country; the demographics are changing. It's not a traditional America anymore. And there are 50 percent of the voting public who want stuff, they want things. And who is going to give them things? President Obama. He knows it, and he ran on it. And, whereby 20 years ago President Obama would have been roundly defeated by an establishment candidate like Mitt Romney, the white establishment is now the minority.[22]

Nor did Obama's exit from the scene and Trump's election to the White House calm these sentiments. If anything, it unleashed them. The lesson conservative broadcasters took from Trump was to say the quiet part loud, and they did. In 2018, Laura Ingraham said:

In some parts of the country, it does seem like the America that we know and love doesn't exist anymore. Massive demographic changes have been foisted upon the American people. And they're changes that none of us ever voted for and most of us don't like. From Virginia to California, we see stark examples of how radically in some ways the country has changed. Now much of this is related to both illegal, and in some cases, legal immigration that, of course, progressives love.

Read that again. *It does seem like the America that we know and love doesn't exist anymore.* Let it sink in. But her colleague Tucker Carlson wasn't saying anything different:

How precisely is diversity our strength? Since you've made this our new national motto, please be specific as you explain it. Can you think, for example, of other institutions such as, I don't know, marriage or military units, in which the less people have in common the more cohesive they are? Do you get along better with your neighbors or your co-workers if you can't understand each other or share no common values? . . . How about this question, after spending two centuries overcoming our country's painful history of racial discrimination and hatred, why is it once again acceptable, even encouraged to attack people on the basis of their skin color?

Just so we're all on the same page: the skin color Carlson is saying it's okay to attack is white. He is, indeed, making an explicit comparison between the "racial discrimination and hatred" faced by white Americans in 2019 and that faced by black Americans through American history.

It would be easy to dismiss these comments as the over-the-top rantings of pundits, but Limbaugh, O'Reilly, Ingraham, and Carlson's views are widely shared. A 2016 Public Religion Research Institute poll found that 57 percent of whites agreed that "discrimination against whites is as big a problem today as discrimination against blacks and other minorities."[23] A 2017

GenForward poll of white millennials found 48 percent agreed with a similar statement, showing that the sentiment isn't confined or even concentrated among older whites.

In 2012, Romney chose to run a campaign mainly based on class identity, pitting his vision of the heroic entrepreneur against Obama's emphasis on the screwed-over worker. He lost, buried under surging nonwhite turnout. In the aftermath of his defeat, Republicans began obsessing over how to win nonwhite voters. The Republican National Committee even commissioned an "autopsy" of the election, which concluded:

> If Hispanic Americans perceive that a GOP nominee or candidate does not want them in the United States (i.e. self-deportation), they will not pay attention to our next sentence. It does not matter what we say about education, jobs or the economy; if Hispanics think we do not want them here, they will close their ears to our policies. In the last election, Governor Romney received just 27 percent of the Hispanic vote. Other minority communities, including Asian and Pacific Islander Americans, also view the Party as unwelcoming. President Bush got 44 percent of the Asian vote in 2004; our presidential nominee received only 26 percent in 2012.

The report went on to recommend embracing comprehensive immigration reform, elevating Hispanic leaders inside the Republican Party, and being "inclusive and welcoming" in both "fact and deed." Otherwise, it warned, "our Party's appeal will continue to shrink to its core constituencies only."

But there were dissenting voices. The political analyst Sean Trende wrote an influential analysis of the results in Real Clear Politics, arguing that "almost 7 million fewer whites voted in 2012 than in 2008."[24] It was mobilizing these "missing white voters,"

Trende said, that offered Republicans a quicker path back to power. That was the path Trump chose—but he was following a trail that was already cut into the electorate.

You can think of politics as a market and powerful, primal forces like white identity as representing a market opportunity. Eventually, someone was going to come along and give the Republican base what they wanted. If Trump hadn't done it in 2016, another politician would have in 2020 or 2024. The pressure was just going to keep building.

Ashley Jardina is a political scientist at Duke University who studies racial identity. In her book *White Identity Politics*, she argues that generations of scholars have taken African American, Hispanic, and Asian identity seriously but assumed there was no such thing as white identity. "When considering whether white Americans feel a sense of anxiety about the status of their racial group, or whether whites possess a sense of racial identity that has political consequences, for the past fifty years, the answer generally has been 'no,'" she writes. "For the most part, scholars have argued that racial solidarity among whites has been invisible and politically inconsequential. Whites, by nature of their dominant status and numerical majority, have largely been able to take their race for granted."[25]

Jardina shows that this was wrong. White political identity is conditional. It emerges in periods of threat and challenges—periods like this one. Demographic change, the election of the first black president, and the downstream cultural and political consequences of both have "led a sizeable proportion of whites to believe that their racial group, and the benefits that group enjoys, are endangered. As a result, this racial solidarity now plays a central role in the way many whites orient themselves to the political and social world."

There is a nuance to Jardina's research worth noting. A sense of racial identity can be based on in-group favoritism or out-group hostility. Both can be, and often are, present, but Jardina repeatedly finds that much of the strengthening of white political identity is a defense of white political privilege without an attendant rise in racist attitudes. To some, this will sound like a distinction without a difference, but it's meaningful in how people experience their own politics and what kinds of appeals and messages they respond to.

Jardina finds that about 30 to 40 percent of the white population feels a strong (and growing) sense of racial solidarity, but most of them feel it without an accompanying sense of racial hostility. That helps explain a strength and a weakness in Trump's political approach: his cocktail of white identity politics and outright bigotry mixes popular components, like a focus on protecting native-born whites from both immigrant competition and foreign competition, with unpopular displays of racism and bigotry. A savvier politician than Trump could focus on defending white privileges without constantly crossing into outright racism, and prove far more politically formidable.

There are lessons here for Trump's opponents, too—you can craft a message and policies to calm the fears powering white identity politics, or you can mobilize your base in ways that aggravate white voters. In 2006, Nyla Branscombe, Michael Schmitt, and Kristin Schiffhauer published a fascinating paper called "Racial Attitudes in Response to Thoughts of White Privilege." They found that priming white college students to think about the concept of white privilege led them to express more racial resentment in subsequent surveys.

The simplest way to activate someone's identity is to threaten it, to tell them they don't deserve what they have, to make them consider that it might be taken away. The experience of losing status—and being told your loss of status is part of society's march to justice—is itself radicalizing.

There's a quote I occasionally see ricochet around social media. "When you're accustomed to privilege, equality feels like oppression."*26 There's truth to this line, but it cuts both ways. To the extent that it's true that a loss of privilege *feels* like oppression, that feeling needs to be taken seriously, both because it's real, and because, left to fester, it can be weaponized by demagogues and reactionaries.

In her book *Talking to Strangers*, Harvard political theorist Danielle Allen writes that "the hard truth of democracy is that some citizens are always giving things up for others." These sacrifices, she argues, are subjective, but they need to be treated as significant, and met with a spirit of "political friendship." In a conversation I had with her for my podcast, Allen expanded on the point. We need "to give each other space to negotiate around experiences of loss," she said. But "more is demanded of winners in any given political moment, it is the job of the winner to make the ongoing possibility of a political friendship real."

What makes that such a difficult principle to adhere to is that the question of who counts as a "winner" at any given moment is hard to answer, and American politics is often a chorus of contradictory voices persuasively claiming victimhood at the same time. Most of us are winners in some ways and losers in others, and we feel the losses more acutely than the victories. Making matters worse, the losses that stem from demographic change are difficult to talk about, and they are often cloaked in more socially acceptable, and politically defensible, language.

---

* The origination of this quote is unclear, but ironically, given how popular the line has become as a feminist riposte, the earliest antecedent that Quote Investigator could find was from a 1997 Usenet message board missive by Mike Jebbett, which read, "Women like her are suffering from a condition I call 'Advanced Pedestalism.' Which basically means that they [women] have been living on the high side for so long, equality looks like oppression."

How demographic threat drives economic anxiety

Talk of white identity politics makes many uncomfortable. There is another explanation some prefer for Trump's rise, an explanation that accounts for the turmoil of our politics without forcing us into uncomfortable conversations about race, power, and resentment. That explanation? It's the economy, stupid.

As the argument goes, the financial crisis, the rise of automation, the wreckage of globalization, the pain of the Great Recession, the shocking run-up in inequality—all of that was more than enough to upend our politics; you don't need to reach for racialized explanations. A bitter debate erupted after the 2016 election between those who blame our politics on economic anxiety and those who see a country riven by racial resentment. In its aftermath, a popular synthesis has emerged: economic anxiety activated racial resentment, which means, comfortingly, that a better economy will calm our divisions.

The best evidence we have suggests the synthesis is right, but we're getting the causality backward. In their book *Identity Crisis: The 2016 Presidential Campaign and the Battle for the Meaning of America*, political scientists John Sides, Michael Tesler, and Lynn Vavreck analyze reams of data and show that racial resentment activated economic anxiety, rather than the other way around:

Before Obama's presidency, how Americans felt about black people did not much affect their perceptions of the economy. After Obama, this changed. In December 2007, racial resentment—which captures whether Americans think deficiencies in black culture are the main reason for racial inequality—was not related to whites' perceptions of whether the economy was getting better or worse, after accounting for partisanship and ideology. But when these exact same people were re-interviewed in July 2012, racial resentment was a powerful predictor of economic perceptions: the greater someone's level of racial resentment, the worse they believed the economy was doing.[27]

This is unnerving data, as we tend to imagine the economy as a rare subject on which objective facts, rather than group conflicts, drive opinions. Sadly, no. Sides, Tesler, and Vavreck analyzed polling on economic sentiment and found that "Republicans in the highest income quintile, those making more than $100,000 per year, were actually slightly *less satisfied* than Democrats in the lowest income quintile, those making less than $20,000 per year." In general, economic anxiety did not predict which candidate people voted for, and what relationship did exist was no stronger in 2016 than in 2012.

This was borne out in the election's aftermath. According to Gallup's polls, Trump's election led to a remarkable 80-point jump in economic confidence among Republicans and a 37-point fall among Democrats. The economy since Trump took office has mostly shown the same trends from the final years of Obama— job growth, in fact, has been slightly slower—but his coalition's confidence continued to soar, even as they lived under much the same economy that so depressed them in 2016. Indeed, new data collected by Tesler shows that the most racially resentful are now the most economically optimistic.

This pattern holds internationally, too. The rise of the populist Right is not a uniquely American phenomenon, and it did not begin in 2016. It has manifested in countries across the Western world. It has gathered force in good economic times and bad, in countries with generous social safety nets and stingy ones. "Far-right party platforms differ from country to country, including on major social issues like feminism and economic issues like the size of the welfare state," wrote Vox's Zack Beauchamp in a careful review of the literature. "The one issue every single one agrees on is hostility to immigration, particularly when the immigrants are nonwhite and Muslim."[28]

Another problem for the economic anxiety hypothesis is that the victories of the populist Right have been much more striking and widespread than those of the populist Left. Plenty of countries feature political parties offering ambitious economic agendas designed in response to the financial crisis. It takes a special kind of condescension to believe voters suffering economically are so distracted by the identity politics of the Right that they have overlooked the direct solutions to the economic problems offered by the Left.

"Anyone who wants to explain what's happening in the West needs to answer two simple questions," writes the political scientist Eric Kaufmann in his book *Whiteshift: Populism, Immigration, and the Future of White Majorities*. "First, why are right-wing populists doing better than left-wing ones? Second, why did the migration crisis boost populist-right numbers sharply while the economic crisis had no overall effect? If we stick to data, the answer is crystal clear. Demography and culture, not economic and political developments, hold the key to understanding the populist moment."[29]

None of this takes away from the fact that economic anxiety is real, or that more broadly shared economic growth would be good for our politics. But it does suggest economic anxiety cannot explain away our political or cultural divisions.

Indeed, Trump himself is proof of this: he calls the economy under his watch a "miracle," but that has not led him or his supporters toward a gentler stance on immigration or less concern over NFL players kneeling to protest police brutality. A better economy would be good for the country because a better economy would always be good for the country. But it will not allow us to vault over the difficulties of a browning, secularizing America.

What the political correctness wars are really about

There's a story Jennifer Richeson, the Yale psychologist responsible for some of the studies discussed above, told me about the building she works in. "My lab is an old engineering building and there's exactly one women's bathroom," she said with a laugh. "No one noticed that, or at least no faculty members did."[30] And then, slowly, Yale began adding women to the department, and they noticed it. They complained. Now there was friction. What had gone unnoticed by those with power in one era was unacceptable to those gaining power in another. "When new people show up, they notice new things and start asking questions and begin making demands," she says.

There's been an obsessive interest in recent years in conflicts over political correctness. Tune in to Fox News on any given night and you'll find yourself dropped into a controversy on some liberal arts college somewhere. The connective tissue of the "intellectual dark web"—the anxiety that has made a coalition of new atheist Sam Harris, conservative pundit Ben Shapiro, Canadian psychologist Jordan Peterson, and others—is fear that the boundaries of acceptable discourse are being narrowed, that PC culture and identity politics are choking free speech. There's a whole subgenre of punditry arguing that Trump's rise is a regrettable, but predictable, backlash to political correctness, and thus the blame for his emergence properly belongs to campus activists and Black Lives Matter protesters.

These fears can seem bizarre at first glance. Given all the other things available to worry about in the world, who cares what happened at this or that college? But the speed with which these clashes go viral on Twitter and Facebook, the enthusiasm with which they're covered on cable news and traffic-hungry websites and celebrated podcasts, all reflect the reality that something deeper and more fearful in us is being activated. These are proxy wars for bigger, more fundamental concerns over the direction of the culture. The theory is that as go elite college campuses, so goes the nation. This is particularly true for those who make a portion of their income giving speeches on college campuses.

Whatever you think of that theory, the issues being raised are fundamental. What can you say without being criticized? Protested? Punished? Who gets forgiven and who gets ostracized? What are the lines, and who gets to decide where they're drawn?

Trump harnessed these sentiments during the campaign. "I think the big problem this country has is being politically correct," he said. "I've been challenged by so many people, and I don't, frankly, have time for total political correctness. And to be honest with you, this country doesn't have time, either."

Much of this debate has played out under false pretenses. The idea that college campuses have ever been bastions of free speech is a fiction. In October 2017, Sean Decatur, the first African American president of Kenyon College, noted that American colleges have always believed the regulation of civility and behavioral norms to be part of their mandate. He quoted Kenyon's statement of student responsibilities from the 1960s, which warned that any behavior that "offends the sensibilities of others (whether students, faculty members or visitors) . . . will result in disciplinary action . . . vulgar behavior, obscene language or disorderly conduct are not tolerated."[31]

This was, he continued, "far stricter than anything that 21st-century critics of higher education see as a product of 'political correctness.'" So what's changed? The answer, Decatur suggested, is who gets to decide what counts as offensive behavior:

> The demographics of elite, residential colleges has changed drastically in the last 50 years and, as a result, the definition of civility has begun to change. There are many, including myself, who see the act of whites dressing in blackface as a disrespectful act. Reminding students of the norms of civil, respectful behavior, including refraining from blackface, is in line with the actions of colleges historically. What has changed is not the expectation that colleges define norms for civility, but rather the definition of civility.
>
> There are behaviors on college campuses in general, and at Kenyon in particular, that may have passed a standard for civility 50 years ago—when the institution was all-male and almost all-white—that would not be considered civil today.[32]

It is easy to read that as pure progress, but for those who dominated the discourse before, it represents real loss, and for everyone involved, it carries confusion and upheaval. New lines are being drawn, but no one is quite sure where they are or who is doing the drawing. The power to define the boundaries of acceptable behavior and polite discourse is profound, and right now, it is contested.

"I call it the democratization of discomfort," says Richeson. "There were whole swaths of people uncomfortable all of the time. Now we're democratizing it. Now more people across different races and religions feel uncomfortable."

The point here is not that college activists never go too far—of course they do, that's almost the point of being a college activist. The point is that we typically don't care what happens on college campuses. In this case, campus conflict is a window into the larger conflicts cutting through our society. It's a hothouse atmosphere where fights take place with particular clarity, as the moderating forces of non-college life—keeping your job, barely having time to go to the gym much less to political protests—are lifted. But on all sides, the debate over PC culture is really about the core questions of not just politics but life: Whose grievances get heard? Who gets to be referred to by the names and labels and pronouns they choose? Who grants respectability, and who takes it away? Put more simply, in a changing America, who holds power?

New York Times columnist Bret Stephens is a good example. He's written column after column slamming the delicate sensitivities of the campus Left. He's tweeted that "the right to offend is the most precious right. Without it, free speech is meaningless."[33] He's lamented the way millennials exact "professional destruction" as the price for "emotional upset."[34] But then the *New York Times* got a bedbug infestation, and George Washington University professor Dave Karpf sent a little-noticed tweet joking that "The bedbugs are a metaphor. The bedbugs are Bret Stephens."[35] Furious, the columnist sent an angry email to Karpf, cc'ing his provost, and sent a separate email to the director of GWU's School of Media and Public Affairs.[36] It was the definition of trying to exact professional destruction as vengeance for emotional upset.

Stephens's overreaction was hypocritical and unwise. He quit Twitter shortly thereafter. But the outburst was the culmination of hurts Stephens had been nurturing for years. Stephens's columns frequently offend the *Times*'s liberal readers, and he's a constant target of mockery on Twitter. In May 2019, Stephens struck back with a column entitled "Dear Millennials: The Feeling Is Mutual," where he wrote that "no faction on the Democratic side more richly deserves rebuking" than "these younger generations that specialize in histrionic self-pity and moral self-righteousness, usually communicated via social media with maximum snark."[37] The personal is political, indeed.

Stephens had far more power and clout than his critics, but humans are social animals, exquisitely tuned to agonize over criticism and obsess over insult. Stephens had been vibrating with fury at how he was treated online. He wanted some higher authority to enforce a more civil tone toward him, personally. The right to offend may be precious, but the endless experience of offense is crushing. In a past decade, Stephens's role at the *Times* might have insulated him from this kind of public assault—he wielded a national platform, while his daily critics would've been left penning angry letters to the editor—but those days had passed. For Stephens, as for so many others in this era, the objective fact of his power did not translate into him feeling powerful. But when he tried to act on his experience of being bullied, he proved the bully. Thus are the disorientations of the age.

It's become common to mock students demanding safe spaces, but look carefully at the collisions in American politics right now and you find that everyone is demanding safe spaces—the fear is not that the government is regulating speech but that protesters are chilling speech, that Twitter mobs rove the land looking for an errant word or misfired joke. In our eagerness to discount our opponents as easily triggered snowflakes, we've lost sight of the animating impulse behind much of politics and, indeed, much of life: the desire to feel safe, to know you can say what you want without fear. In a telling postscript, Stephens initially agreed to a debate with Karpf at George Washington University on the topic of civility in the media, but pulled out when GWU insisted on making the debate open to the public.[38]

How demographic change changes our parties

As America changes, so, too, do the issues America chooses to confront and the ways it chooses to confront them. In 1996, as President Clinton swept to reelection, the Democratic Party platform included a section on immigration that sounds as if it could have been released by the Trump administration today:

> Today's Democratic Party also believes we must remain a nation of laws. We cannot tolerate illegal immigration and we must stop it. For years before Bill Clinton became President, Washington talked tough but failed to act. In 1992, our borders might as well not have existed. The border was under-patrolled, and what patrols there were, were under-equipped. Drugs flowed freely. Illegal immigration was rampant. Criminal immigrants, deported after committing crimes in America, returned the very next day to commit crimes again.
>
> President Clinton is making our border a place where the law is respected and drugs and illegal immigrants are turned away. We have increased the Border Patrol by over 40 percent; in El Paso, our Border Patrol agents are so close together they can see each other. Last year alone, the Clinton Administration removed thousands of illegal workers from jobs across the country. Just since January of 1995, we have arrested more than 1,700 criminal aliens and prosecuted them on federal

felony charges because they returned to America after having been deported.

Fast-forward to the 2016 Democratic Party platform: another Clinton was running for president, but the party was much more reliant on Hispanic votes.

> Democrats believe we need to urgently fix our broken immigration system—which tears families apart and keeps workers in the shadows—and create a path to citizenship for law-abiding families who are here, making a better life for their families and contributing to their communities and our country. . . .
>
> [W]e will defend and implement President Obama's Deferred Action for Childhood Arrivals and Deferred Action for Parents of Americans executive actions to help DREAMers, parents of citizens, and lawful permanent residents avoid deportation. We will build on these actions to provide relief for others, such as parents of DREAMers. . . .
>
> We believe immigration enforcement must be humane and consistent with our values. We should prioritize those who pose a threat to the safety of our communities, not hardworking families who are contributing to their communities. We will end raids and roundups of children and families, which unnecessarily sow fear in immigrant communities.

In 1996, white voters were more closely split between the two parties, the Hispanic vote was smaller, and both parties were more skeptical of immigration. In 2016, white voters were concentrated in the Republican Party, Hispanic voters were far more powerful, and this cut a political schism in which Democrats became friendlier to immigrants and Republicans nominated Trump.

This is a dynamic Tesler describes well. "In the post–civil rights era, Democrats needed to maintain their nonwhite base without alienating white voters," he told me. "So their incentive was silence. And Republicans needed to win over white voters without appearing racist. So their incentive was to speak about race in code. The shifts now have made it so Democrats' incentive is to make explicitly pro–racial equality appeals and Republicans now have an incentive to make more explicit anti-minority appeals."[39]

But it's not just that Democrats need a racial justice agenda to appeal to their nonwhite base. In another example of the way stacking identities and changing demographics shift opinion, they increasingly need it to appeal to their white base, too.

In 1994, 39 percent of Democrats and 26 percent of Republicans said discrimination was the main reason "black people can't get ahead these days." By 2017, 64 percent of Democrats believed that, but only 14 percent of Republicans. Much of this trend has been driven by white Democrats. "In the past five years, white liberals have moved so far to the left on questions of race and racism that they are now, on these issues, to the left of even the typical black voter," writes Vox's Matt Yglesias, in an analysis of what he calls the "Great Awokening."[40] Strikingly, "white liberals are now *less* likely than African Americans to say that black people should be able to get ahead without any special help." Part of being a Democrat today—and particularly a white Democrat—is a commitment to racial equality, built on an understanding of systemic racism as a central scourge. As political demography changes, so do political identities.

Take that idea and extend it out into the coming decades of American politics. The Democratic Party will not be able to win elections without an excited, diverse coalition. The Republican Party will not be able to win elections without an enthused white base. Democrats will need to build a platform that's even more explicit in its pursuit of racial and gender equality, while Republicans will need to design a politics even more responsive to a coalition that feels itself losing power.

This dynamic is behind much of the panic about "identity politics." When a single group dominates the political agenda, its grievances and demands are just coded as politics, and the vast majority of policy is designed in response to its concerns. But that changes when no one group can control the agenda but many groups can push items onto it; then the competition among identity-based groups becomes visible. It wasn't called identity politics when every cabinet member of every administration was a white male. It's only identity politics when there's pressure to diversify appointments. And yet that process doesn't reflect a strengthening of a particular identity group's hold on politics but a weakening of it.

In June of 2018, I went to Los Angeles to interview Mayor Eric Garcetti. I asked him how, in a diverse polity, he dealt with the tensions of what some call identity politics and what some just call politics. His answer? Talk less, act more. "I came in here as mayor," he said, "and I looked at the boards and commissions that I appointed[,] about 300 people to oversee our departments. And within six months, I made them, for the first time, over 50 percent women. I think it was 53 or 54 percent women. And then we could get back to business."[41]

But imagine that at the national level, attempted by the first female president, with a polarized media looking for conflict. Many would celebrate it. Others would see discrimination, threat, loss. Think back to Limbaugh saying, "How do you get promoted in a Barack Obama administration? By hating white people." Think of Jordan Peterson labeling Canadian prime minister Justin Trudeau's efforts to promote gender equality a "murderous equity doctrine."[42]

The world is not zero-sum, but it is sometimes zero-sum. A world in which 50 percent of government appointees are female is a world in which fewer are male. Those losses will be felt and fought. Powerful social movements will arise to protect what is being taken, to justify the way things were before. Society often appears calm when fundamental injustices go unchallenged, but even if that were desirable—and it's not—it will be impossible as historically marginalized groups gain the power to demand their share of the American dream.

As we navigate these sensitivities, we can do so with more or less care. Richeson believes it would be wise for demographers to stop using terms like "majority-minority America"—after all, whites will still be a plurality, and what good can come of framing America's trajectory in a way that leaves the single largest group feeling maximally threatened? It sounds like "a force of nonwhite people who are coming and they are working as a coalition to overturn white people and whiteness," Richeson says. "That's a problem."[43]

Richeson's research shows that if you can add reassurance to discussions of demographic change—telling people, for instance, that the shifts are unlikely to upend existing power or economic arrangements—the sense of threat, and the tilt toward racial and political conservatism, vanishes. The problem, she admits, is "we can't say, 'Don't worry, white people, you'll be okay and you'll get to run everything forever!'"

The other problem is that the conversation about, and the experience of, a browning America will not be driven by demographers and social psychologists; it will be driven by politicians looking for an edge, by political pundits looking for ratings, by outrageous stories going viral on social media, by cultural controversies like Gamergate and Roseanne Barr getting fired. It will absorb even figures who might prefer not to talk much about race.

Bernie Sanders is a good example here. In 2016, he centered his campaign on class and was criticized for a tin ear on race.

Ultimately, he won slightly more white votes than Clinton, but was swamped by her 50-point margin among African Americans.[44] In 2020, Sanders has run a more race-conscious campaign, emphasizing his past as a civil rights activist. "I protested housing discrimination, was arrested for protesting school segregation, and one of the proudest days of my life was attending the March on Washington for Jobs and Freedom led by Dr. Martin Luther King Jr.," he said in his announcement speech. His campaign has hired more nonwhite staffers, worked harder to build relationships with black political leaders, and released plans to "address the five central types of violence waged against black, brown and indigenous Americans: physical, political, legal, economic and environmental."[45]

Nor is it just race. Sanders had long been skeptical of immigration's effect on native-born workers. He opposed a 2007 bill that included a path to citizenship for undocumented immigrants on the grounds that it permitted too many guest workers who would compete with Americans for jobs. In 2015, while interviewing Sanders, I asked him about open borders, a policy that many democratic socialists support, even if only aspirationally. Sanders responded with disgust. "Open borders? No, that's a Koch brothers proposal. That's a right-wing proposal, which says essentially there is no United States. It would make everybody in America poorer."[46] Open borders is usually seen as a left-wing idea, but Sanders's dismissal reflected a long-standing skepticism of overly liberal immigration policies as bad for American workers. In the 2020 primary, however, Sanders endorsed decriminalizing unauthorized border entry and providing public health insurance to unauthorized immigrants.

Sanders's evolution on these issues reflects both the broader trajectory of white American liberals and the strategic incentives facing any candidate trying to win the Democratic primary. Joe

Biden, for his part, spent much of the early primary praising Obama's leadership while distancing himself from the Obama administration's early deportations (a policy Obama himself had disavowed by the end of his presidency). Being a national Democrat in 2020 means holding positions on race and immigration that would've been considered lethal as recently as 2008.

To say American politics is in for demographic turbulence is not to say we are in for dissolution. A majority of Americans—though not of Republicans—believe the browning of America is a good thing for the country. And we have watched states like California and Texas transition into majority-minority status without falling to pieces. Politicians able to articulate a vision of this future that is inclusive, inspiring, and nonthreatening—the mixture Obama sought in 2008—will reap massive rewards.

But as Obama found after he was elected, leadership in this era requires delivering for diverse coalitions, taking sides in charged cultural battles, and thus becoming part of the very conflict you're trying to calm. The cycle of unity giving way to conflict, of hope about the future activating fear about the present, is likely to continue. And as long as much of the country feels threatened by the changes they see, there will be a continuing, and perhaps growing, market for politicians like Trump.

Interlude

What I've tried to do in the first half of this book is build a model of what's driven American politics into its current place of bitter polarization. Let's take a moment to put it all together.

The human mind is exquisitely tuned to group affiliation and group difference. It takes almost nothing for us to form a group identity, and once that happens, we naturally assume ourselves in competition with other groups. The deeper our commitment to our group becomes, the more determined we become to make sure our group wins. Making matters worse, winning is positional, not material; we often prefer outcomes that are worse for everyone so long as they maximize our group's advantage over other groups.

The parties used to be scrambled, both ideologically and demographically, in ways that curbed their power as identities and lowered the partisan stakes of politics. But these ideologically mixed parties were an unstable equilibrium reflecting America's peculiar, and often abhorrent, racial politics. The success of the civil rights movement, and its alliance with the national

135

Democratic Party, broke that equilibrium, destroyed the Dixie-crat wing of the Democratic Party, and triggered an era of party sorting.

That sorting has been ideological. Democrat now means liberal and Republican now means conservative in a way that wasn't true in, say, 1955. The rise in partisanship is, in part, a rational response to the rise in party difference—if the two sides hated and feared each other less fifty years ago, well, that makes sense; they were more similar fifty years ago.

But that sorting has also been demographic. Today, the parties are sharply split across racial, religious, geographic, cultural, and psychological lines. There are many, many powerful identities lurking in that list, and they are fusing together, stacking atop one another, so a conflict or threat that activates one activates all. And since these mega-identities stretch across so many aspects of our society, they are constantly being activated, and that means they are constantly being reinforced.

All this is happening in an era of profound, powerful social change. A majority of infants born today are nonwhite. The fastest-growing religious identity is no religious identity at all. Women make up majorities on college campuses. Soon, a record proportion of America's population will be foreign born. Groups that are rising in power want their needs reflected in politics and culture, groups that feel themselves losing power want to protect the status and privileges they've had, and this conflict is sorting itself neatly into two parties. Obama's presidency was an example of the younger, more diverse coalition taking power; Trump's presidency represented the older, whiter coalition taking it back.

The second half of the book is about the relationship between a more polarized public and more polarized political institutions. In particular, I want to show the feedback loop of polarization: institutions polarize to appeal to a more polarized public, which further polarizes the public, which forces the institutions to polarize further, and so on.

Polarization isn't something that happened to American politics. It's something that's happening to American politics. And it's getting worse.

Chapter 6

The Media Divide
beyond Left-Right

I 've been a political journalist for more than fifteen years. In that time, I've been a blogger, a newspaper reporter, a magazine writer, a long-form editor, an opinion columnist, a cable news host, a social media personality, a viral video star, a podcaster, and a media entrepreneur. I launched *Wonkblog*, the online policy vertical at the *Washington Post*, and I was a cofounder and the first editor in chief of the explanatory news organization Vox, which now reaches more than 50 million people each month.

When I was launching Vox, I often got asked who our competitors were.* The answer people expected me to give was other politics-heavy news and analysis sites. The *Atlantic*. Nate Silver's FiveThirtyEight. The *Washington Post*. But the truth was that other news sites were less competitors than they were collaborators in a shared effort to engage people in politics. If Silver converted a sports fan into a politics junkie, that person

---

* Vox is a general-interest news site that covers science, culture, technology, and much more. But this is a book about American politics, so in this section I'm going to be mainly talking about our political coverage.

became instantly more likely to read Vox's political coverage. But if someone wasn't interested in politics, or was just sufficiently more interested in, for example, gardening tips or rewatching old *Friends* clips on YouTube, then that person was lost to us.

I say all this to give my next sentence some weight. The central truth I've learned about the audience in each and every one of those places is almost no one is forced to follow politics. There are some lobbyists and government affairs professionals who need to stay on the cutting edge of legislative and regulatory developments to do their jobs. But most people who follow politics do so as a hobby; they follow it in the way they follow a sport or a band.

We can't rely on people to read us out of duty; we have to compete with literally everything else for their attention. Rachel Maddow is at war with reruns of *The Big Bang Theory*. Vox's You-Tube channel competes with Xbox games. Time spent reading this book is time not spent listening to the podcast *Serial*. The logic of this extends to the very edges of our conscious life and beyond. Netflix's CEO Reed Hastings famously said his biggest competitor is sleep. This is the context in which modern political journalism is produced and absorbed: an all-out war for the time of an audience that has more choices than at any point in history.

This is another moment when I need to stop and state: this is new. As banal and inevitable as a competitive media market feels to those of us existing within it, it's never existed before, not like this.

Consider the options available to eager political news consumers in 1995. They might have had a hometown paper or two, a handful of radio stations, the three nightly newscasts, the newly launched CNN, and, if they were really hard-core, a couple of magazine subscriptions.

Fast-forward a decade. Those same consumers could fire up Internet Explorer and read almost any newspaper in the country—

and most of the major newspapers of the world—online. For political opinion, they had a dizzying array of magazines, any op-ed page they chose, and, all of a sudden, a countless number of blogs. On television, CNN had been joined by Fox News and MSNBC. On radio, satellite began crowding the airwaves with more political commentary. In pockets, the launch of the iPod kicked off the age of podcasting.

This smorgasbord of news about the present was nothing compared with the explosion of information about the past. Prior to the digital revolution, virtually all available political news was remorselessly ephemeral: a newspaper article, magazine feature, or news broadcast from six months ago might be preserved in some library somewhere, but so far as the average news consumer was concerned, it was gone. If you heard a term you didn't know or caught a reference to a historical event you were hazy on, there were few options for snap enlightenment. The information in front of you, and physically located nearby, was all the instant information you had.

By the mid-aughts, that was no longer true: media organizations had uploaded vast archives, they were linking back to old stories, they had internal search engines, and, more important, they had made everything available to Google. If you wanted to read up on something that happened a year ago or ten years ago, it was all there for you, even if all you knew was some general words pointing toward the subject. Never in human history had it been remotely possible to be this politically informed.

In most models of democratic politics, information is the constraint. Voters don't have the time or energy to read thick tomes of political theory and keep themselves updated on every act of Congress, so they're dependent on the political professionals— elected officials, campaign operatives, party staffers, lobbyists, pundits—who do. What follows from this model is tantalizing:

if information ceases to be scarce, if it becomes freely and easily available to all, the fundamental problem afflicting democratic systems would be solved.

And then the dreams of democratic theorists everywhere actually came true. The internet made information abundant. The rise of online news gave Americans access to more information—vastly more information, orders of magnitude more information—than they had ever had before. And yet surveys showed we weren't, on average, any more politically informed. Nor were we any more involved: voter participation didn't show a boost from the democratization of political information. Why?

In the early aughts, Princeton political scientist Markus Prior set out to unravel this apparent paradox. The way he resolved the problem is, in retrospect, obvious. What the digital information revolution offered wasn't just more information but more choice of information. Yes, there were now more cable news channels, but they were dwarfed in number by the channels that had no interest whatsoever in news—channels that served up round-the-clock cooking, home repair, travel, comedy, cartoons, tech, classic films. Yes, you could read the political coverage of any newspaper or magazine in the country online, but you could also read so much more nonpolitical coverage—the explosion in political media was more than matched by the explosion in media covering music, television, diets, health, video games, rock climbing, spirituality, celebrity breakups, sports, gardening, cat pictures, genealogical records—really, everything.

The key factor now, Prior argued, was not access to political information, but interest in political information. He made his point by comparing it to television. Like the internet, television multiplied the amount of information available to people, and it spread like wildfire. But unlike the internet, television, at least in its early years, offered little choice. "For decades the networks' scheduling ruled out situations in which viewers had to choose between entertainment and news," Prior wrote in his paper "News vs. Entertainment." "Largely unexposed to entertainment competition, news had its place in the early evening and again before the late-night shows. Today, as both entertainment and news are available around the clock on numerous cable channels and web sites, people's content preferences determine more of what those with cable or Internet access watch, read, and hear."[1]

Politics had once been bundled alongside everything else, and even the uninterested were pushed to consume political news. You might subscribe to the newspaper for the sports page, but that meant seeing the political stories on A1. You might own a television because you refused to miss *I Love Lucy*, but if you had the TV on in the evening, you ended up sitting through the news anyway. The digital revolution offered access to unimaginably vast vistas of information, but just as important, it offered access to unimaginably more choice. And that explosion of choice widened that interested-uninterested divide. Greater choices lets the junkies learn more and the disinterested know less.

To test this, Prior surveyed more than 2,300 people about their content preferences and their political knowledge. And because he was conducting this survey in 2002 and 2003, the early years of the internet and still reasonably early for cable, he was able to survey people who had internet access, those who had cable access, those who had both, and those who had neither.

Content preferences—which is to say, how much people wanted to consume political information versus how much they wanted to consume other forms of entertainment—had little effect on the knowledge of those without cable and internet access. Even if you wanted more political information, you didn't have easy access to it, so the interest didn't translate cleanly into information. But among those with cable and internet access, the difference in political knowledge between those with the highest and lowest interest in cable news was 27 percent. That dwarfed the difference in political knowledge between people with the highest and lowest levels of schooling. "In a high-choice environment, people's content preferences become better predictors of political learning than even their level of education," Prior wrote.

We talk a lot about the left-right polarization in the political news. We don't talk enough about the divide that precedes it: the chasm separating the interested from the uninterested. But you can't understand one without the other. To a large degree, one exists because of the other. And remember: Prior was conducting this research in the early 2000s, before Facebook and Twitter, before mobile internet and YouTube algorithms, before MSNBC's leftward turn, before *BuzzFeed* and *HuffPost*, before Breitbart and the alt-right. The internet has become much better at learning what we want and giving us more of it since then. The competition for audience, and the threat to journalistic business models, has become much more intense since then. And all of this has changed both how political news is produced and how it's consumed.

Political media is for the politically invested

In *All the News That's Fit to Sell: How the Market Transforms Information into News*, economist James Hamilton writes, "News emerges not from individuals seeking to improve the functioning of democracy but from readers seeking diversion, reporters forging careers, and owners searching for profits."[2] That's a bit more cynical than I'd be—a lot of us really do want to improve the functioning of democracy—but as a description of the overall economic system that surrounds our work, it's accurate. And as much as we might want to, it's malpractice to try to understand the news without understanding the financial and audience forces that shape it.

In an age of choice, political journalism is a business that serves people interested in political news and that tries to create more people interested in political news. That wasn't the business model when political news was just one part of a monopolistic bundle; when we were attached to the one newspaper in the city or to the three networks given access to public airwaves, the business model was about appealing to as wide an audience as possible, but it wasn't necessarily about serving an audience intensely interested in politics.

The rise of a more opinionated press is a return to an older media equilibrium. For much of American history, most newspapers were explicitly partisan, often including "Democrat" or "Republican" in the name to signal their lean—some of them, like the *Arkansas Democrat-Gazette*, and the *Arizona Republic* (which was, until 1930, the *Arizona Republican*), still carry that legacy on their mastheads. In 1870, 54 percent of metropolitan dailies were affiliated with the Republican Party, 33 percent were Democratic, and 13 percent claimed independence from party.[3]

Hamilton argues that the transition to a news industry that prized independence from party and ideology was driven by technological advances that changed the business model of newspapers. "The development of presses with runs of 25,000 sheets or more per hour meant a single newspaper could supply a significant portion of a city's readers," he writes. Alongside a drop in the price of paper, newspapers became cheaper, which meant their potential audience became larger, which meant the prices advertisers would pay to reach that audience multiplied. The money really started rolling in if you could dominate a market, because then you could set the rates advertisers paid. But you couldn't dominate a market if you were explicitly serving one political persuasion and offending the other. Thus, newspapers, and other forms of news media, began building an ethic of nonpartisanship, one that both protected their businesses and served important editorial goals.

The explosion of choice and competition carried by digital news upended this calculation again. If the strategy of the monopolistic business model was to be enough things to all people, the strategy of the digital business model is to be the most appealing thing to some people. So the question becomes: What makes people interested in political news? It's that they are rooting for a side, for a set of outcomes. This is not a new insight. Columnist Walter Lippmann put it sharply in his 1922 book *Public Opinion*:

> This is the plight of the reader of the general news. If he is to read it at all he must be interested, that is to say, he must enter into the situation and care about the outcome. . . . The more passionately involved he becomes, the more he will tend to resent not only a different view, but a disturbing bit of news. That is why many a newspaper finds that, having honestly evoked the partisanship of its readers, it can not easily, supposing the editor believes the facts warrant it, change position.

To be interested in politics is to choose a side. How could it be otherwise? The differences between the parties and their coalitions are profound. They are ideological, geographic, demographic, temperamental. Whether your side wins or loses is a literal matter of life and death—perhaps not for you, but given the stakes for health insurance and foreign policy, certainly for someone. Whether your side wins or loses is also a matter of identity and group status. Think back to the magazine covers that follow presidential elections, the ones that make sweeping pronouncements about what kind of nation we truly are based on whether 3 percent of the Midwest vote swung left or right, or the predictable postelection screeds in which liberals discuss moving to Canada and conservatives wonder if Texas should secede; elections feel like they decide whether our country belongs to us and whether we belong in it.

In the less polarized media sphere that preceded cable news and the internet, this focus on whether your side would win or lose expressed itself in an overemphasis on horse race journalism— journalism literally about whether Democrats or Republicans would win or lose the next election. In a media committed to the appearance of neutrality, horse race coverage let them focus on the questions that most animated the audience without tipping ideologically to one side or the other. It's considered biased to say one party's health plan is better than the other's, but it's not considered biased to say one candidate's campaign is better run than the other's. Take it from a practitioner: political journalism is weird.

In today's media sphere, where the explosion of choices has made it possible to get the political media you really want, it's expressed itself in polarized media that attaches to political identity, conflict, and celebrity. That is to say, it expresses itself in journalism and commentary that is more directly about the question of why your side should win and the other side should lose.

I don't want to denigrate this kind of journalism. I've produced much of it myself. I cover politics because I think policy is important, which is to say, because I think who wins and who loses policy fights is important. And, obviously, my views on those questions are rational, judicious, disinterested, and objectively correct. The problem is lots of other people are doing that kind of work, too, and some of them come to different conclusions than I do. So what I want to do here is step back and look at how a political media system increasingly organized around that axis deepens political identity, hardens polarization, and raises the political stakes.

The simplest measure for assessing political journalism is whether it's giving those who follow it a more accurate understanding of American politics. As one disturbing window into this question, consider "The Parties in Our Head: Misperceptions About Party Composition and Their Consequences," a fascinating study published by Douglas Ahler and Gaurav Sood in 2018. In it, Ahler and Sood observe that the intensity of partisan feeling is increasing as the parties become more demographically different from each other, but the level of animosity seems to far outpace the level of difference. After all, they write, "majorities of both parties' supporters are white, middle class, and heterosexual, and both parties' modal supporters are middle aged, nonevangelical Christians."[4] So what's going on?

The answer, they say, is that the parties we perceive are quite different from the parties that exist. To test the theory, they conducted a survey asking people "to estimate the percentage of Democrats who are black, atheist or agnostic, union members, and gay, lesbian, or bisexual, and the percentage of Republicans who are evangelical, 65 or older, Southern, and earn over $250,000 per year." They were asking, in other words, how much people thought the composition of the parties fit the caricatures of the parties.

Misperceptions were high among everyone, but they were particularly exaggerated when people were asked to describe the other party. Democrats believed 44 percent of Republicans earned over $250,000 a year; it's actually 2 percent. Republicans believed that 38 percent of Democrats were gay, lesbian, or bisexual; the correct answer is about 6 percent. Democrats believed that more than four out of every ten Republicans are seniors; in truth, seniors make up about 20 percent of the GOP. Republicans believed that 46 percent of Democrats are black and 44 percent belong to a union; in reality, about 24 percent of Democrats are African American and less than 11 percent belong to a union.

But what was telling about these results is that the more interested in politics people were, the more political media they consumed, the more mistaken they were about the other party (the one exception was the income category: high levels of political knowledge led to more accurate answers about the percentage of Republicans earning more than $250,000). This is a damning result: the more political media you consume, the more warped your perspective of the other side becomes.

But it makes sense if you think about the incentives driving media outlets. Fox News doesn't get Facebook shares by reporting on some banal comments made by Bob Casey, the understated Democratic senator from Pennsylvania. It focuses on Minnesota Representative Ilhan Omar, a liberal, confrontational Muslim American who wears a hijab and speaks with a soft, Somalian accent. Similar dynamics hold on MSNBC and, honestly, everywhere in the media. Representative Steve King, the racist Republican from Iowa, holds little power in the House but receives far more coverage than Representative Greg Walden, the top Republican on the powerful House Energy and Commerce Committee.

The old line on local reporting was: "If it bleeds, it leads." For political reporting, the principle is: "If it outrages, it leads." And outrage is deeply connected to identity—we are outraged when members of other groups threaten our group and violate our values. As such, polarized media doesn't emphasize commonalities, it weaponizes differences; it doesn't focus on the best of the other side, it threatens you with the worst.

As that last paragraph suggests, I'm about to step into some dangerous territory, so let me say this clearly: I'm not asserting moral equivalence, and I'll have much more to say in future chapters about the ways and reasons the Left and the Right—including their media spheres—have diverged. But virtually everyone in political media is competing for audience attention and loyalty amid a cacophony of other choices. We all make different decisions about how to compete for that audience, but since we are all trying to attract other human beings, there are certain similarities in our approach.

Why audience-driven media is identitarian media

Krista Tippett, host of the humane and wise public radio show *On Being*, once told me the media often looks to her like "a conspiracy to surface the loudest voices."[5] She's right, but it's no conspiracy. It's more like the reason the food and restaurant industries pack products with salt and fat and sugar: that's what the market demands. And market demand in media has become a more powerful and more precise force.

I've already discussed the way the audience didn't have much choice in media as recently as a few decades ago. But just as important, the media didn't have much information about the audience. The networks had ratings. The newspapers had subscription renewals. Everyone received letters. But that was really it.

The combination of direct competition and constant access to audience analytics transformed newsrooms. I used to regularly guest host on cable news, and the emotional rhythm of that workday crested around four p.m., when the Nielsen numbers came out, and everyone stopped to compare how their show did against the competition. If you beat your competitors—both inside and outside the network—you could rest easy. If you didn't, you had to worry. And if you lost a few times in a row, you'd start getting calls from upstairs. Maybe your programming should stick closer to the news of the day. Maybe you needed shorter intros, or longer intros, or more guests, or more heat. The numbers were broken up by the quarter hour, so you could even try to decide whether your B block was superior to your D block. The data wasn't good enough to truly answer those questions, but it was good enough to decide whether you were to be celebrated, left alone, or subjected to concerned scrutiny. Cable news is journalism, but it's also a business, and the business runs on ratings. Chris Hayes, who anchors MSNBC's eight p.m. newscast and is among the most thoughtful, civic-minded journalists in the industry, put it this way on his podcast:

> We have very strong metrics we get every day about how many people are watching our show. It is our job to get people's attention and to keep it. And getting people's attention and keeping it can sometimes be in tension with giving them information. There's an amazing Will Ferrell line in *Anchorman 2*, in which he says, "What if instead of telling people the things they need to know, we tell them what they *want* to know?" Which is like the creation story of cable news.[6]

"At some level," he continues, "we're wedding DJs. And the wedding DJ's job is to get you on the floor." The point is not that this leaves no room for serious journalism. As Hayes says, there are good wedding DJs, and bad wedding DJs, and the work of being a cable news host is making sure you're one of the good ones. But this is the business context in which cable news decisions are made.

Then came the rise of real-time digital analytics. Every newsroom in the country subscribes to some service or another that tracks traffic in a gamified, constantly updating interface. The most influential is Chartbeat, which shows you every article on your site, indicates the number of people on each article at any given second, and colors the dots representing those people to tell you how they found the article. Green dots mean they found you through a search engine. Purple dots mean they came from a social network, usually Facebook, Twitter, or Reddit. Walk through a modern newsroom and you'll see the Chartbeat display dotting computer screens: it's addicting to watch people read your work. It's pure pleasure to watch the display for an article you worked hard on fill with dots.

But we don't just want people to read our work. We want people to spread our work—to be so moved by what we wrote or said that they log on to Facebook and share it with their friends or head over to Reddit and try to tell the world. That's how you get those dots to multiply. But people don't share quiet voices. They share loud voices. They share work that moves them, that helps them express to their friends who they are and how they feel. Social platforms are about curating and expressing a public-facing identity. They're about saying I'm a person who cares about this, likes that, and loathes this other thing. They are about signaling the groups you belong to and, just as important, the groups you don't belong to.

The rise of *BuzzFeed* made this subtext into text. Its cofounder and CEO, Jonah Peretti, helped launch the *Huffington Post* (now *HuffPost*), and he built *BuzzFeed* on the side as a skunk works for experimenting with how viral content spread online. The answer soon became clear: identity was the slingshot. And the key insight was there were more identities that people felt strongly about than anyone had ever imagined. People weren't just Republican or Democrat, black or white, gay or straight. They were '90s kids, Alabama football fans, Beyoncé stans, cat lovers, obsessive compulsives. And there was nothing as pleasurable as drawing the boundaries of your group, as sending out a signal that only other members would understand.

BuzzFeed was successful as a laboratory for discovering the principles and drivers of social sharing, and the kind of content it created reflected the discoveries it made. "A classic early *BuzzFeed* post, and later video, was '13 Struggles All Left Handers Know to Be True,'" Peretti tells me. "Another early classic was 'Signs You Were Raised by Immigrant Parents.' That one's a racial identity but also an immigrant identity."

There are so many more. One of *BuzzFeed*'s most popular series was "X Things Only a Y Would Understand." A Google search for those key words brings up articles like "14 Things Only Anxious People Will Understand," "19 Things Only People with Fibromyalgia Will Understand," "53 Things Only '80s Girls Can Understand," "30 Things Everyone Who Went to College Will Understand," "27 Struggles You'll Only Understand if You Were Born Before 1995," "38 Things Only Someone Who Was a Scout Would Know," "19 Comics Only Night Owls Will Understand," "19 Things You'll Only Understand if You Had Strict Parents," "18 Photos That Only People Who Had Braces Will Understand."

I could go on.

This is identity media in its purest form. When you share "38 Things Only Someone Who Was a Scout Would Know," you're saying you were a Scout, and you were a serious enough Scout to understand the signifiers and experiences that only Scouts had. To post that article on Facebook is to make a statement about who you are, who your group is, and, just as important, who is excluded.

The rise of *BuzzFeed*'s quizzes reflected a similar learning. Quizzes revealing—and then letting you share—the answer to questions like "What State Do You Actually Belong In?," "Which Disney Princess Are You?," "What Level of Introvert Are You?," and "Which Hogwarts House Do You Belong In?"* are all about identity. They spit back an expression of your personality, alongside the group you belong to, and let you display that to your friends.

Long before *BuzzFeed*, the internet was enabling people with niche interests to find one another and build communities around shared passions. IRC message boards were fractal worlds spinning off into ever smaller subgroups; history nerds would subdivide into medieval history nerds would subdivide into medieval history reenactors all the way until it was, inevitably, just three dudes looking at esoteric porn. If you go back and read early journalism on the internet, this is what much of it's about: the internet as a place for people to link up with others who share their interests.

But much of what the media thought were interests were actually identities. That shift is subtle but important. Peretti thinks it's inherent in having an actual relationship with your audience. You feed an interest with information; you build an identity through socialization. "The fact that people will watch a cooking show on the Food Network wouldn't necessarily make you think there is an identity and a community there," he says. "But when people are engaged on a YouTube channel with cooking, there's all these comments, people are saying, 'I made this and I made that'—there's feedback and it's shaping the content. You start to realize that this is for a particular type of person. Then the content starts representing identity more."

---

* Gryffindor, duh.

The forces *BuzzFeed* found and followed are shaping political news and conversation, too. They are not reflected quite so literally in headlines, of course. "27 Facts About Health Care Only Liberals Will Know" would not be such a good—actually, no, that would be a great headline, and it would do monster social traffic. But most of the time, the way identity is affirmed and activated in political headlines is more oblique: this public figure that you and everyone in your group loathes said something awful. This poll came out saying you and your group are going to win or, better yet, that your out-group is going to lose. This slashing column explains why you're right about everything and why your opponents are wrong.

A lot of these pieces are true and useful. Mostly the ones I agree with or personally wrote. A lot of them are garbage. But cumulatively, it's a sharp change from the days in which most political content people saw was self-consciously trying to avoid offending anyone. The stories that thrive when your business model is a local monopoly that needs a news product that's appealing to every kind of person who might shop at a department store is different from the stories that thrive when your business model is people who strongly agree with your stories sharing them with their friends.

There are two ways of thinking about how this change in media changes us. One is to imagine identities as static and preexisting. If that's true, then the rise of digital media was simply revealing what was already there. In this telling, we used to have a limited number of media outlets, and they were almost all run by wealthy white men, so the market was simply ill served and waiting for correction. This is clearly part of the story. In the absence of social media and audience analytics, I doubt that newsrooms run by white men would've devoted blanket coverage to the events in Ferguson, Missouri, and their aftermath. And I say that as a white man who was running a newsroom at that time—this is the way analytics and social media improve our work, by giving us truer, broader information about the audience's interests.

But the other perspective takes identities as living, malleable things. They can be activated or left dormant, strengthened or weakened, created or left in the void. In this telling, all this identity-oriented content will deepen the identities it repeatedly triggers, confirms, or threatens. It will turn interests or opinions into identities.

When I was in high school, I began smoking pot. When I started reading about it online, I quickly fell into drug legalization communities that turned my interest in getting high into an activist identity, complete with a rich community of people I believed in, enemies I was mad at. I subscribed to a newsletter full of stories I never would've seen but that now pissed me off and made me more committed to the cause. I don't say this to dismiss my younger self or criticize the process of identity formation. I think my high school self was right about pot legalization. I think developing an activist identity was healthy. The point is simply that this process is far easier in the age of the internet than it was before.

The digital scholar Zeynep Tufekci has tracked the way YouTube's recommendation algorithm serves as an engine of radicalization. She noticed that videos of Trump rallies led to recommendations for videos of alt-right content. Videos of Hillary Clinton speeches eventually served up leftist conspiracies. As she widened her analysis, she found it wasn't just politics. "Videos about vegetarianism led to videos about veganism. Videos about jogging led to videos about running ultramarathons. It seems as if you are never 'hard core' enough for YouTube's recommendation algorithm. It promotes, recommends and disseminates videos in a manner that appears to constantly up the stakes."[7]

That algorithm isn't just an engine of radicalization; it's an engine of identity. As Peretti observed, interests become identities as they socialize you into a community. YouTube's algorithm is constantly trying to lure you into new communities, populated by charismatic YouTube stars who cultivate tight-knit audiences. When I was a teenager smoking pot, I had to search out a newsletter about pot legalization, and I had no sense of who wrote it or who read it. Today, I would be algorithmically invited into communities of legalization activists, whose names and faces I would quickly come to know.

Many of us who wrote about politics on the internet before the rise of social media lament the feeling that something has been lost, that a space that once felt fresh and generative now feels toxic and narrow. In her book *Trick Mirror*, Jia Tolentino offers a description of what changed that feels right to me, which is that social media shifted the "organizing principle" of online discourse:

> The early internet had been constructed around lines of affinity and openness. But when the internet moved to an organizing principle of opposition, much of what had formerly been surprising and rewarding and curious became tedious, noxious, and grim.
>
> This shift partly reflects basic social physics. Having a mutual enemy is a quick way to make a friend—we learn this as early as elementary school—and politically, it's much easier to organize people against something than it is to unite them in an affirmative vision. And, within the economy of attention, conflict always gets more people to look.[8]

Few realized, early on, that the way to win the war for attention was to harness the power of community to create identity, and the simplest way to do that, particularly in politics, was to focus on enemies. But the winners emerged quickly, often using techniques whose mechanisms they didn't fully understand—witness the reckoning Facebook has had to undergo facing up to the behavior their core product rewarded—and triggering an explosion of digital identities.

When I entered journalism, the term of art for pieces infused with perspective was "opinion journalism." The point of the work was to convey an opinion. Nowadays, I think a lot of it is closer to "identity journalism"—the effect of the work, given the social channels through which it's consumed, is to reinforce an identity. But an identity, once adopted, is harder to change than an opinion. An identity that binds you into a community you care about is costly and painful to abandon, and the mind will go to great lengths to avoid abandoning it. So the more media people see that encourages them to think of themselves as part of a group, and the more they publicly proclaim—through sharing and liking and following and subscribing—that they are part of a group, the deeper that identity roots and the more resistant the underlying views become to change.

Reading the other side doesn't change our minds, it deepens our certainty

When I interviewed Obama, he put particular focus on the role of the media in polarization. "I'm not the first to observe this, but you've got the Fox News/Rush Limbaugh folks and then you've got the MSNBC folks and the—I don't know where Vox falls into that, but you guys are, I guess, for the brainiac-nerd types. But the point is that technology which brings the world to us also allows us to narrow our point of view."[*9] You can call this the echo chamber theory of polarization: we've cocooned ourselves into hearing information that only tells us how right we are, and that's making us more extreme.

There is an optimistic theory embedded in this story: people are open to counterevidence, but they're just not getting much of it. We watch MSNBC if we're liberal, Fox News if we're conservative, and CNN if we just want to see people fight; Facebook and Twitter serve us up the news they've learned we like, which means the angriest voices we already agree with; we don't see or hear from the other side, so of course we're becoming more polarized. This story suggests a straightforward solution: if only we crossed the informational aisle, if only the liberals would watch a bit of Fox and the conservatives would spend some time with Maddow, we would realize the other side is more like us than we thought, that it makes some good points, too, and our enmity and polarization would ebb.

Beginning in October 2017, a group of political scientists and sociologists decided to test this theory. In the largest study of its kind ever conducted, they paid 1,220 regular Twitter users who identified as either Democrats or Republicans to follow a bot retweeting elected officials, media figures, and opinion leaders from the other side. The participants took regular surveys asking about their views on ten issues ranging from immigration to government waste to corporate profits to LGBT acceptance.

The researchers were testing the collision between two pop-

---

* Obama is onto something with that description of Vox. "Brainiac-nerd type" is a kind of identity people hold, and it's one we try to activate both in our brand and our coverage. We do that in part because we think it's a healthy identity that aligns well with producing rigorous journalism. That we can choose to activate more productive identities is a theme I will return to later.

ular models. In one, "a vast literature indicates contact between opposing groups can challenge stereotypes that develop in the absence of positive interactions between them."[10] In the other, exposure to those with opposing political views can "exacerbate political polarization," as being told you're wrong by someone you already don't like triggers annoyance, not reflection.

In this case, the pessimists won the day. The result of the monthlong exposure to popular, authoritative voices from the other side of the aisle was an increase in issue-based polarization. "We find that Republicans who followed a liberal Twitter bot became substantially more conservative posttreatment," write the authors. "Democrats exhibited slight increases in liberal attitudes after following a conservative Twitter bot, although these effects are not statistically significant."

The difference between the Democratic and Republican responses is interesting and merits more study. But the key finding is that neither group responded to exposure to the other side by moderating its own views. In both cases, hearing contrary opinions drove partisans not just to a deeper certainty in the rightness of their cause, but more polarized policy positions—that is to say, Republicans became more conservative rather than more liberal, and Democrats, if anything happened at all, became more liberal rather than more conservative.

I spoke to Christopher Bail, one of the study's authors and the head of Duke University's Polarization Lab. "For a long time, people have been assuming that exposing people to opposing views creates the opportunity for moderation," he told me. "If I could humbly claim to figure out one thing, it's that that's not a simple process. If Twitter tweaks its algorithms to put one Republican for every nine Democrats in your Twitter feed, that won't increase moderation."[11]

Imagine you're a liberal browsing Twitter and you're suddenly confronted with a Trump tweet slamming "Sleepy Joe Biden" for destroying America. Your response isn't to think, "Hmm, that Trump makes some good points." It's to instantly come up with an argument for why he's wrong or to dismiss him as a bully. If you're a conservative who comes across Representative Alexandria Ocasio-Cortez railing against the GOP's corrupt, racist agenda, you're likely to be offended, not convinced. In both cases, exposure to the other side's attacks is likely to trigger rebuttal, not reflection—identity-protective cognition, remember?

There is evidence that structuring positive, collaborative interactions can promote understanding. But very little in either political media or social media is designed for positive interactions with the other side. Most political media isn't even designed for persuasion. Some is—Ross Douthat's column at the *New York Times* is a conservative trying to persuade a liberal audience, for instance—but, for all the reasons we've discussed, the bulk of opinionated political media is written for the side that already agrees with the author, and most partisan elected officials are tweeting to their supporters, who follow them and fund-raise for them, rather than to their critics, who don't.

Ironically, this same dynamic limits the polarizing effect of opinionated media, at least on its direct audience. After years in which people worried over the polarizing effects of cable news, Kevin Arceneaux and Martin Johnson decided to test it in something closer to real-world conditions. In a series of experiments, they forced one group to watch either politically friendly or unfriendly cable news content, but let another choose between political news and entertainment channels.[12]

Sure enough, if you forced people to watch cable news that agreed with them, they became more polarized, and if you forced them to sit through cable news that disagreed with them, it either did nothing or backfired. But if you gave them the remote and allowed them to change the channel, the effect dissipated entirely. It turned out the polarization was coming from forcing people who were persuadable to watch political news, which they didn't want to do. Once you gave them the choice to opt out, it was just preaching to the choir.

Tellingly, this was under conditions that were unusually favorable to cable news: political channels were a third to half of all available content in the experimental conditions, as opposed to a tiny fraction of all available content, as is true on our actual televisions. But even that bare level of choice permitted the persuadable to wander off—or, if you prefer, flee elsewhere. "Political news shows cannot directly affect those who refuse to watch them," Arcenaux and Martin conclude.

I don't take this to prove cable news and other forms of politicized and social media aren't polarizing, even on those who don't watch or tweet. Many of us, myself included, have watched an older family member retire and swing sharply right as Fox News comes to fill their days. And a number of studies show that Fox News increased Republican vote share as it rolled out across the country, suggesting a genuine persuasive effect compared to the pre–Fox News equilibrium.[13] But the reality is these networks command modest audiences. The key to their influence is that they have the right audiences. A polarized media environment can polarize the country through its effect on political elites and party activists. Virtually every congressional office on the Hill has its televisions tuned to cable news. Politicians are increasingly addicted to Twitter, with the president being only the most prominent example.

To the extent that political elites have cocooned themselves into more polarized informational worlds—and they have—they behave in more polarized ways, which in turn polarizes the system. Fox News has whipped the Republican Party into a number of government shutdowns, and much of Trump's most offensive rhetoric comes on a direct conveyor from conservative media feeding him conspiracies that he transforms into presidential proclamations. Indeed, the impeachment effort House Democrats launched against Trump stems from Trump believing a set of anti-Biden conspiracies pushed by Breitbart editor-at-large Peter Schweizer and heavily promoted on Fox News.[14] Most Americans had never heard of Hunter Biden, much less followed vague insinuations about Ukrainian prosecutors. But the president was sufficiently persuaded that he threw the weight of his administration into an investigation, setting off a chain of events that changed American political history. You don't need a big audience when you have the right audience.

Politics is, first and foremost, driven by the people who pay the most attention and wield the most power—and those people opt in to extraordinarily politicized media. They then create the political system they perceive. The rest of the country then has to choose from more polarized options, and that in turn polarizes them—remember, the larger the difference between the parties, the more compelling it becomes for even the uninterested to choose a side.

Journalists are hardly immune to these forces. We become more polarized, and more polarizing, when we start spending our time in polarizing environments. I have seen it in myself, and I have watched it in others: when we're going for retweets, or when our main form of audience feedback is coming from partisan junkies on social media, it subtly but importantly warps our news judgment. It changes who we cover and what stories we chase. And when we cover politics in a more polarized way, anticipating or absorbing the tastes of a more polarized audience, we create a more polarized political reality.

The media creates, it doesn't just reflect

The news is supposed to be a mirror held up to the world, but the world is far too vast to fit in our mirror. The fundamental thing the media does all day, every day, is decide what to cover—decide, that is, what is newsworthy.

Here's the dilemma: to decide what to cover is to become the shaper of the news rather than a mirror held up to the news. It makes journalists actors rather than observers. It annihilates our fundamental conception of ourselves. And yet it's the most important decision we make. If we decide to give more coverage to Hillary Clinton's emails than to her policy proposals—which is what we did—then we make her emails more important to the public's understanding of her character and potential presidency than her policy proposals. In doing so, we shape not just the news but the election, and thus the country.

While I'm critical of the specific decision my industry made in that case, this problem is inescapable. The news media isn't just an actor in politics. It's arguably the most powerful actor in politics.* It's the primary intermediary between what politicians do and what the public knows. The way we try to get around this is by conceptually outsourcing the decisions about what we cover to the idea of newsworthiness. If we simply cover what's newsworthy, then we're not the ones making those decisions at

* Speaking of the news media as a singular entity is, of course, problematic. The *New York Times* and the *Baltimore Sun* and the *Washington Examiner* and NPR and Vox do not make coverage decisions as a cartel. But the news media exhibits enough herdlike behavior, and responds to similar enough incentives, that I don't think it's any more problematic than talking about "Wall Street," "Silicon Valley," or "America."

all—it's the neutral, external judgment of newsworthiness that bears responsibility. The problem is that no one, anywhere, has a rigorous definition of newsworthiness, much less a definition that they actually follow.

A simple example comes in the treatment of presidential and pre-presidential rhetoric. On some level, anything that the president says, or that a plausible candidate for president says, is newsworthy. And yet, only a small minority of what is said by presidential candidates, or even presidents, gets covered as major news.

When President Obama gave a speech on manufacturing policy at an Ohio steel mill and when Senator Marco Rubio held a town hall discussing higher education costs in New Hampshire, they struggled to get the press to take notice. Trump, meanwhile, routinely gets cable networks to air his rallies live—and he was able to command that kind of coverage even before he became president. Indeed, there's a good argument to be made that this is why he became president.

In *Identity Crisis*, Sides, Vavreck, and Tesler find that "from May 1, 2015, to April 30, 2016, Trump's median share of cable news mentions was 52 percent." There were seventeen Republican candidates running for president, so Trump was getting more than half of all the media coverage, with the other sixteen candidates splitting the remainder.[15]

It gets worse. "Trump received 78 percent of all coverage on CNN between Aug. 24 and Sept. 4, 2015," and by November 2015, "Trump had received more evening network news coverage—234 minutes—than the entire Democratic field. By contrast, Ted Cruz had received seven minutes."[16] This was a choice the media made, and it is not one, in retrospect, that I think many would defend. In February of 2016, for instance, the chairman of CBS said of Donald Trump's candidacy, and the ratings it drew, "it may not be good for America, but it's damn good for CBS. . . . It's a terrible thing to say, but bring it on, Donald. Keep going." I suspect he would not make the same comments today.

Sides, Vavreck, and Tesler argue that in a chaotic, crowded primary, the media coverage Trump received was crucial to legitimizing his campaign. "Republican voters had received no clear signal about who the front-runner was or should be. The resulting uncertainty meant that this signal needed to come from somewhere else. It was news media coverage that would fill this void."[17] The coverage of Trump also made it impossible for his challengers to get their messages heard.

But why did the media give Trump so much coverage? Why does he continue to get so much coverage? That he led the polls then or is president now isn't good enough. Trump got that coverage before he led the polls; he then got more coverage than other front-runners in past primaries and he gets more coverage than past presidents. As president, his rambling mono-logues, which are unusually detached both from factual rigor and from his own administration's policy-making decisions, are treated as worthier of airtime than the more careful, factual, and policy-predictive speeches of his predecessors. I remember the Bush and Obama administrations begging the press to pay attention to this or that policy announcement. But when Trump sends out a misspelled tweet slamming Elizabeth Warren, it dominates cable for the rest of the day. The answer, simply, is that Trump understands what newsworthy really means, and he uses it to his advantage.

In theory, newsworthiness means something roughly like "important." The most newsworthy story is the most important story. But if that were true, front pages and cable news shows would look very different from how they do now: more malaria, fewer celebrities (including political celebrities). In practice, newsworthiness is some combination of important, new, outrageous, conflict-oriented, secret, or interesting.

"Journalism academics have always known that newsworthiness, as the American press defines it, isn't a system with any coherence to it," Jay Rosen, a journalism professor at New York University, told me "It doesn't make any sense. It's just a list of factors that occasionally come together to produce news. There's no real logic to it, other than it's a list of things that can make something news. The advantage of it is that it leaves maximum leeway for editors to say, 'This is news,' and, 'That's not news,' and so it's news if a journalist decides it's news."[18]

But journalists don't want to decide what's newsworthy, because we don't want to be seen influencing politics so profoundly. If we began saying, for instance, that education policy announcements were only half as newsworthy as national security announcements, the outcry would be immense. The point is to obscure the fact that the decisions being made are decisions at all. It's best if newsworthiness feels like a quality external to journalistic judgment, as if it were a weight attached to each story and measurable with proper instrumentation.

Because of that, judgments of newsworthiness are often contagious; nothing obscures the fact that a decision is being made quite like everyone else making it, too. Thus, a shortcut to newsworthiness has always been whether other news organizations are covering a story—if they are, then it's newsworthy by definition. In the modern era, a shortcut to newsworthiness is social media virality; if people are already talking about a story or a tweet, that makes it newsworthy almost by definition. In both cases, the presence of other outlets and other voices serves to build a fortress of tautology: whatever everyone is covering is newsworthy because everyone is covering it.

This can lead the country into odd, angry cul-de-sacs. I remember returning from an offline vacation only to find the entire political media at war over a viral video in which students from Covington Catholic High School wearing MAGA hats appeared to harass Nathan Phillips, a Native American elder playing a drum. In the original video, which took place during a protest at the National Mall, the teens were seen mocking, smirking, and making Tomahawk chop motions at Phillips. A longer video muddied the waters, offering evidence that the teens were themselves harassed by members of the fringe Black Israelites group beforehand. Soon enough, the media was filled with takes and counter-takes, and President Trump himself was weighing in. "Nick Sandmann and the students of Covington have become symbols of Fake News and how evil it can be," he tweeted.[19]

What was striking, walking into this debate without the (dis) advantage of being present for its initial escalation, was how angry everyone was over something that objectively didn't matter at all. Who cared about an unpleasant—but ultimately nonviolent— confrontation at a protest that few even knew was happening in the first place? How was this newsworthy? The answer was that it had been dominating social media all weekend and that had made it newsworthy. And why had it dominated social media? Because it was a perfect collision of political identities: MAGA-hatted teenagers against a peaceful, drumming Native American elder. Liberal news outlets turning the country against conservative, Christian children from a religious school. As my colleague Zack Beauchamp wrote, it was like a "skeleton key to our increasingly identity-focused politics."[20] But more than that, it was an object lesson in how social media's preference for identitarian conflict focuses the media on identitarian conflicts, even when those collisions are almost comically obscure.

These are dynamics that Trump, who is masterful at seeding social media with identitarian conflict, exploits daily. He weaponizes outrageousness, offensiveness, and identity cues to capture a share of political coverage unknown in the modern era. He's shown that in a competitive media environment—particularly one responsive to social platforms—you can dominate the media by lobbing grenades into our deepest social divides. If you announce your campaign by calling Mexican immigrants rapists and criminals, you'll dominate mindshare among both the people who hate you, whose identity and group you're threatening, and the people who've been waiting eagerly for someone to descend a golden escalator and finally stand up for them and their beliefs. To put it simply, in a media driven by identity and passion, identitarian candidates who arouse the strongest passions have an advantage. You can arouse that passion through inspiration, as Obama did, or through conflict, as Trump did. What you can't do is be boring.

Trump understood this and deprived his competitors of the media oxygen necessary to get their own messages heard. How do you knock Trump off the polls if you can't get a word in edgewise? On December 7, 2015, the first poll was released showing Trump falling to second place in Iowa, behind Cruz. Later that same day, Trump took the stage and read, unusually, from a prepared statement. "Donald J. Trump is calling for a total and complete shutdown of Muslims entering the United States until our country's representatives can figure out what is going on," he said. It was a shocking, unconstitutional proposal—and it gave Trump complete control of a media narrative that might otherwise have emphasized Cruz's candidacy and Trump's slipping numbers.

The media doesn't just reflect the politics we have; it shapes it, even creates it. For all the talk of Trump's Twitter feed, the demographics of his voters are the precise inverse of the demographics of Twitter users. Twitter is used by the young; Trump won atop the votes of the old. His Twitter feed matters because it sets the agenda for every political news outlet in the country.

The media is how most Americans get their information about politics and politicians, and if the media is tilting, or being tilted, toward certain kinds of political stories and figures, then the political system will tilt in that direction, too.

Trump is a product of the tilting, but he is not the first, and he will not be the last. The political media is biased, but not toward the Left or Right so much as toward loud, outrageous, colorful, inspirational, confrontational. It is biased toward the political stories and figures who activate our identities, because it is biased toward and dependent on the fraction of the country with the most intense political identities.

Oh, and funny thing. So, too, is everyone else in politics.

Chapter 7

Post-Persuasion Elections

Before he worked for George W. Bush, first as Bush's director of polling and planning in 2000 and then as Bush's chief campaign strategist in 2004, Matthew Dowd had been a Democratic campaign consultant. He was that rarest of creatures: a persuadable voter. Perhaps that's why he was able to recognize, poring through the results of the 2000 election, that he was going extinct.

"One of the first things I looked at after 2000 was what was the real Republican vote and what was the real Democratic vote," he recalled in an extensive interview to PBS's *Frontline*, "not just who said they were Republicans and Democrats, but independents, how they really voted, whether or not they voted straight ticket or not. And I took a look at that in 2000, and then I took a look at what it was over the last five elections or six elections."[1]

What Dowd found was that the share of true independents—the number of people who were actually undecided and could vote for either party—had plummeted in recent elections, going from, in his calculations, about 22 percent of the electorate to 7 percent. The implications of this were "fairly revolutionary, because everybody up until that time had said, 'Swing voters, swing voters, swing voters, swing voters, swing voters.'"

Dowd realized, looking at his chart, that presidential campaigns were conceptualizing elections all wrong. They had imagined the bulk of the electorate as open to persuasion and had been "putting 80 percent of our resources into persuasion and 20 percent into base motivation." In reality, though, almost all voters now had their minds made up. You didn't need to persuade them of whom to vote for—indeed, you *couldn't* persuade them of whom to vote for. What you needed to do was excite the group of them who, if they were going to vote, were going to vote for you. Those people had to register, they had to remember where their polling place was, they had to take time out of their day to go cast a ballot. America isn't like Australia, where voting is compulsory. We make it both optional and, in many places, difficult, so a winning campaign needs not just supporters but motivated supporters.

In 2000, Bush ran as "a uniter, not a divider." One reason Ralph Nader's third-party candidacy attracted so much support was that he convinced many Americans that the choice between Bush and Gore was a choice between "Tweedledum and Tweedledee." History proved Nader profoundly wrong about that, but the message worked because Bush and Gore were running to win over the persuadable middle, and that meant sanding off their ideological rough edges. Gore was a New Democrat. Bush was a compassionate conservative. Gore ran on fiscal responsibility, promising to protect the Social Security Trust Fund with his lockbox. Bush ran as a Republican who cared, promising to close the racial achievement gap in schools.

The 2004 election, coming in the polarized aftermath of the Iraq War, was about sharpening the differences between the parties. Mark McKinnon, who worked as a media strategist on

Bush's campaigns, told *Frontline* that "it struck me as a political consultant as something radical, because for years we had always talked about that persuadable middle electorate, and that's what it was all about. You ignored everything else. All your resources went into that persuadable vote."[2] No longer. You still needed to win over swing voters, but the top priority was mobilizing the base. This strategy, Dowd said, "influenced everything that we did. It influenced how we targeted mail, how we targeted phones, how we targeted media, how we traveled, the travel that the president and the vice president did to certain areas, how we did organization, where we had staff."

So in 2004, the issues the Bush campaign emphasized, the commercials it ran, the identities it activated—all of it was oriented toward brightening the distinctions between Republicans and Democrats and turning out the voters who were on their side. If Bush's 2000 message was that he was a Republican Democrats could feel good about, his 2004 message was he was a Republican Republicans could feel great about. It worked. Bush went from losing the popular vote in 2000 to winning it in 2004. Republicans expanded their majorities in the House and Senate. Most tellingly, the share of the electorate that self-identified as Republican matched that of Democrats for the first time in history, as the Bush team's effort to turn out Republicans bore fruit. The base mobilization strategy had been a risk, but it had paid off. "Thank goodness, it was the right decision," says Dowd.

That presidential campaigns have shifted their focus toward base mobilization is backed up by the amusingly named "All About That Base," a study conducted by Northeastern University political scientist Costas Panagopoulos. The American National Election Survey has been asking voters whether a campaign contacted them going all the way back to 1956. Panagopoulos realized you could break those responses down by different types of voters and see whether independents, weak partisans, or strong partisans were getting the most outreach.

In 1956, 20 percent of independents and 17 percent of strong partisans reported being contacted by a campaign. By 2012, the last year in Panagopoulos's data set, 32 percent of independents and 45 percent of strong partisans said they'd heard from a campaign. Notably, Panagopoulos finds that 2000, not 2004, was the break point when base mobilization began outpacing persuasion—that year, the Bush campaign contacted 17 percent of independents and 39 percent of strong Republican partisans. Either way, the trend has been clear: "presidential campaign strategies have shifted in recent years reflecting a stronger emphasis on base mobilization compared to persuading independent, undecided or swing voters."[3]

We have lived through a transformation in our elections. As the parties sorted, both demographically and philosophically, it became harder and stranger to remain undecided. It's easy to be in the middle of a muddle; it's harder to be in the middle of a chasm. But a more polarized electorate changes the strategies candidates use to get elected. Those more polarized strategies further polarize the electorate. And then the cycle continues.

The Democratic presidents who bookended Bush are, in some ways, even starker examples. After losing three presidential elections in a row, Democrats were desperate to win in 1992 and convinced that the path back to power ran through persuasion, so they nominated a white, southern centrist named Bill Clinton who promised to reform welfare and balance the budget. After Bush's successful 2004 campaign, however, the Democratic Party was operating in the era of base mobilization, and it nominated someone who thrilled liberals and reflected the more diverse Democratic coalition: a young, charismatic, liberal African American senator from Chicago.

From a political identity perspective, Clinton was a candidate designed to cross-pressure the electorate: he was a Democrat who could appeal to Democrats through party and some policy and appeal to non-Democrats through region, race, gender, and style. Clinton often made a show of challenging the party's left wing, of signaling that he both heard and shared the qualms undecided voters had about the party's most liberal voices and ideas. He promised to "end welfare as we know it" and said abortion "should be safe, legal, and rare." Obama, by contrast, was a candidate for an age of identity stacking: his strength wasn't in converting Republicans but in mobilizing Democratic constituencies to vote at unheard-of rates.

When Hillary Clinton ran for president, she ran more like Obama than her husband. If anything, she ran to Obama's left. Lacking Obama's easy rapport with the young, nonwhite voters who had powered his rise, she had to say much of what he left unsaid, to promise much of what he let voters assume. So while Obama was reticent to discuss race, and careful to reflect white anxieties when he did, Clinton was eager to discuss it and aimed her comments at winning over voters of color. "Ending systemic racism requires contributions from all of us, especially those of us who haven't experienced it ourselves," Clinton said, becoming the first major-party candidate to use the term "systemic racism" in a speech. Where Obama made a point of increasing deportations in his first term in office as part of a bid to win moderates over to immigration reform, Clinton promised not to deport any undocumented immigrants save for violent criminals or terrorists, a position well to Obama's left.

It's to cast no judgment on either side to say that the choice between the party of Hillary Clinton and the party of Donald Trump is sharper than the choice between the parties of Bill Clinton and George H. W. Bush. It is easier to know if you agree with the Democrats in the age of Hillary Clinton than of Bill Clinton, just as it was easier to know where you stood with George W. Bush than his father. But in offering policies, drawing contrasts, and choosing candidates meant to mobilize a polarized electorate, both parties are further polarizing that electorate. Clearer choices mean fewer undecided voters to persuade, which further reinforces the incentives to focus on base mobilization. Here, as elsewhere, polarization begets polarization; it's a flywheel, not a switch.

Strong partisans, weak parties, and broken primaries

The decline of persuadable voters sounds like good news for political parties. How much easier to focus on the swath of the electorate that agrees with them, that already believes what they believe, than the mushy middle. But parties, too, are in decline.

"The defining characteristic of our moment is that parties are weak while partisanship is strong," wrote Marquette University political scientist Julia Azari.[4] She's right, and it's one of the most important insights for understanding the rise of Trump, the success of more ideologically extreme candidates, and the American political system's deepening vulnerability to charismatic demagogues. At the beginning of the book, I posed a question: How did a candidate as abnormal as Trump win the Republican primary and end up with such a normal share of the general election vote? Weak parties and strong partisanship is the answer.

Trump's win would have been impossible in the strong party system we had fifty years ago. Elites within the Republican Party viewed him with horror. His primary opponents spoke of him in apocalyptic terms. Ted Cruz called Trump a "pathological liar," "utterly amoral," and "a narcissist at a level I don't think this country's ever seen." Rick Perry said Trump's candidacy was "a cancer on conservatism, and it must be clearly diagnosed, excised, and discarded." Rand Paul said Trump is "a delusional narcissist and an orange-faced windbag. A speck of dirt is way more qualified to be president." Marco Rubio called him "dangerous" and warned that we should not hand "the nuclear codes of the United States to an erratic individual."

And then every single one of those Republicans endorsed Trump. Cruz told Americans to vote for the pathological liar. Perry urged people to elect the cancer on conservatism and then later served as its secretary of energy. Paul backed the delusional narcissist. Rubio campaigned to hand the nuclear codes of the United States to an erratic individual. The list goes on. Paul Ryan, the Republican Speaker of the House of Representatives, endorsed Trump, as did Mitch McConnell, the Senate majority leader, and Reince Priebus, the head of the Republican National Committee. Mike Pence, the governor of Indiana, commiserated with Dan Senor, a former Bush adviser, over the fact that Trump was "unacceptable"—and then signed on as Trump's vice president.[5]

With that kind of elite support, it's little wonder Trump managed to consolidate Republican-leaning voters behind him. Whether you were a Trump Republican or a Cruz Republican or a Ryan Republican or just someone who didn't like Hillary Clinton, the choice was clear: vote Trump. Trump would appoint Republican judges, pass Republican tax cuts, fight Republican enemies. The decision to endorse Trump was "binary," Ryan told CNN. It was either Trump or Clinton, and Ryan knew where he fell. "In the balance of things, the good clearly outweighs the things I don't agree with. . . . We don't have people who run for office who 100 percent reflect all of our views. It doesn't work like that."[6]

Fifty years ago, Republican Party elites would've stopped Trump long before the choice collapsed into the binary of him or Clinton. Up until the 1970s, party nominations were controlled by party officials. The only way to win a presidential nomination was to win the delegates at the national convention. That meant convincing party bosses who cared more for their own power than ideology and who prioritized, above all, being able to work with whoever took office. The horse-trading to win a nomination could be intense, particularly when no candidate entered with a commanding majority of delegates: in 1924, Democratic delegates went through more than a hundred ballots before nominating John W. Davis. It's from brokered conventions like these that we get the modern metaphor of smoke-filled back rooms.

Both parties have since turned their presidential nomination processes over to party primaries, which means that the measure of a candidate isn't whether he or she can win over party bosses but whether he or she can win over the intense minority of party supporters who turn out to vote in primaries (in 2016, for instance, less than 30 percent of eligible voters participated in primaries—and that was unusually high). This has made parties weaker, partisans stronger, and the American political system more vulnerable to demagogues.

As Steven Levitsky and Daniel Ziblatt argue in *How Democracies Die*, American politics has long given rise to demagogic showmen with intense bases of support. The anti-Semitic priest and radio star Father Coughlin fits this description, as does Henry Ford and Louisiana governor Huey Long. But even if 20 or 30 percent of the population loved them, they had no chance at winning a party convention:

> The convention system was an effective gatekeeper, in that it systematically filtered out dangerous candidates. Party insiders

provided what political scientists called "peer review." Mayors, senators, and congressional representatives knew the candidates personally. They had worked with them, under diverse conditions, over the years and were thus well-positioned to evaluate their character, judgment, and ability to operate under stress. Smoke-filled back rooms therefore served as a screening mechanism, helping to keep out the kind of demagogues and extremists who derailed democracy elsewhere in the world. American party gatekeeping was so effective that outsiders simply couldn't win. As a result, most didn't even try.[7]

Today, though, the path to a nomination runs through primaries and caucuses, both of which favor candidates with intense supporters, even if they're not the candidates with the broadest support. After all, you can't win a caucus on a rainy, cold night in January unless you have supporters willing to go out in the wet and spend hours caucusing for you. We've flipped from a system that selected candidates who were broadly appealing to party officials to a system that selects candidates who are adored by base voters. Put differently, neither Donald Trump nor Bernie Sanders would've had a prayer in the 1956 presidential primaries, but one of them won and the other nearly won the 2016 presidential primaries.

Threaded through that change is a strange fact in American political life: we consider party officials exercising influence over party nominating processes as illegitimate. You can see a stark version of this in the battle over Democratic "superdelegates." In 2016, about 85 percent of delegates to the party convention were normal delegates, bound by the results of primaries and caucuses; but about 15 percent were so-called superdelegates, who could vote however they wanted. These superdelegates were elected officials or other high-up party functionaries, and they became a focal point for Sanders supporters, who worried that they'd throw the nomination to Clinton even if Sanders won the most primaries and caucuses.

In theory, this was plausible. In New Hampshire, Sanders won the primary by more than 20 points, netting fifteen of the state's regular delegates to Clinton's nine. But New Hampshire also had eight superdelegates, six of whom endorsed Clinton before the primary even happened, meaning that Clinton emerged from the primary with a loss in the vote but a tie in delegates. It didn't end up mattering because Clinton won more primary votes and regular delegates nationally than Sanders did, but the existence of the superdelegates enraged Sanders's supporters. It seemed ugly and undemocratic that a bunch of party officials could swing the nomination to the runner-up in the primaries. The DNC heeded the outcry and changed the rules in 2018: now only normal delegates can vote on the convention's first ballot.

You might think this an odd change to make in the aftermath of an election where elite weakness on the Republican side led to Trump's nomination. Shouldn't that have proven there is a role for party officials to play in blocking unqualified demagogues, even if they are able to win some primaries? But the truth is that even if party officials had the power to act as a check on their base's will, they no longer had the popular legitimacy to use it: the resulting backlash would split the party in two. Parties aren't weak because the rules have changed. The rules have changed because parties are weak.

What's true at the presidential level is also true at the congressional level. Ideological primary challenges have become more common in recent decades, particularly in the Republican Party. Clark University political scientist Robert Boatright found that the share of Republican primary challenges that are based around the incumbent not being conservative enough has shot from less than 25 percent in the 1970s to more than 40 percent in the 2010s; among Democrats, ideological primary challenges have gone from a bit under 10 percent to a bit over 10 percent (Democratic primary challenges are likelier to focus on social identity than ideology).[8]

While it remains rare for politicians to lose a primary challenge, it happens often enough, and in high-profile enough cases, that no member of Congress can afford to rest easily. Every Republican realizes he could share the fate of former House majority leader Eric Cantor, who lost in a shocking upset to conservative challenger Dave Brat. And every Democrat realizes he could end up like former representative Joe Crowley, widely believed to be a future House Speaker, before Alexandria Ocasio-Cortez ended his career.

All of this has eroded the power of party elites and amplified the power of primary voters, who are a much more polarized group than general election voters. And it has forced members of Congress, who mostly occupy safe seats, to pursue more polarized political strategies in order to keep themselves secure. Of course, political security is a resource you can at least partially purchase, so long as you can raise the funds. And money is another place where parties are weakening, partisans are strengthening, and polarizing candidates are prospering.

Institutional donors are corrupting, small donors are polarizing

On September 9, 2009, President Obama gathered a joint session of Congress for a rare, nationally televised speech about health

care. The speech, which came at a moment of peril for the Affordable Care Act, is largely forgotten today. But there is a moment
in it that has passed into the political lore and meme of the era.
Obama had made the case for his plan and turned to trying to
rebut the distortions that had snaked into the national conversation. "There are also those who claim that our reform effort will
insure illegal immigrants," he said. "This, too, is false—the reforms
I'm proposing would not apply to those who are here illegally."
Sitting in the audience, Congressman Joe Wilson, a South Carolina Republican, couldn't contain himself. "You lie!" he shouted.

Obama wasn't lying. The legislative text barred the undocumented from benefits. But it was Wilson's breach of decorum,
not his more banal abuse of the truth, that stunned even his
colleagues. "Totally disrespectful," said Senator John McCain,
just months out from losing the election to Obama. Republican
leadership leaned on Wilson to apologize, which he kind of, sort
of, did. "I let my emotions get the best of me when listening to
the President's remarks regarding the coverage of illegal immigrants in the health care bill," he said in a statement. But if the
Republican Party wasn't happy with Wilson's outburst, Republican voters sure were. Within a few weeks, Wilson raised almost
$2 million from conservatives thrilled by his comments—and
he went, overnight, from House backbencher to GOP celebrity.
It wasn't just that Wilson was raising money; it was that other
Republicans were begging him to come help them raise money.
"I've received hundreds of invitations," he said. "I've had dozens
of members of Congress ask me to appear in their districts. (Rep.)
Michele Bachmann said, 'Joe, you're a hero in Minnesota.' "[9]

In becoming a hero to Bachmann's supporters, Wilson had
become a villain to Obama's. His opponent in the upcoming 2010
election, Rob Miller, also began fund-raising off Wilson's notoriety.
"He should be doing an apology tour," he said of Wilson, who had

embarked on a thank-you tour in the incident's aftermath. "He should be apologizing to every teacher, every law enforcement official, every man, woman and child in South Carolina for being disrespectful to the president." Miller nationalized that argument and raised $1.5 million in the weeks after Wilson went viral. "The game has changed," he said of his haul. "The campaign has changed."[10] Wilson and Miller went on to raise and spend more than twice as much as any other House race in South Carolina that year, much of it from out-of-state donors. (For all that, Wilson won by about the same margin he posted in 2008.)

There was an important lesson buried in the Wilson drama, but it had nothing to do with health care. It had to do with money, how the trend toward national networks of highly ideological small donors is changing the way campaigns are funded and the way candidates compete for those funds.

In their book *Campaign Finance and Political Polarization: When Purists Prevail*, Raymond La Raja and Brian Schaffner argue regulations don't keep money out of politics so much as redirect the channels through which money gets into politics. Slap limits on donations to political parties, and people begin giving to candidates. Slap them on candidates, and they give to super PACs. That means you can use the different regulations of different states to learn quite a bit about how different fund-raising rules change politics. In particular, you can compare states where the parties raise huge amounts of money that they distribute to candidates with states where the candidates have to fund-raise for themselves. So La Raja and Schaffner gathered data for all fifty states from 1990 to 2010, looking at how restrictions on giving to parties affected polarization.

The lesson was clear: the more powerful the parties were, the less polarization the state legislatures showed. These results were biggest in the states where money mattered most and just plain large overall. Looking at the thirty-six "professional" legislatures—that is, the states where being a member of the legislature is a real, paid job—La Raja and Schaffner compared the states that limited party contributions between 1997 and 2007 with those that didn't. "The increase in polarization was nearly three times as large in the 28 chambers that limited party contributions as it was in the 8 chambers that allowed for unlimited contributions," they write.[11]

I'm doubtful that campaign finance laws explain the entirety of those results, but it's still a telling finding—and relevant to national politics, which sharply curtailed party fund-raising with the McCain-Feingold Act. The big picture, as La Raja and Schaffner see it, is that parties want to win and are willing to support more moderate candidates to notch those victories. But it may go beyond that: a criticism more ideological activists make of the party committees is that they prize moderation even when it is unlikely to influence electability, and the data backs them up: research by Florida State University political scientist Hans Hassell showed that party networks supported more moderate candidates even in safe seats.[12] Whatever the motivation, if you're a candidate who wants to fund your campaign in a state where the party controls the money, your incentive is to convince your party that you can win, and that often means convincing it of your ideological and temperamental moderation.

But if you have to raise the money yourself, your incentives change. Most people, and most groups, don't give money to politicians. Those who do give are, predictably, more polarized, more partisan, or they want something. You motivate them through inspiration, outrage, or transaction. Put differently, you appeal to them through ideology, identity, or corruption.

La Raja and Schaffner cut this divide into "pragmatists" and "purists." Politics, they argue, is a war between pragmatists "concerned primarily with staying in power" and "policy-demanding" purists, who care above all about getting their agenda passed. Defunding parties empowers the purists over the pragmatists.

I think this typology misses the powerful role of political identity and negative partisanship. Here, as elsewhere, political conflict isn't just about policy, and it's not just about power. It's about group conflict. That is different, to be clear, from it being about winning. If it was just about winning, people would give to the closest races, based on expert opinion about flipping seats. But people often give to the races where they're most ideologically invested, no matter the chances of success (look at the amount of money Democrats spent on the Texas Senate race in 2018, their loathing of Ted Cruz overwhelming the lure of more winnable elections against less hated incumbents). Wilson didn't raise his millions because of a purer policy agenda or because he represents a swing seat. He raised them because conservatives hated Obama, and he became, momentarily, their champion, no matter where they lived.

That's another difference between party-centric fund-raising and candidate-centric fund-raising. Parties know who's running for office where. They pay a phalanx of staffers to research which districts are vulnerable, which candidates are capable, which races deserve money. But voters don't have a full-time staff picking through candidate résumés six days a week. So candidates who want to raise big money from individuals need to somehow get known by those individuals. You can do it by being a generational political talent, like Obama when he ran for Senate in 2004. You can do it by running against someone whom your party really hates, as O'Rourke did in taking on Cruz. You can do it by pulling a controversial stunt that makes you the center of a national firestorm, like Wilson did. You can do it by going viral on social media, as Ocasio-Cortez does, or getting yourself regularly interviewed constantly on the news, as Senator Chuck Schumer was famous for in New York. You can do it by renting lists of past party donors and trying to send them fund-raising emails or making fund-raising calls that get their attention. But somehow or another, you need to stand out. You have to get noticed, retweeted, booked. And, in general, loud gets noticed. Extreme gets noticed. Confrontational gets noticed. Moderate, conciliatory, judicious—not so much.

Here, political trends are being compounded by technological ones. I was an intern on Howard Dean's 2004 presidential campaign, which was the first to use the internet to find supporters, organize them into a movement, and use them to finance a campaign. I was there, stunned like everyone else, when the big red thermometer tracking individual donations before the third-quarter deadline nearly reached $15 million. No one had ever done that before. And they hadn't done it before because they couldn't do it before. Prior to email—this was before the social media revolution, and yes, I do feel old—it was costly for campaigns to communicate with supporters, even if they had them, and difficult for supporters to donate to campaigns, even if they wanted to. Mail is expensive at the scale of millions and too slow to take advantage of a momentary outrage dominating the news cycle. But digital tools are instant, and if not costless, pretty close to it. You can ping backers constantly, track them closely, let them connect to one another in ways that deepen their connection to you.

God, we were idealistic about what it all meant. Joe Trippi, Dean's campaign manager, published a memoir/manifesto entitled *The Revolution Will Not Be Televised*. Subtitle: *Democracy, the Internet, and the Overthrow of Everything*, which sounded more hopeful and less sinister at the time. "This was nothing less than the first shot in America's second revolution," Trippi wrote, "nothing less than the people taking the first step to reclaiming a system that had long ago forgotten they existed."[13] Small-donor democracy was going to save us! It would wring the corruption out of politics, permit new kinds of candidates to run and win, engage voters who'd been ignored in favor of deep-pocketed donors. It was thrilling. It was even partly true.

But we didn't see the dark side clearly. Dean, the little-known governor of Vermont, electrified the campaign by being willing to say what too many leading Democrats wouldn't: the Iraq war was a mistake and Bush's presidency was a disaster. He was right. Subsequent candidates would, like Dean, find that you could raise tremendous amounts of money and excite huge crowds of people by saying the things that millions of Americans wanted said, even if the parties didn't want their leading figures saying them. There is real value here. But it's a channel through which racist lies and xenophobic demagoguery can travel as easily as overdue truths. The overthrow of everything, indeed.

As these tools, rules, trends, and technologies matured, small-donor fund-raising exploded. Political scientists Karen Sebold and Andrew Dowdle looked at small-donor donations to presidential campaigns during the all-important year leading up to the primary. This is both the crucial period for campaigns looking to build support and well before the press and most voters turn their attention to presidential politics. Sebold and Dowdle found that "the total number of small contributions rose from 55,000 in 2000 to more than 566,000 in 2016," a more than ten-fold increase.[14] As it's become easier to fund campaigns through individual contributions, more candidates have done it. But that's also changed the kinds of candidates who prosper in primaries.

In 2016, Bernie Sanders smashed small-donor fund-raising records, raising more than $130 million from small donors and far outpacing Hillary Clinton and Martin O'Malley. On the

Republican side, Donald Trump also raked in small-donor cash,[15] crushing John McCain's and Mitt Romney's campaign totals months before the election. I don't consider Trump and Sanders morally equivalent politicians, but both represent the weakening hold of political parties.

The nationalization of politics is both a cause and consequence of these trends. As Daniel Hopkins shows in his book *The Increasingly United States: How and Why American Political Behavior Nationalized*, the share of itemized political giving—that is to say, contributions over $200, which have to be reported to the Federal Election Commission—that goes to in-state political candidates has fallen from two-thirds in 1990 to one-third in 2012. That's a sharp drop, but it makes sense. As political media becomes more nationalized and less local, we hear more about national candidates. Hopkins finds, tellingly, that the share of Americans who can name their governor has been declining, even as the share that can name the vice president has held steady. He also finds that when asked to name the politician they hate most, only 15 percent name someone in their own state. And we all know that voter turnout is massively higher in presidential elections than other years, but Hopkins shows that Senate elections, which are framed as part of the national political story, have recently passed gubernatorial elections as a turnout driver, too. We hear more about national candidates, controversies, and conflicts. Those are the stories we're invested in. Our donations follow our attention.

It is worth pausing on this point a moment, because it illuminates one of the fundamental debates in politics and a thread of this book. Under materialist theories of political engagement, where people participate because they're trying to maximize their share of the resources politicians control, this engagement pattern doesn't make sense. State and local political decisions matter more for most people's daily lives than the debates that drive national politics. People have far more power to influence their mayor, state senator, or governor than they have to influence the president. People should be most engaged in the tangible stakes of the politics nearest to their experience, not the more abstract collisions of the national scene.

But under an identity model of political engagement, where people participate to express who they are, who they support, and who they loathe, it makes perfect sense. Of course you're likelier to donate to defeat the politician who serves as the villain in the political dramas you watch rather than some local legislator whose name you can't remember. Of course the stakes of national politics, with their titanic clashes over good and evil, their story lines omnipresent on social media and late-night comedy, are more gripping than local bond ordinances. But as we give more to national candidates and less to local candidates, that creates incentives for candidates to nationalize themselves, focusing on the polarizing issues that energize donors in every zip code rather than the local issues that specifically matter in their states and districts. The rewards here, as viral superstars of both parties routinely discover, are massive. You don't become a national figure by being boring.

Of course, neither Trump nor Sanders actually raised the most money in the 2016 primary. And that's because small donors—and even individual donors—aren't the whole picture. There's also the endless flood of cash from "access-oriented" donors. In an interesting paper, Michael Barber exploits another difference in state campaign finance laws and compares states that limit individual contributions to candidates with states that limit PAC contributions to candidates.[16] Where the rules push toward individual donations, he finds candidates are more polarized. Where the rules open the floodgates to PAC money, the candidates are more moderate. Individual donors want to fall in love or express their hate. They're comfortable supporting candidates who offer less chance of victory but more affirmation of identity. Institutional donors are more pragmatic. They want candidates who will win, and they want candidates who, after they win, will get things done.

This is less benign than it sounds. Institutional donors want government to work, it's true—but they want it to work in their favor. If individual donors give money as a form of identity expression, institutional donors give money as a form of investment. Individual donors are polarizing. Institutional donors are corrupting. American politics, thus, is responsive to two types of people: the polarized and the rich.

In physics, there are different rules at different scales (stay with me). The quirks of quantum physics dominate the very small and the rules of special relativity describe the very large. So, too, with money in politics. In my experience, transactional giving drives the bills no one has heard of, the provisions few people read, the regulatory processes the public and the media tend to ignore. But at the macro level—the level of presidential politics and legislative fights that lead front pages day after day—it's partisan dollars that dominate outcomes. If the business community could purchase its preferences in all things, immigration reform and infrastructure investment would've passed long ago and Jeb Bush would be president. Once an issue becomes a red-blue collision, corporate cash often loses out to the zero-sum logic of partisanship or the fury of the base. But that isn't to dismiss the power of access-based money: we don't hear about most of what politicians do, leaving a truly vast space for the corruptions of transactional fund-raising to warp policy. And there are moments when the transactionalists and the polarizers settle into alliance with each other: that's often been the story of the Trump administration, which tweets about kneeling NFL players in the morning and passes corporate tax cuts in the evening.

The Supreme Court, in a series of rulings dating back to the '70s, has decided that political spending is constitutionally protected speech, so you can't regulate it out of politics. But that means that the workable reforms tend to toss us between plans that amplify the powers of small donors, which worsen the problems of polarization, or plans that permit institutional money to flood the system, with all the attendant corruption. So long as politics runs on private donations, you're left with the inescapable problem that the people who donate want something different from the people who don't.

The fall of the parties, the rise of the partisans

Donald Trump didn't win the Republican Party over gently. It was a hostile takeover. George W. Bush was "a lousy president," he tweeted. As for John McCain, "I like people who weren't captured," Trump said. He called Mitt Romney "one of the dumbest and worst candidates in the history of Republican politics."

It wasn't just Republican candidates Trump assailed. It was Republican policies. He promised to preserve Medicare, Medicaid, and Social Security, to raise taxes on people like himself (he was lying). He promised health care for everyone (also a lie), an end to free trade, a softer line on Russia, a wall across the border. Much of this polled well and drove support for Trump. But it also alienated large swaths of the GOP that either liked the people Trump was slandering, the ideological commitments he was betraying, or both. It was a strategy to mobilize an alienated minority of the Republican base in order to prevail in a crowded, fractured field, and though it worked in the primary, everyone knew, or thought they knew, that a party divided against itself could not win a general election. Punditry was thick with predictions of a Republican wipeout, followed by an intraparty civil war. "I think the GOP as a national party will have to be reconstituted," Matthew Dowd told *Politico*. "There doesn't seem a good way to put this all together."[17]

These predictions were based on an old understanding of politics, one in which partisanship was weaker and deviations in candidate choice were punished more severely. In 1964, Barry Goldwater ran hard to the right, and Republicans paid for it. Goldwater carried five Deep South states and his home state of Arizona. He received 7 million fewer votes than Richard Nixon had gotten four years prior. And as historian Geoffrey Kabaservice points out in *Rule and Ruin*, "the real carnage was further down the ticket. The party dropped thirty-eight seats in the House, reducing Republican representation to its lowest level since the 1936 election. . . . [I]n the state legislatures the party lost some ninety members of the upper houses and almost four hundred and fifty members of the lower houses, again reducing Republican numbers to levels they had not touched since the Depression."

Democrats faced a similar wipeout after shifting to the left in 1972. That year, George McGovern won the Democratic primary even though much of the Democratic Party viewed him with suspicion and even fear. Major Democratic interest groups, like the AFL-CIO, refused to endorse him in the general election, and top Democrats, including former governors of Florida, Texas, and Virginia, organized "Democrats for Nixon." McGovern went on to lose with less than 40 percent of the vote, a dismal showing driven by Democrats who abandoned a nominee they considered unacceptable.

None of this happened to Trump. And it's not because there weren't Republicans repulsed by his behavior or interest groups unnerved by his heterodoxies. It's because the parties are more polarized, so the alternative—Hillary Clinton—was unimaginable. This is the key to the weak parties/strong partisanship dichotomy: threat is as powerful a political motivator as love. This was true among Trump's supporters in 2016. Exit polls showed that Clinton won 53 percent of voters who said their vote was motivated by "strong support" for the candidate they favored, but Trump had an 11-point margin among voters who said they were primarily voting against the other side. Trump's win, in other words, depended heavily on voters who were actually just voting against Clinton—indeed, some preelection polls showed a majority of Trump supporters said they were motivated more by fear of Clinton than admiration of Trump.

If you were a liberal, you didn't have to like Clinton to vote for her; everything Trump did and said was evidence that the GOP had lost its mind and had to be kept from power at all costs. Much of Clinton's campaign proceeded in that frame: it was less about why she should be president than why he shouldn't be. But Clinton herself served that same purpose for conservatives. She is one of the most polarizing political figures of the modern era. She won her primary by running to Bernie Sanders's left on race and gender, and the entire Republican campaign was built around painting her as a criminal who deserved to be literally "locked up"—if you leaned Republican, or simply found yourself uncomfortable with the browner coalition Democrats seemed to be building to win power, you didn't have to like Trump to vote against Clinton.

This is true in Congress, too. In his 2019 paper "Man Bites Blue Dog," Stephen Utych looked at congressional races and concluded that "while moderates have historically enjoyed an advantage over ideologically extreme candidates," that "gap has disappeared in recent years."[18] Today, Utych found, "moderates and ideologically extreme candidates are equally likely to be elected." As party affiliation becomes more important, individual candidate traits lose their power. You might prefer a moderate Republican to a fire-breathing conservative, but given what the Left looks like to you these days, you'll take either over a Democrat.

I should say that there's dispute over this finding. In his book *Who Wants to Run? How the Devaluing of Political Office Drives Polarization*, Andrew Hall concluded that moderates still enjoy an advantage over more ideologically polarized candidates when they run, albeit a declining one. But the reason that Hall found moderates more electable is interesting: nominating an extreme candidate drives up turnout among the *other* party—negative partisanship, once again. What has changed, Hall finds, is that moderates are increasingly disgusted by the political system, by the compromises and fund-raising necessary to be a candidate, so fewer moderates are running in the first place. It's an interesting debate, but I don't think it changes the fundamental story here: we're seeing less variation in voting patterns due to ideology and more stability due to partisanship. Which makes sense.

When you vote for a candidate, you're not just voting for him or her. You are voting for, well, everything we have discussed up till now. You're voting for your side to beat the other side. You're voting to express your identity. You're voting for your members of Congress to be able to pass bills. You're voting for the judges your side would appoint. You're voting so those smug jerks you fight with in comment sections don't win, so that aunt or uncle you argue with at Thanksgiving can't lord it over you. You're voting to say your group is right and worthy and the other group is wrong and unworthy. That's bigger than any one candidate for president. It's true even if the personal characteristics of the other party's nominee leave your standard-bearer looking like a decadent sleazebag.

When you vote, you're voting to keep a candidate, a coalition, a movement, a media ecosystem, a set of donors, and a universe of people you don't like and maybe even fear out of power. All of that gives you reason to learn to like your candidate and, if you can't do that, to justify voting for him anyway. It's perfectly rational to care more about the party label than a candidate's character. Politics is about parties, not individuals.

But look where that leaves us: parties, and particularly the Republican Party, are losing control of whom they nominate. But once a party nominates someone—once it nominates anyone— that person is guaranteed the support of both the party's elites and its voters. Unlike in Goldwater's or McGovern's day, when ticket-splitting was common, any candidate able to win his party's presidential primary can now count on his party's support and has a damn good chance of winning the presidency.

Perhaps scarier, these dynamics gather even more force once a demagogic candidate has won the presidency. In January of 2016, the *National Review*, long the closest thing conservatism has had to a gatekeeper, published an issue entitled "Against Trump." In it, the editors asked, "If Trump were to become the president, the Republican nominee, or even a failed candidate with strong conservative support, what would that say about conservatives? The movement that ground down the Soviet Union and took the shine, at least temporarily, off socialism would have fallen in behind a huckster. The movement concerned with such 'permanent things' as constitutional government, marriage, and the right to life would have become a claque for a Twitter feed."[19]

In November 2019, as the House impeachment inquiry was proceeding, Rich Lowry, the editor of the *National Review*, explained to my Vox colleague Sean Illing how his views had evolved. Trump, he said, been steadfast "on pro-life stuff, on conscience rights, on judges." The downside, Lowry admitted, is "he doesn't respect the separation of powers in our government, he doesn't think constitutionally, and says and does things no president should do or say." That seems like a pretty big downside! But, Lowry continued, "at the end of the day, we're asked to either favor Trump or root for Elizabeth Warren or Bernie Sanders or Joe Biden or Mayor Pete, who oppose us on basically everything. So it's a pretty simple calculation."[20]

I've come to think of this as the central flaw in our electoral software. In an era of high polarization, weak parties, and strong partisanship, it's easy to see how extremists and, more than that, demagogues penetrate the system. America was lucky, if that's the right word, that Trump proved himself, once in office, distractible, lazy, and uninterested in following through on his most authoritarian rhetoric. He's done plenty of damage, but he's not emerged as a dictator in control of American political institutions, as many liberals feared in the direct aftermath of the election. But the world also produces clever, disciplined demagogues. They are the ones who truly threaten republics, and they are watching.

Chapter 8

When Bipartisanship Becomes Irrational

O n February 13, 2016, Justice Antonin Scalia died. Scalia was the pugnacious, literary anchor of the Supreme Court's 5–4 conservative majority. A brilliant writer, he was the rare judge whose prose attained a popular audience; in 2004, a book of his decisions, called *Scalia Dissents*, was published. What gained Scalia his public following wasn't merely his legal reasoning but his slashing style, the way he flayed his enemies, the ferocity with which he championed conservatism from the bench.

Scalia was appointed to the Supreme Court by President Reagan in 1986 and unanimously confirmed by the Senate. Like many conservative theorists of the era, his jurisprudence was formed in the shadow of the Warren Court, which saw the Constitution as a living document that evolved alongside the country it founded. The Warren Court, and its successors, looked inside the Constitution and found protections that previous generations had missed: for African Americans, for women seeking abortions, for men who loved other men.

Scalia thought this preposterous. The Constitution, he said, is "not a living document. It's dead, dead, dead."[1] He believed, or said he believed, in originalism:[2] the Constitution meant only what he understood it to have meant to the men who wrote it, at the time at which they wrote it. As such, while all sorts of protections might be read into the glittering language on the page, Scalia found them absent in the minds of the document's authors and thus absent from the law.

Scalia was always a conservative, but he reveled in his status as a culture warrior as he aged. In 2013, he told *New York* magazine that he had canceled his subscriptions to the *Washington Post* and the *New York Times*. "It was the treatment of almost any conservative issue," he said. "It was slanted and often nasty. And, you know, why should I get upset every morning?"[3] He got his news, he admitted, from more congenial sources: the *Washington Times*, the *Wall Street Journal*, and right-wing talk radio hosts like Bill Bennett.

Supreme Court justices are appointed for life. That means their retirements are typically planned—they step down when the time is right, when their friends and allies can name their replacement. But Scalia's unexpected passing threw all this into chaos; it deprived the Court of both its most powerful conservative voice and its conservative majority, and it did so with a Democrat, President Obama, in the White House. But Obama's power over Scalia's replacement was not absolute. The Constitution gives the Senate advise-and-consent authority over judicial appointments, and in 2014 Republicans had won back the gavel. So Obama sought a conciliatory pick: Merrick Garland, the chief judge on the District of Columbia's Court of Appeals.

Garland's name had come up before: in 2010, Republican Senator Orrin Hatch, a former chairman of the Judiciary Committee, had recommended Garland as a "consensus nominee" whose nomination could calm the bitter partisanship that had turned

Supreme Court appointments into outright partisan warfare. "I have no doubts that Garland would get a lot of votes," Hatch said. "And I will do my best to help him get them."[4]

But that was in 2010, when Democrats held the Senate. In 2016, with his own party in control, Hatch did not help Garland get the votes. Instead, Senate Republicans refused to take a vote on or even hold a hearing for Garland's nomination. The issue, Majority Leader Mitch McConnell said, was that it was an election year, and it would be absurd to fill a Supreme Court seat in an election year. No, the choice properly belonged to whoever succeeded Obama, so the Senate wouldn't consider any nomination Obama made to Scalia's seat, no matter how qualified or moderate the candidate might be. This wasn't about Garland; it was about democracy.

It was also unprecedented. "There have been 103 prior cases in which—like the case of President Obama's nomination of Judge Garland—an elected President has faced an actual vacancy on the Supreme Court and began an appointment process prior to the election of a successor," wrote law professors Robin Bradley Kar and Jason Mazzone. "In all 103 cases, the President was able to both nominate and appoint a replacement Justice, by and with the advice and consent of the Senate. This is true even of all eight such cases where the nomination process began during an election year."[5]

McConnell's bet paid off. Trump won the 2016 election—indeed, there's a reasonable argument that conservative mobilization around the vacancy was what pushed Trump over the finish line—and conservative jurist Neil Gorsuch was named to the open seat, preserving the GOP's 5-4 majority. "One of my proudest moments was when I looked Barack Obama in the eye and I said, 'Mr. President, you will not fill the Supreme Court vacancy,'" McConnell said.[6]

The Garland affair remains an open wound to liberals, an example of how Republicans will stop at nothing to gain and retain power. "I'm the longest-serving senator. I've never seen anything like that with either the Republicans or the Democrats," said Patrick Leahy, the Democrat from Vermont. "We all take an oath to uphold the Constitution. The Constitution says the president shall nominate, says we shall advise and consent. The president followed the Constitution. The Senate violated it."[7]

McConnell, for his part, gave up the game in 2019. Speaking at a Chamber of Commerce luncheon in Kentucky, he was asked what he'd do if a Supreme Court vacancy opened in 2020, the year of the next presidential election. CNN's Ted Barrett reported what happened next: "The leader took a long sip of what appeared to be iced tea before announcing with a smile, 'Oh, we'd fill it,' triggering loud laughter from the audience."[8] There was no mystery to McConnell's reasoning, but he laid it bare anyway. The simplest way for politicians to have a "long-lasting positive impact" was to appoint judges. "Everything else changes," McConnell said, but judges serve for life.

The hard question isn't why McConnell blocked the Garland nomination. It's why anyone ever expected him—or anyone else—to do anything different.

America's unstable form of government

The most powerful critique of America's political system was published in 1990 by a Spanish political sociologist named Juan Linz.

Linz was an outsider to American politics and, more important, to its self-serving mythologies. Born in the Weimar Republic in 1927 and raised in Spain under the Francoist dictatorship, Linz both lived through and studied the circumstances in which political systems fail. The causes of collapse were often encoded in the architecture of the government: he showed that systems based around an independent president tended to dissolve, as conflicts between the executive and the legislature were often irresolvable, and irresolvable conflicts end in crisis and collapse.

But America's political system posed a puzzle for Linz. As an outside observer, he was free from the quasi-religious reverence we afford our founding documents. He knew that the American political system had failed wherever else it had been tried. He knew that America itself was loath to impose its system on other nations—for all our nation-building adventurism, we never give any country developing into a democracy a system that works like ours. But he also knew that in America, the American political system had worked.

In 1990, in a paper entitled "The Perils of Presidentialism," Linz explained why. The "vast majority of the stable democracies" in the world were parliamentary regimes, where whoever wins legislative power also wins executive power.[9] America, however, was a presidential democracy: the president is elected separately from the Congress and can often be at odds with it. This system had been tried before. America, worryingly, was the only place where it had survived.

The problem is straightforward. In parliamentary systems, the prime minister is the leader of the coalition that controls the legislature. If that coalition loses an election, it loses power. But at any given moment, only one party or coalition holds power. In presidential systems, by contrast, one party can control the legislature and another can control the presidency. Both parties, then, have a claim to democratic legitimacy. "Under such circumstances," asked Linz, "who has the stronger claim to speak on behalf of the people: the president or the legislative majority that opposes his policies?"

It gets worse. What happens when the majorities that the president and the Congress represent are different majorities, who voted at different times and through different methods? Linz noted that presidents tend to be elected by voters but legislatures tend to reflect geography, with small towns and rural areas given outsized power. It's hard enough resolving a democratic disagreement that plays out among a single electorate. What do you do when you're facing a disagreement that reflects different kinds of electorates?

It's a question with no answer. In general, we assume a system like this encourages compromise, and that's true, when the competing political coalitions are open to compromise. But a system like this can also encourage crisis—crises where, in other countries, "the armed forces were often tempted to intervene as a mediating power."[10]

This is why there are no long-standing presidential democracies save for the United States. And it's why America doesn't impose its specific form of government on others. "Think about Germany, Japan, Italy, and Austria," wrote Vox's Matt Yglesias.

> These are countries that were defeated by American military forces during the Second World War and given constitutions written by local leaders operating in close collaboration with occupation authorities. It's striking that even though the US Constitution is treated as a sacred text in America's political culture, we did not push any of these countries to adopt our basic framework of government.[11]

Linz admitted that he couldn't fully answer the question of why America was different. He suspected that "the uniquely diffuse character of American political parties—which, ironically, exasperates many American political scientists and leads them to call for responsible, ideologically disciplined parties—has something to do with it." Whatever the explanation, Linz continued, "the American case seems to be an exception; the development of modern political parties, particularly in socially and ideologically polarized countries, generally exacerbates, rather than moderates, conflicts between the legislative and the executive."[12]

Linz was writing in 1990, when America's political parties were far more exceptional, far more mixed and moderated, than they are today. But what read in 1990 like an explanation of what made America's political system different now reads like an analysis of why America's system is in crisis. The Garland affair is a perfect example. For all the fury over McConnell's behavior, what, exactly, did he do wrong?

In the 2014 election, Republicans took control of the Senate with a decisive fifty-four-vote majority. True, the 2014 election had the lowest turnout in seventy years, and sure, only a third of Senate seats are up for election in any given year, and yes, the Senate is a noxiously undemocratic institution that gives a voter in Wyoming sixty-six times as much power as a voter in California, but the rules are what they are. McConnell was leader of a Republican majority in the US Senate. He had the votes to block any nominations Obama might make—why shouldn't he have used them? Did the voters who gave him that majority really want him to let Obama replace Scalia with a Democratic justice, no matter how moderate? Wouldn't it have been more of a betrayal of his voters if he'd led a new Republican majority in the Senate to help Obama flip the Supreme Court to a 5–4 liberal split?

You can argue, as many did, that Obama represented a more

legitimate democratic majority. He won a national election, with much higher voter turnout, in 2012. He was president of the United States of America. He had nominated a clearly qualified candidate, in accordance with the historical norm. McConnell's behavior was both unprecedented and dangerous: in flatly refusing to consider any candidates nominated by a president of the other party, McConnell established a principle that could destroy the Supreme Court. Given the Senate's small-state bias, it's easy enough to imagine extended periods of divided control, and given McConnell's successful deployment of absolute obstruction, it's easy enough to imagine vacancies on the Court going continuously unfilled.

But why is that McConnell's problem? Why should he have been the one to fold? Perhaps Obama should have bowed to the winners of the most recent election and nominated a Scalia-esque conservative to fill Scalia's seat. It may sound ridiculous, but both McConnell and Obama represented legitimate electoral majorities, and there was no obvious way to resolve their differences.

Ideological differences are easier to resolve when they are smaller. That's why Linz put "the uniquely diffuse character of American political parties" at the center of America's unusual political success. In the twentieth century, the ideological and demographic diversity of the Republican and Democratic coalitions lowered the stakes of partisan political disagreement considerably. Our core cleavages played out within the two parties rather than just between them. But those days are gone.

McConnell's obstructive innovations are a cause of our current divisions, but they are also a consequence of them. The question that Supreme Court vacancies pose in the modern era is different from the question they posed in previous eras. That's because a more polarized political system has led to a more polarized Supreme Court (which, as with the Garland case, is further polarizing the political system—remember, everything is a feed-back loop!).

In an analysis published after Justice Anthony Kennedy retired, law professors Lee Epstein and Eric Posner wrote in the *New York Times* that in the '50s and '60s, "the ideological biases of Republican appointees and Democratic appointees were rela-tively modest."[13] Even as late as the '90s, justices regularly voted in "ideologically unpredictable ways." In the 1991 term, for instance, Byron White, a Democratic appointee, "voted more conservatively than all but two of the Republican appointees, Antonin Scalia and William Rehnquist."

But that's changed. Over the past decade, "justices have hardly ever voted against the ideology of the president who appointed them," Epstein and Posner find. "Only Justice Kennedy, named to the court by Ronald Reagan, did so with any regularity." Their chart is striking:

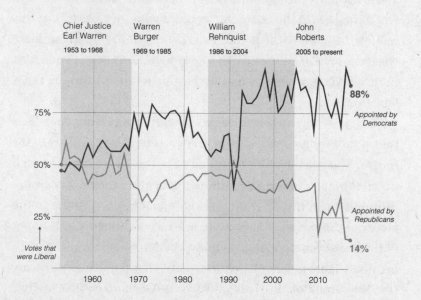

The Supreme Court is a powerful institution in American life, and it has often been a controversial institution in American life, but it has not always been a politically polarized institution in American life. As the parties have become more ideological, however, their expectations for Supreme Court justices followed suit.

It's easy to read an analysis like this and think the authors are describing a golden age. But it's all a matter of perspective. The eras of relative moderation are considered eras of failure and betrayal by the political parties responsible for them. Republicans lament the heterodoxies of justices like Earl Warren, John Paul Stevens, David Souter, and Anthony Kennedy—indeed, it's precisely in response to these unpredictable appointments that the parties began to develop more ideological and reliable methods of sourcing judges.

Scalia was one of those more ideological justices, and he made the case for his approach explicitly. "It really enrages me to hear people refer to it as a politicized court," he said in 2012. "Maybe the legislature and the president are not as stupid as you think. They assuredly picked those people because of who they are and when they get to the court they remain who they were."[14] In this telling, the point of the nomination process is to find a candidate who will vote in concert with the expectations of his sponsors. Future divergence isn't a feature of independent thinking but a flaw in vetting.

Today, candidates considered for Supreme Court vacancies have a vanishingly small chance of surprising their sponsors in the future. The path to being nominated to the Court runs through decades of ideological and professional party service. Kennedy's ultimate replacement, Brett Kavanaugh, was a top staffer in the George W. Bush administration in addition to being a member of the conservative legal group the Federalist Society.

It's not just that more ideologically reliable candidates raise the stakes around Supreme Court nominations. Deeper political divides are leading to more partisan cases: consider the Right's multiyear effort to convince the Court to destroy Obamacare, a campaign with no corollary in the aftermath of, say, Medicare's or Medicaid's passage. Partisan disagreement and paralysis in Congress are making the Court's judgments more consequential, as when the Court throws out a bill or invalidates a program; legislators rarely have the bipartisan consensus or partisan power to revisit the legislation and answer the Court through modifications.

This is the context for the Garland collision. Yes, McConnell broke with past practice in refusing to even consider qualified Democratic candidates. But he was operating in an era when the Supreme Court had become a more partisan institution rendering more partisan decisions on more partisan cases. The idea that nominees should be judged on professional merit rather than philosophical alignment had long since ceased to reflect the real workings of the system. There is perhaps no single vote members of the US Senate take with as much long-term ideological importance than that of a lifetime appointment to the Supreme Court, and asking them to keep that vote, and that vote alone, separate from the ideological promises they make to their voters, and to themselves, is bizarre.

This is a problem that afflicts much in American governance. The rules, as set down in the Constitution and our institutions, push toward partisan dysfunction, conflict, and even collapse. The system works not through formal mechanisms that ensure the settlement of intractable disputes but through informal norms of compromise, forbearance, and moderation that collapse the moment the stakes rise high enough. McConnell didn't break any laws or devise any new powers to stop Garland; he just led his party to break with the historical practice of appointing Supreme Court justices they didn't agree with ideologically—a historical practice that forces parties to regularly cross their ideologies and voters for the good of the system. In breaking with that precedent, he was doing precisely what his voters wanted, and they rewarded him for it in the next election. Why should any of his successors do anything different?

But now imagine a world where Republicans, due to their advantages in small states, routinely hold the Senate while Democrats, who've won the popular vote in six of the last seven presidential elections, routinely hold the White House. What happens to the Supreme Court in that world? Do vacancies just go unfilled? What if Democrats then come to see the Supreme Court as fundamentally illegitimate, as its conservative majority relies on Republicans refusing to consider Democratic nominees? Do Democrats continue abiding by its rulings?

As Linz argued, a presidential political system in which power is divided among different branches works when the parties that control those branches are ideologically mixed enough to cooperate with one another, and that was, for much of the twentieth century, the secret to the American political system's success. But now America's political parties are ideologically polarized. They are also, importantly, nationalized.

All politics isn't local

Nebraska senator Ben Nelson was the final, crucial vote on the Affordable Care Act. Nelson was an old-school Democratic centrist, a transactional, silver-haired former insurance executive who held on in a red state through acts of ostentatious moderation and a laser-like focus on Cornhusker interests. But he was in a bind. The choice on Obamacare was yes/no. Democrats needed his vote to pass the law. Nelson wanted the law to pass. But Obamacare was unpopular back home, and Nelson was up for reelection in 2012. He was caught between his career, his party, and his conscience.

Nelson's solution was to split the ideological interests of Nebraska's Republicans from the financial interests of Nebraskans. Obamacare's Medicaid expansion was built with an unusual structure. Typically, Medicaid is funded by a roughly 60:40 split between the federal government and the states. The Affordable Care Act, however, promised that the federal government would pay 100 percent of the law's new Medicaid costs for three years, before phasing down to a 90:10 split by 2020. But some conservatives said that even the 10 percent states were being asked to pay was too much. This was, in particular, a charge levied by Nebraska's popular Republican governor, Dave Heineman. So Nelson negotiated a special deal on the state's behalf: for Nebraska, the federal government would carry 100 percent of the Medicaid expansion's bill, a subsidy worth more than $100 million.

Nelson was doing what members of Congress have done since the dawn of the republic: winning support for a polarizing national policy by extracting a material concession for his state. The American political system is built on a deep sense of place. The House isn't meant to host the meeting of two parties but of 435 districts; the Senate is not meant to represent red and blue but to balance the interests of fifty states. This reflects the Founders' belief—true in their time—that our political identities were rooted in our cities and states, not the more abstract bonds of nationhood. "Many considerations . . . seem to place it beyond doubt that the first and most natural attachment of the people will be to the governments of their respective States," wrote James Madison in *Federalist* 46.

The centrality of state and local political concerns in national politics has been one of the American political system's brakes on polarization. The zero-sum forces of two-party competition were moderated by the regional interests of politicians rooted, first and foremost, in a particular place. Sure, you may be a Republican, and that bill might be pushed by Democrats, but you're a Republican from Oklahoma, dammit, and that bill is good for Oklahoma. Catering to a member of Congress's particularistic interests, either through the direct design of the legislation or through earmarks offering unrelated benefits, gave congressional leaders ways to build coalitions that the logic of partisanship denied. Your party might not want you to vote for that bill, but if you vote for it, your district will get money for a bridge it desperately needs, and putting your name on that bridge is worth more than keeping your copartisans happy.

At least, it was.

In his book *The Increasingly United States*, Daniel Hopkins tracks the troubling nationalization of American politics. At the core of that nationalization is an inversion of the Founders' most self-evident assumption: that we will identify more deeply with our home state than with our country. Hopkins traces the change here in a variety of clever ways. He ran a text analysis of digitized books going back to 1800, comparing use of the phrase "I am American" with "I am a [Californian/Virginian/New Yorker/etc.]." Prior to the Civil War, expressions of state identity were far more common than expressions of national identity. National identity took the lead in the run-up to World War I, the two traded places for a while in the early twentieth century, and then, around 1968, expressions of national identity raced ahead and never looked back. He shows that when you ask Americans to rank their most important identities in surveys, almost everyone lists nationality in their top three, while the number listing their state, city, or neighborhood lags far behind. He finds that people are likelier to feel insulted when America is being criticized than when their state or city comes in for scorn. He shows that when asked to explain why they are proud of their nation or their state, they routinely express national pride in terms of politically relevant values, while state pride tends to focus on geographic features. I love America because of freedom; I love California because of beaches.

If all of this seems obvious—if you take the centrality of national identity for granted—that's the point: what was unimaginable to the Founders is self-evident to us.

As goes identity, so goes politics. In an analysis of more than 1,600 state party platforms dating back to 1918, Hopkins finds while "the platforms in earlier eras focused more on state-specific topics," modern platforms "now emphasize whatever topics dominate the national agenda." Similarly, he shows that in 1972, "knowing which way a state leaned in presidential politics told one nothing about the likely outcome in the gubernatorial race."[15] Today, it tells you most of what you need to know.

The culprit here is obvious. In recent decades, the media and political environments have both nationalized. Voters following politics today get constant cues to think about national politics, but coverage of state and local politics is declining. For instance, growing up, I read the *Los Angeles Times* and listened to LA's public radio station, KCRW, which fed me national political stories but also state and local stories. I developed, as a result, a pretty strong identity around California politics, which was less polarized than national politics and focused on very different questions. What I never did was read the *New York Times*, because we didn't get it, or listen to national political podcasts, because they didn't exist.

If I were growing up outside Los Angeles today, perhaps I'd be reading the newly revitalized LA *Times*, but it's likelier, as a political junkie, that I'd be reading the *New York Times* and the *Washington Post* and Vox, listening to political podcasts, and watching cable news. All of that would be civic-minded and informative, but it would be pounding away at my national political identity and underdeveloping the parts of my political psyche rooted in the place I actually lived. A nationalized media means nationalized political identities.

States used to have different political cultures from that of the nation as a whole. That gave members of Congress cross-cutting incentives from what the national parties wanted. Now those incentives are, like so many others, stacked. As Hopkins writes, "Rather than asking, 'How will this particular bill affect my district?' legislators in a nationalized polity come to ask, 'Is my party for or against this bill?' That makes coalition building more difficult, as legislators all evaluate proposed legislation through the same partisan lens." A more nationalized politics is a more polarized politics.

Here's an easy way to realize the truth of Hopkins's point: if local interests drove voting patterns, you could predict how a member of Congress would vote on the Affordable Care Act by knowing whether the uninsured rate among his or her constituents was above or below the national average. The ACA was, above all else, a direct subsidy to areas with larger uninsured populations from areas with smaller ones. But how a member of Congress voted on the ACA was almost perfectly predicted by party affiliation—as evidenced by the fact that not a single Senate Republican voted for it and not a single Senate Democrat voted against it. State conditions predicted nothing.

A weird thing happened as we nationalized our politics. We became disgusted with the ways that local politics played out nationally. Take earmarks, the small addenda members of Congress would add on to bills to fund a road, a hospital, or a job-training bill back home. Earmarks were a way that bipartisan cooperation was, yes, bought. The Congress reporter Jon Allen described how it worked in a 2015 Vox article:

In 2003, I asked Jack Murtha, the Democratic defense appro-
priator who controlled about $4 billion in earmarks each year,
about Tom DeLay, the Republican leader known as "The Ham-
mer" for his ability to nail down votes. Murtha sat in the far
corner of the Democratic side of the House, out of view from
the press galleries, and DeLay would sometimes come to visit
him before a tight vote. When DeLay needed a few Democrats
to secure a win on the floor, Murtha said, "He comes over to the
corner, and we work it out." Murtha's earmarking power meant
that he had a roster of people who owed him favors. For a little
more money, he could easily swing a small bloc of votes to help
DeLay pass a bill. Murtha and DeLay didn't agree on much,
but earmarks kept them talking, and working with each other.[16]

In 2011, Congress got rid of earmarks entirely. They were
considered a corrupt, and a corrupting, form of politics. Much
better to have Congress run on pure principle and partisanship
than the grimy work of negotiating something tangible for your
constituents. To ideologues, transactional politics always looks
dirty. To the transactional, ideologues look self-destructive.

That is, in the end, what happened to Nelson. Rather than
being celebrated back home for cutting Nebraska such a sweet
deal, conservative media pounced on him. His concession got
branded the "Cornhusker Kickback," and his own governor told
him to turn it down. "Now it's a matter of principle," Heineman
told *Politico*. "The federal government can keep that money."[17]
Nelson called him "foolish" but backed down. The provision
was stripped from the bill. Nelson, seeing the writing on the
wall, declined to run for reelection in 2012 and was replaced by
a Republican.

That same year, Heineman cautioned his constituents against
accepting the Medicaid expansion they could've had for free. "If

this unfunded Medicaid expansion is implemented, state aid to education and funding for the University of Nebraska will be cut or taxes will be increased," he warned.[18]

More competition, more problems

There was, perhaps, another secret to the system's success, one that I didn't appreciate until I read Princeton University political scientist Frances Lee's book *Insecure Majorities*. American politics, for most of its history, simply wasn't very competitive. And contrary to what the conventional wisdom holds, perhaps that was a good thing, or at least, given the idiosyncrasies of our system, a necessary one.

This is not what I learned in civics class. Close competition means voters have real choices, that politicians have accountability, that both sides need to keep public opinion and the common good in mind. Absent real competition, even a well-structured democracy rots into a corrupt autocracy.

But here's the thing, Lee says. For most of American history, including the eras of cooperative, farsighted governance our civics textbooks remember most fondly, American politics wasn't competitive.[19] Writing in 1965, Samuel Lubell said, "Our political solar system . . . has been characterized not by two equally competing suns, but by a sun and a moon."[20] The Republican Party ran American politics for most of the late nineteenth and early twentieth centuries. Democrats held the reins in the decades following the Great Depression and World War II. And majorities, both in terms of presidential vote totals and congressional control, were often lopsided.

Consider Lee's chart, which combines share of the national two-party presidential vote, share of House seats, and share of Senate seats. The farther the line stretches left, the larger the Democrats' advantage. The farther it plunges right, the stronger the GOP's lock on political power.

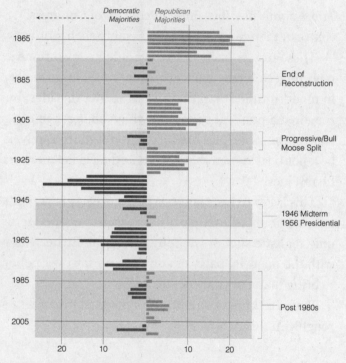

A history of party control

The durability of party control in America's past is easy to miss because our political histories tend to be presidential histories, and the presidency has tended to be more competitive than control of Congress. But when you view political power through a broader lens, our era is an aberration. In this 150-year time frame, there's no period where political control has been as tenuous as in the last four decades. And that's true whether you're looking at how often control of the government switches or how much power the majority party wields when it's on top.

The stability of American politics extended to the media's coverage of American politics. Lee swept the *New York Times*'s archive between 1958 and 2014 and found that "before 1982, in only two election years was there speculation in the *New York Times* about possible shifts in control of Congress." In 2010, by contrast, there were more than seventy such stories.

These results likely reflect changing conventions in political reporting. News sections carry more speculation about outcomes in modern times than they did in earlier decades, but the fact remains: a political system in which changes in congressional control are rarer, and are talked about more rarely, is going to be a political system that both is and feels far more stable in its hierarchies.

This is key to Lee's point. When one party is perpetually dominant, the subordinate party has reason to cooperate, as that's its only realistic shot at wielding influence. Either you work well with the majority party or you have no say over policy, nothing to bring home to your constituents.

You can think of a politician's political priorities as running roughly in this order:

1. Win reelection
2. Win the majority
3. Shape governance as much as possible

Governing comes third not because politicians are cynical, though they often are, but because you can't govern at all if you don't win reelection, and you can't govern effectively from the minority.

Even so, if winning the majority becomes impossible, then the priorities look like this:

1. Win reelection
2. Shape governance as much as possible

Indeed, in this ranking, both priorities work together, because you're likelier to win reelection, at least in past eras in American politics, if you're bringing money home to your district and can brag about bills with your name on them. But for those priorities to work together, you have to cultivate a good relationship with the majority party. You can't be engaged in a constant campaign of obstruction and sabotage.

Lee's argument is that close competition, where "neither party perceives itself as a permanent majority or permanent minority," breeds all-out partisan combat. When winning the majority becomes possible, the logic of cooperation dissolves. If you're signing on to the majority's bills and boasting about the provisions you added to their legislation, then you're part of their reelection strategy. If you're keeping the majority from passing anything and making sure people are fed up with the state of politics, then the voters are likelier to make a change.

This is the paradox of bipartisanship: what Bob Michel, the leader of the House Republicans in the 1980s, called the "subservient, timid mentality of the permanent minority"[21] makes it easier to work with the majority but harder to win back the majority. Governing and campaigning conflict.

Once a political party has decided the path to governing is retaking the majority, not working with the existing majority, the incentives transform. Instead of cultivating a good relationship with your colleagues across the aisle, you need to destroy them, because you need to convince the voters to destroy them, too.

Dick Cheney, then a member of the House of Representatives, put it sharply in 1985. "Confrontation fits our strategy," he said. "Polarization often has very beneficial results. If everything is handled through compromise and conciliation, if there are no real issues dividing us from the Democrats, why should the country change and make us the majority?"[22]

There's nothing particularly unusual about this. It's the logic of zero-sum contests everywhere. But America's political system is unusual in that it permits divided government and is full of tools minorities can use to obstruct governance.

Imagine you work in an office where your boss, who you think is a jerk, needs your help to finish his projects. If you help him, he keeps his job and maybe even gets a promotion. If you refuse to help him, you become his boss, and he may get fired. Now add in a deep dose of disagreement—you hate his projects, believe them to be bad for the company and even the world—and a bunch of colleagues who also hate your boss and will be mad at you if you help him. Think you'll help him under those conditions?

That's basically American politics right now. Bipartisan cooperation is often necessary for governance but irrational for the minority party to offer. It's a helluva way to run a railroad.

This bizarre structure worked during much of American history because one party was usually dominant enough to make cooperation worth it for the minority. Lee quotes Theodore Lowi's 1963 analysis, "Towards Functionalism in Political Science," where he says that the party system that best fits America's weird political structure "is not a competitive two-party system but a system in which the second party is very weak: that is, a 'modified one-party system.'" But we've not had that system for almost forty years now, and there's no obvious way to return to it even if we wanted to. The age of cooperation is over. The disagreements run too deep, the debates are too nationalized, the coalitions are too different, the political identities are too powerful. So what's happening now is the norms and understandings that made the informal system work are collapsing, and the underlying, dysfunctional structure is coming clear, with disastrous consequences for day-to-day governance.

Take, for instance, the filibuster.

Breaking Congress to control it

Here's the thing about the Senate filibuster: it wasn't supposed to exist. Sarah Binder, author, alongside Steven Smith, of *Politics or Principle: Filibustering in the United States Senate*, dug deep into the rule's origins and found there was no real origin at all.

Originally, both the House and the Senate had what's called a "previous question motion," which allows a member of the body to move off whatever point is being debated—the previous question, in parliamentary parlance—and demand an actual vote. That's the provision the House uses to end discussion even today. The Senate used to have that rule, too. And then it got rid of it, and created the filibuster as an unintended consequence.

"In 1805, Aaron Burr has just killed Alexander Hamilton," Binder told me. "He comes back to the Senate and gives his farewell address. Burr basically says that you are a great body. You are conscientious and wise, you do not give in to the whims of passion. But your rules are a mess. And he goes through the rulebook pointing out duplicates and things that are unclear."[23]

This is, it's worth saying, a famous speech. It's recorded that Burr, not always known as a great speaker and fresh from murdering another major politician in a duel, literally brought members of the Senate to tears in the delivery. It's easy to inspire when you're telling people how great they are and how magnificent their legacies will be when given history's due consideration.

One of Burr's suggestions was to cut the "previous question motion," so they did, apparently without realizing that they just made it impossible to cut off debate. "We say the Senate developed the filibuster to protect minorities and the right to debate," says Binder. "That's hogwash! It's a mistake. Believe me, I would've loved to find the smoking gun where the Senate decides to create a deliberative body. But it takes years before anyone figures out that the filibuster has just been created."

The filibuster then was not like the filibuster now. Today, the filibuster can be shut down with sixty votes, a process known as cloture. Then, the filibuster was unstoppable so long as a senator or group of senators was willing to hold the floor. You could have every member of the body but one desperate to take a vote and there wasn't a damn thing they could do about it. As such, past filibusters were a war of physical endurance and tactical gamesmanship.

In 1908, for instance, Senator Thomas Gore was filibustering a currency bill, with the support of his compatriot Senator William Stone. Gore tried to yield the floor to Stone. But Gore, who was blind, didn't realize Stone had stepped out of the chamber. The majority did, and they used the mistake to take back the floor and call the vote.[24] Brutal.

It wasn't until 1917, when a group of senators filibustered President Woodrow Wilson's bill to arm American merchant ships against German submarines for twenty-three days, that Wilson, a trained political scientist with strong views about proper parliamentary procedure, convinced the Senate to adopt a cloture rule allowing filibusters to be broken by a two-thirds majority of the body. And it wasn't until 1975 that the threshold was lowered to its current three-fifths level.

Given the way today's weakened filibuster paralyzes the US Senate, how did the body survive, and even thrive, in this long era of unbreakable filibusters? The answer is that though the rules made the filibuster far more powerful for most of American history, the norms made it weaker. The filibuster was barely used. Just because a senator, a group of senators, or a party full of senators could filibuster didn't mean they would. After all, if everyone was filibustering all the time, how would the Senate ever get anything done?

My favorite example of this comes from a letter written by President Lyndon Johnson's Senate liaison, Mike Manatos, after the 1964 election, assessing how the results changed Medicare's chances of passage. After ticking through the winners and losers, Manatos concluded, "If all our supporters are present and voting we would win by a vote of 55 to 45."[25] Imagine that. In living memory, the Senate could consider a bill as consequential as Medicare without anyone expecting a filibuster.

The filibuster rule is used to make more obscure mischief, too. A cloture vote isn't costless: it carries at least thirty hours of additional debate, which means that even if the minority knows it will lose, it can still use cloture votes to slow the majority down, tie up the Senate floor, and keep other business from getting done. There are examples of judicial nominees being filibustered only to subsequently pass unanimously. In 2009, then senator Tom Harkin, a Democrat from Iowa, told me about a particularly egregious example, coming as it did deep in the throes of the financial crisis. "We had an extension on unemployment insurance," Harkin said. "We had a filibuster that lasted over three weeks. They held up everything. And in the end, the vote was 97 to one."[26] Filibustering isn't a way lone senators make an unpopular argument heard, but a way the minority party in the US Senate sabotages the majority's ability to govern, in the hopes that voters will punish the party that seems to be in charge.

Filibusters were rare in past Senates (with one gruesome exception: they were used routinely to block anti-lynching and civil rights legislation). According to official records, from 1917 to 1970, the Senate took forty-nine votes to break filibusters. That's an average of slightly less than one each year. From 2013 to 2014, it had to take 218. That might've been a high mark of Senate obstruction, but there was no subsequent retreat to the rare filibusters of yesteryear: the 2015–2016 Senate session saw 123 cloture votes, and the 2017–2018 session hosted 168.

This is exactly what Linz's and Lee's research would predict. Back when American politics was less competitive and less polarized, filibusters were rare. They were rare in part because the parties were ideologically diverse, which prevented the internal agreement that leads to coordinated and strategic obstruction, and in part because the minority party saw little chance of regaining power, which left it cautious about antagonizing the majority. But now that the disagreements between the parties run deep and control of the Senate teeters on a knife's edge, the filibuster is a constant. This is American politics shifting to align with the more confrontational, zero-sum strategies the formal rules would suggest, rather than the more cooperative, tolerant approaches the informal norms encouraged.

Another good example of this dynamic is the debt ceiling—perhaps the strangest, most dangerous booby trap in American policy making. The way it works is this: Congress and the president routinely make spending decisions that carry, as a predictable consequence, additional federal borrowing. But rather than authorizing that borrowing when the spending decision is made, Congress holds separate votes, at separate times, permitting the federal government to borrow the money necessary to keep paying its bills.

This might seem like a small bit of dysfunction, but it's actually a bomb resting in the center of the global financial system. US Treasury bonds are considered the safest asset on the planet. They're held in massive numbers by governments, pension funds, hedge funds, investment banks, even ordinary investors, and they always play the same purpose: a riskless asset, the one financial product you can always count on to pay off. As such, much of the rest of the financial system is built on top of US Treasury bonds: the interest rate they pay is called "the riskless rate of return," and other products, from mortgages to auto loans, use it as their benchmark and then add the risk they calculate in their loans on top of it.

A simple definition of financial crises is that they occur when an important class of assets that people think is worth X actually proves to be worth something very different from X, and the market realizes that prices are wrong all throughout the system. Markets are built on information, and if the core information collapses into chaos all at once, the results can be catastrophic. That's roughly what happened in 2008, when the subprime mortgage bonds that the markets thought to be low risk turned out to be high risk, and credit markets convulsed in the aftermath.

If the US government failed to pass a debt ceiling increase and thus stopped paying its debts, the markets would have to reevaluate the most core piece of financial information of them all. The result would be a global financial crisis, sparked by congressional infighting.

Debt ceiling bills have always been used to embarrass the other side, but they've never been used as actual leverage because the consequences were simply too dire. That changed in 2011, when the newly elected Tea Party class of Republicans refused to increase the debt ceiling in order to increase their leverage to force spending cuts (a bit of anti-deficit dogmatism that tellingly evaporated the moment a Republican won the White House). The resulting crisis shook financial markets and led the Standard & Poor's credit agency to downgrade US government debt.

Congressional Republicans weren't wrong that the debt ceiling gave them power to demand concessions. Congress could have simply chosen to tie borrowing and spending decisions together, so there was never the possibility of legislators forcing a default. Instead, they left it hanging out there, a cocked gun that reckless legislators could use to hold their own country hostage unless they got what they want. That had never been done before because that just wasn't how things were done in American politics. Now it is.

You see these dynamics everywhere in the American political system now. Norms of cooperation and deference are breaking down and crises, paralysis, and polarization are the result. Shutdowns have become more common, judicial nominations have stopped relying on home-state senators' consent, rules have evolved to limit amendment processes and committee debate. This is all rational and maybe even inevitable: Why shouldn't both sides use and, when possible, change the rules to maximize their advantage? The problem is that we have a political system where the rules create irresolvable conflict, gridlock, and even global financial crises.

"This is dangerous," Senator Michael Bennet, a Colorado Democrat known for his bipartisan bent, told me. "We are a democratic republic. If we can't make decisions because of structural issues in our political system, or because of a habit of mind that doesn't allow us to believe other people deserve to be on the playing field, we cannot govern ourselves. That is an existential threat to the next generation of Americans."[27]

Chapter 9

The Difference between Democrats and Republicans

When I moved to Washington, in 2005, Thomas Mann and Norm Ornstein had risen to the most rarified heights in political journalism: they had become clichés. Mann and Ornstein—the coauthors were always referred to as a duo, like Sonny and Cher—had been the Beltway's go-to experts on Congress for a generation. They knew everything, talked to everyone, were everywhere. They became so ubiquitous that I knew of publications barring reporters from quoting the two scholars just to get some new voices into their stories.

A key reason for the duo's preeminence is they were relentlessly, ostentatiously balanced. Mann made his home at the center-left Brookings Institution. Ornstein hung his hat at the more forthrightly conservative American Enterprise Institute. Thus, in addition to their deep knowledge of Congress and their talent for offering the perfect quote on deadline, they embodied a fundamental assumption of American politics: the two parties were ideologically opposed but otherwise equivalent. Their presence in an article was a meta-message about nonpartisanship.

But Mann and Ornstein grew queasy. They might have been balanced, but the political system they were paid to understand had grown imbalanced. Worse, they believed the media's fetishization of the very thing they represented was obscuring the truth of American politics. So Mann and Ornstein decided to speak it themselves.

Few acts of political analysis are truly courageous, but this one was. Mann and Ornstein spent a lifetime of accumulated political capital, detonating a carefully constructed brand, to try to force a reckoning with what the Republican Party had become—and the role the media had played. In 2012, the two scholars published *It's Even Worse Than It Looks*, and in it, they minced no words:

> Today's Republican Party . . . is an insurgent outlier. It has become ideologically extreme; contemptuous of the inherited social and economic policy regime; scornful of compromise; unpersuaded by conventional understanding of facts, evidence, and science; and dismissive of the legitimacy of its political opposition, all but declaring war on the government. The Democratic Party, while no paragon of civic virtue, is more ideologically centered and diverse, protective of the government's role as it developed over the course of the last century, open to incremental changes in policy fashioned through bargaining with the Republicans, and less disposed to or adept at take-no-prisoners conflict between the parties. This asymmetry between the parties, which journalists and scholars often brush aside or whitewash in a quest for "balance," constitutes a huge obstacle to effective governance.[1]

Mann and Ornstein's diagnosis was controversial at the time, and the scholars found themselves disinvited from the Sunday shows that used to book them so regularly, ignored by the reporters who used to call them so eagerly. Liberals loved their book, of course, but now the media saw quoting Mann and Ornstein as signaling something entirely different: they had gone from representing the cherished assumption of party equivalence to representing the controversial rejection of it.

A few years later, Trump emerged like a golem summoned by Mann and Ornstein's words. He was their description of the GOP given a shock of orange hair, a cardiovascular system, and a Twitter account. In August 2015, when a Trump nomination—to say nothing of a Trump presidency—still sounded like a ridiculous prediction, Ornstein argued in the *Atlantic* that Trump really could win, that his candidacy and its triumph was predicted by a cycle of radicalization that was afflicting the Republican Party at every level:

> I have seen a GOP Congress in which the establishment, itself very conservative, has lost the battle to co-opt the Tea Party radicals, and itself has been largely co-opted or, at minimum, cowed by them.
>
> As the congressional party has transformed, so has the activist component of the party outside Washington. In state legislatures, state party apparatuses, and state party platforms, there are regular statements or positions that make the most extreme lawmakers in Washington seem mild.
>
> Egged on by talk radio, cable news, right-wing blogs, and social media, the activist voters who make up the primary and caucus electorates have become angrier and angrier, not just at the Kenyan Socialist president but also at their own leaders.[2]

Most observers saw Trump as a radical break from the Republican Party's traditions and narratives. Ornstein saw him as the logical next step for a party that was transforming itself, its institutions, and its leadership into vessels of revanchist rage.

Conservatives were choosing, again and again, the path of maximum confrontation and disruption, rallying behind the voices
that promised to go where their predecessors hadn't, to speak
the words that had previously been whispered, to embrace the
tactics that had once been shunned.

Trump wasn't a break with this Republican Party. He was the
most authentic expression of its modern psychology. The primary
would prove Ornstein right.

This is not a story you can tell about the Democratic Party,
which, though it has moved ideologically left, has remained tethered to traditional institutions and behaviors. You can get way in
the weeds of the data showing congressional Republicans have
moved further left than Democrats have moved right—believe
me, I have—but the simple fact is that Republicans nominated
Donald Trump in 2016 and Democrats nominated Hillary Clinton.
That is to say, one party nominated a candidate contemptuous of
established norms, obsessed with locking up political opponents,
and possessed by conspiracy theories. The other party . . . didn't.

Nor was the presidency a one-off. Between 2012 and 2018,
House Republicans drove John Boehner from the speakership
for being insufficiently radical and then made Paul Ryan's life so
miserable he resigned the post after only three years. By contrast,
as of 2019, House Democrats were led by the same leadership
team they elected in 2006.

During Bill Clinton's administration, Republicans pursued an
unpopular and bizarre impeachment campaign. During Barack
Obama's presidency, Republicans nearly breached the debt ceiling,
almost causing another global financial crisis, in an attempt to
bring the Democrat to heel. During both presidencies, Republicans
repeatedly shut down the federal government. In all these cases, top
Republicans expressed unease with the path they had chosen but
seemed helpless to do anything but channel the fury of their base.

For all the rage Democrats felt toward George W. Bush in 2006 and Donald Trump in 2018, they have have not attempted to gain leverage by endangering the global financial system. When Democrats took the House in 2006, Pelosi resisted calls to defund the Iraq War. Weirdly and tellingly, the longest government shutdown of the Trump era began when Republicans held Congress and Trump himself forced a shutdown over a Republican spending compromise that didn't fund his wall.

Make no mistake: plenty of liberals will read this capsule history as a recounting of Democratic weakness. The difference here is not that liberal activists haven't wanted the Democratic Party to escalate its tactics in opposition; it's that elected Democrats have largely been able to resist their demands.

The polarizing forces I have described throughout this book are acting on both coalitions. So why has the Democratic Party weathered them in a way the Republican Party hasn't? Why are the two parties so different? The answer is twofold: Democrats have an immune system of diversity and democracy. The Republican Party doesn't. This has not left the Democrats unaffected by the forces of polarization, to be sure. But if polarization has given the Democratic Party the flu, the Republican Party has caught pneumonia.

The benefits of diversity

Early in the 2020 Democratic primary, an interesting thing began happening. The Democratic candidates began getting asked about reparations for slavery. A few of them—notably Kamala Harris and Elizabeth Warren—expressed support. But instead of proposing direct compensation to the descendants of slaves, it turned out the Democrats were pitching policies for, well, everybody. "Harris has proposed monthly payments to qualified citizens of any race in the form of a tax credit," reported the Associated Press in February 2019. "Warren has called for universal child care that would guarantee the benefit from birth until a child enters school." These were universalist programs—programs that would help people of all races—being pitched in particularist ways.[3]

As an act of politics, it was a bizarre, worst-of-both-worlds compromise. "It risks prompting both withering criticism from Republicans and a shrug from black voters and activists if the proposals are seen as an empty gesture that simply renames existing policy ideas as reparations," wrote the AP. Why take a broadly popular policy, like Harris's idea to expand the earned income tax credit, and tie it to a divisive idea like reparations? The reason gets to a deep and underappreciated difference between the parties.

Back in chapter 2, we discussed the ways the two coalitions have sorted by ideology, race, religion, geography, and psychology. But not all sorting is the same. Sorting has made Democrats more diverse and Republicans more homogenous. This is often seen as a weakness for Democrats. They're a collection of interest groups, a party of list makers, an endless roll call. But it's played a crucial role in moderating the party's response to polarization.

Republicans are overwhelmingly dependent on white voters. Democrats are a coalition of liberal whites, African Americans, Hispanics, and Asians. Republicans are overwhelmingly dependent on Christians. Democrats are a coalition of liberal and nonwhite Christians, Jews, Muslims, New Agers, atheists, Buddhists, and so on. On the fixed versus fluid psychological dimensions discussed earlier, Republicans are overwhelmingly the party of fixed voters. But as Hetherington and Weiler note in their book *Prius or Pickup?*, Democrats are psychologically sorted only among white voters. "Communities of color include lots of people who value traditional family hierarchies and top-down authority," they write. "In fact, African Americans are the group most likely to have members with fixed worldviews."[4] But the Republican Party has so repelled nonwhite voters that they tend to be Democrats no matter their psychological makeup.

When we talk about sorting, it can sound symmetrical. Republicans have become the party of white voters, Democrats the party of nonwhite voters. But those are two very different party structures. Sorting has made the Democrats into a coalition of difference and driven Republicans further into sameness. As a result, appealing to Democrats requires appealing to a lot of different kinds of people with different interests. It means winning liberal whites in New Hampshire and traditionalist blacks in South Carolina. It means talking to Irish Catholics in Boston and the karmically curious in California. Democrats need to go broad to win over their party and, as we'll see, they need to reach into right-leaning territory to win power. Republicans can afford to go deep.

You can see this in the polling. The percentage of Americans calling themselves conservative has long dwarfed the percentage who identify as liberal. In 1994, conservatives outnumbered liberals 38–17. That gap has closed in recent years, but as of January 2019, conservatives still lead, 35–26. Three-quarters of Republicans identify as conservative, while only half of Democrats call themselves liberals—and for Democrats, that's a historic high point. Self-identified moderates outnumbered liberals in the Democratic Party until 2008.[5] What that means is Republicans have been able to appeal to their party through ideology. Democrats haven't. They've had to appease a coalition of whites and nonwhites, liberals and moderates, the fixed and the fluid. They've done that by promising different policies to different groups—offering a transactionalist, more than ideological, approach to party building.

In their book *Asymmetric Politics: Ideological Republicans and Group Interest Democrats*, Matt Grossmann and David Hopkins offer the most careful study yet of the differences between the Republican and Democratic coalitions. What they find is that the Democratic Party is a diverse collection of interest groups held together by policy goals, while the Republican Party is built atop a more united base that finds commonality in more abstract, ideological commitments.[6]

Grossmann and Hopkins show this difference in a variety of ways. More than twice as many interest groups make endorsements in Democratic primaries as Republican primaries. In an analysis of presidential debates from 1996 to 2012, "Republican presidential candidates were more than twice as likely as Democrats to mention ideology or principles," while Democrats "cited social, demographic, and interest groups at markedly higher rates than Republicans" and talked more about new policy proposals. In poll after poll, and under both Democratic and Republican presidents, Democrats say they prefer politicians who compromise to get things done, while Republicans say they prefer politicians who stick to their positions.

I differ with Grossmann and Hopkins on a key point. I think they mistake an identitarian movement for an ideological movement. If conservatives believed what they claim to believe about executive power, limited government, and congressional primacy, they would have seen Trump's presidency as a crisis. And for some, it was. George Will, the longtime columnist at the *Washington Post*, left the Republican Party. Representative Mark Sanford, the rock-ribbed conservative from South Carolina, refused to hold his tongue and lost to a primary challenger. Representative Justin Amash, the libertarian Republican from Michigan, called for impeachment proceedings against Trump and renounced his party membership.

But for most conservatives, whether they were prominent pundits or everyday voters, there proved to be no contradiction between conservatism and Trumpism. Quite the opposite, actually. According to a September 2019 Gallup poll, 75 percent of self-identified conservatives and 91 percent of self-identified conservative Republicans approved of the job Trump was doing.[7] This is because conservatism isn't, for most people, an ideology. It's a group identity.

A clever 2018 paper by political scientists Michael Barber and Jeremy Pope tested this experimentally. Trump was constantly adopting contradictory positions on issues, and his reputation for saying and doing anything primed voters to believe he really had said whatever they were told he'd said. "There has never been a president (or any party leader) who shifts back and forth so often between liberal and conservative issue positions," they wrote, and that opened space for a revealing study.[8]

Here's how it worked: Barber and Pope asked voters if they agreed or disagreed with different policies. Because of the, erm, flexibility of Trump's rhetoric, they were able to pick policies where Trump had, at some point, articulated both a liberal policy position and a conservative policy position. They then split their sample into four groups: a control group, a group that got asked about their policy views without any Trump-related information, and then groups that were asked about policy and given either Trump's liberal views or his conservative ones.

If conservatism was an ideology first and foremost, then a stronger attachment to that ideology should provide a stronger mooring against the winds of Trump. Instead, the precise opposite was true. The people who identified as most strongly conservative were the likeliest to move in response to Trump. And the effect was about the same size whether Trump was taking the conservative or liberal position. It was the direction of Trump, not the direction of the policy, that mattered. Interestingly, there wasn't an equal and opposite reaction among strong liberals: they didn't change position much to oppose Trump.*

This is what Trump understood about conservatives that so many of his critics missed: they were an identity group under threat, and so long as you promised them protection and victories, they would follow you to hell and back. Amash, in an interview conducted with Vox's Jane Coaston days before leaving the GOP, put it well.

> A lot of Trump Republicans have this mindset that they have to fight this all out war against the left. And if they have to use big government to do it, they're perfectly fine with that. So when I go to Twitter and talk about overspending or the size of the government, I get a lot of reactions now from Trump supporters saying, "Who cares how big the government is", or "Who cares how much we're spending as long as we're fighting against illegal immigration and pushing back against the left."[9]

The Fox News effect

Crucially, the Democratic Party isn't just more diverse in terms of its members; it's also more diverse in its trusted information sources. In 2014, the Pew Research Center conducted a survey measuring trust in different media sources, giving respondents thirty-six different outlets to consider and asking them to rate their

---

* This doesn't prove liberals wouldn't exhibit the same behavior toward Obama or Sanders. Just that they didn't exhibit it in the negative toward Trump.

trust in each. Respondents who counted as "consistent liberals" trusted a wide variety of media outlets ranging from center-right to left: ABC, Al Jazeera America, the BBC, Bloomberg, CBS, CNN, *The Colbert Report*, *Daily Kos*, *The Daily Show*, the *Economist*, *The Ed Schultz Show*, Google News, the *Guardian*, the *Huffington Post*, *Mother Jones*, MSNBC, NBC, the *New Yorker*, the *New York Times*, NPR, PBS, *Politico*, *Slate*, *USA Today*, the *Wall Street Journal*, the *Washington Post*, and Yahoo!

Consistent conservatives did not. Of the thirty-six outlets named, only a handful of deeply ideological sources commanded more trust than distrust among respondents who counted as consistently conservative: Fox News, Breitbart, the *Wall Street Journal*, the Blaze, the Drudge Report, *The Sean Hannity Show*, *The Glenn Beck Program*, and *The Rush Limbaugh Show*.

Pew also asked consistent liberals and conservatives which outlet served as their "main" news source. Here, too, the difference was stark. For the liberals, there was no dominant news source. CNN was the top choice with 15 percent, followed by NPR with 13 percent, MSNBC with 12 percent, and the *New York Times* with 10 percent. Among consistent conservatives, 47 percent chose Fox News, with the next most popular answer being "local news," at 11 percent.

Two years later, Pew commissioned a similar survey during the 2016 election, measuring where Clinton and Trump voters were getting their news. Among Clinton voters, the most popular choice was CNN, with 18 percent naming it as their main news source, followed by MSNBC, which was the top choice of 9 percent. Among Trump voters, 40 percent named Fox News.[10]

The Pew findings mirror what other researchers have discovered. In "Partisanship, Propaganda, and Disinformation: Online Media and the 2016 U.S. Presidential Election," a study of media dynamics in the 2016 election, six Harvard researchers concluded:

The leading media on the right and left are rooted in different traditions and journalistic practices. On the conservative side, more attention was paid to pro-Trump, highly partisan media outlets. On the liberal side, by contrast, the center of gravity was made up largely of long-standing media organizations steeped in the traditions and practices of objective journalism.[11]

Political parties exist within informational ecosystems. Those ecosystems create the context in which voters make demands, in which politicians make strategic choices, in which presidential aspirants craft messages. The Democratic Party's informational ecosystem combines mainstream sources that seek objectivity, liberal sources that push partiality, and even some center-right sources with excellent reputations, like the *Economist* and the news reporting in the *Wall Street Journal*. On any given question, liberals trust in sources that pull them left and sources that pull them toward the center, in sources oriented toward escalation and sources oriented toward moderation, in sources that root their identity in a political movement and sources that carefully tend a reputation for being antagonistic toward political movements.

There is no similar diversity in the GOP's trusted informational ecosystem, which is entirely built around conservative news sources, many of them propagandistic. Conservatives protest that the media is liberally biased, so they had no choice but to build their alternative network. In my experience, it's true that reporters for mainstream outlets are culturally liberal in their personal politics, though more mixed in their economic and foreign policy views. The newsrooms I know are overwhelmingly pro-choice, but they're also biased toward deficit hawkery and the national security establishment. The dominant ideology, to the extent there is one, tracks *Morning Joe*, not the *Nation*. That said, mainstream newsrooms are built around incentives that are different from, and often contrary to, liberalism as a political movement. The *New York Times* and ABC News fear a liberal reputation—they want to be understood as neutral arbiters of truth—and reporting oppositionally and inconveniently on the Democratic Party is both part of the self-identity and the business model.

Perhaps as important, the intermixing of mainstream and left news sources forces an adherence to professional journalistic practices. MSNBC's reporters and prime-time hosts want to be respected by the *Washington Post*'s reporters. *Slate*'s writers want to do work that will get them hired by the *New York Times*. As such, the business models and reputational ambitions of the mainstream outlets don't just discipline their work; they also discipline the work of the more liberal outlets that admire them.

Conversely, Breitbart, Limbaugh, and the Blaze are operating in a self-contained conservative ecosystem, where part of the appeal is outright hostility to mainstream institutions. Over and over again, you see conservative media working to discredit other forms of media and even other forms of information. Fox News's tagline, "Fair and Balanced," is an insinuation that the rest of the media is unfair and biased. Limbaugh goes even further than that. He calls the media, the scientific community, academia, and the government "the four corners of deceit" and tells his listeners:

> We live in two universes. One universe is a lie. One universe is
> an entire lie. Everything run, dominated, and controlled by the
> left here and around the world is a lie. The other universe is
> where we are, and that's where reality reigns supreme and we
> deal with it. And seldom do these two universes ever overlap.[12]

The conservative movement has spent years battling liberal bias in the media and the academia. Some of their complaints had merit. But rather than reform those institutions or build similarly credible competitors, the right has untethered itself from them and built an informational ecosystem premised on purity rather than process. In their essay "How Information Became Ideological," Grossmann and Hopkins describe the result:

> Only the Republican Party has actively opposed society's central information-gathering-and-disseminating institutions—universities and the news media—while Democrats have remained reliant on those institutions to justify policy choices and engage in political debate, considering them both independent arbiters and allies. Although each party's elites, activists and voters now depend on different sources of knowledge and selectively interpret the messages they receive, the source of this information polarization is the American conservative movement's decades-long battle against institutions that it has deemed irredeemably liberal.[13]

In an essay for Vox, Dave Roberts calls this "tribal epistemology"—when "information is evaluated based not on conformity to common standards of evidence or correspondence to a common understanding of the world, but on whether it supports the tribe's values and goals and is vouchsafed by tribal leaders."[14] You can hear it ring clearly when, for instance, Rep. Lamar Smith, a Texas Republican, says it's "better to get your news directly from the president. In fact, it might be the only way to get the unvarnished truth."[15]

All of this both predates and contextualizes Trump's constant refrain of "FAKE NEWS!" Here, too, Trump isn't a break from recent Republican traditions but a logical extension of them.

An interesting question is why the Right didn't build institutions similar in ethos and practice to the ones they sought to replace, just staffed with conservatives. In 2009, Tucker Carlson mounted the stage at the conservative conference CPAC and warned the Right that it needed a strong journalistic culture of its own. "The *New York Times* is a liberal paper, but it is also . . . a paper that actually cares about accuracy," he said. "Conservatives need to build institutions that mirror those institutions." Riding the hype from that speech, Carlson went on to found the *Daily Caller*, which has fallen from its initial high ideals and today mixes conservative paranoia with slideshows of hot women,*[16] and then to take a prime-time slot on Fox News, where he's the cable news pundit most skilled at catering to white fear of a browning America.

There are examples of strong institutions with conservative cultures in direct competition with the *New York Times*—the Murdoch-owned *Wall Street Journal*, for instance—but they exist as exceptions, not as oft-followed models. I don't have a firm answer as to why, but I suspect it reflects the market available to carve off: because the mainstream media and academia actually aren't that liberal, because they mostly do put truth-seeking ahead of partisanship, there isn't that much demand for alternatives. The audience that is sufficiently alienated by mainstream outlets to present a business opportunity is uniformly conservative, and creating a differentiated enough product to appeal to them means creating a product that chooses to cater to conservative identity, rather than a product that routinely confronts it. But the result is that Democrats rely on a diversity of information sources that discipline their flights of fancy, while Republicans

---

* Examples include, "This Sexy Model Is Blowing Up the Internet [SLIDESHOW]," "This UFC Octagon Girl's Instagram Account Is Sizzling Hot [SLIDESHOW]," and—I kid you not—"13 Syrian Refugees We'd Take Immediately [PHOTOS]," which reads, "While a growing list of governors are claiming they won't allow Syrian refugees to enter their states, we think these women might make them change their minds. They are Syria-sly hot."

rely on a narrower set of media institutions that propel their polarization.

There should be a check on this sort of behavior. A party that narrows the sources it listens to is also narrowing the voters it can speak to. And political parties ultimately want to win elections. Lose enough of them, enough times, and even the most stubborn ideologues will accept reform. Democracy, in other words, should push against polarization. But America isn't a democracy.

America, the undemocratic

"In most democracies," writes political scientist Jonathan Rodden in his book *Why Cities Lose*, "the path to victory is simple: win more votes than your competitors. For the Democratic Party in the United States, however, this is often not good enough."[17]

As I write these words, Republicans control the White House, the Senate, and the Supreme Court. The only national branch under Democratic control is the House. And yet Democrats didn't just win more votes in the House elections. They won more votes in the Senate elections, too. They won more votes in both the 2016 and 2000 presidential elections. If America was a democracy, Democrats would control the House, the Senate, the White House, and, through those victories, a commanding majority on the Supreme Court. Their weakness is the result of geography, not popularity.

The Democrats' problems are, if anything, worse in the states. As Rodden notes, "the Republican Party has controlled the Pennsylvania Senate for almost forty consecutive years, even while losing the statewide popular vote around half of the time. The

Republicans have controlled the Ohio Senate for thirty-five years, during which time Democrats won half of the state's US Senate elections and around one-third of the gubernatorial elections."

America is not a democracy. Our political system is built around geographic units, all of which privilege sparse, rural areas over dense, urban ones. This is most glaringly true in the Senate, where Vermont wields the same power as New York. But it is also true in the House, due to the way districts are drawn, and in the White House, due to the electoral college, and thus it is *also* true in the Supreme Court, which reflects the outcomes of presidential and senatorial elections. And power, of course, begets power. Republicans use their majorities to pass partisan gerrymandering plans, pro-corporate campaign finance laws, strict voter ID requirements, and anti-union legislation, and Supreme Court decisions further weaken Democrats' electoral performance. My point here is not that this is unjust, though I believe it is. Instead, I want to focus on the way this system restrains polarization among Democrats and unleashes it among Republicans.

To win, Democrats don't just need to appeal to the voter in the middle. They need to appeal to voters well to the right of the middle. In the Senate, FiveThirtyEight's Nate Silver estimates the average state is six points more Republican than the average voter.[18] So when Democrats compete for the Senate, they are forced to appeal to an electorate that is far more conservative than the country as a whole. Similarly, it's estimated that Democrats need to win a substantial majority in the House popular vote to take the gavel.[19] And the fact that Democrats have lost two of the last five presidential elections due to the electoral college—the only times that's happened in American history—signals a growing imbalance there also. Indeed, a recent study by Michael Geruso, Dean Spears, and Ishaana Talesara calculates that "Republicans should be expected to win 65% of Presidential contests in which they narrowly lose the popular vote."[20]

The voters who hold the balance of power in American politics are whiter, older, and more Christian than the country as a whole. So for all the talk of democratic socialism and all the star power of Alexandria Ocasio-Cortez, when the dust settled on the 2018 elections, the House's moderate New Democrat Coalition swore in forty new members, making it the largest caucus in the Democratic Party.

The GOP's geographic advantage permits it to run campaigns aimed at a voter well to the right of the median American. It's oft remarked that Republicans have lost the popular vote in six of the last seven elections. If they'd also lost six of the last seven presidential elections, they would have overhauled their message and agenda to become competitive again. If Trump had lost in 2016, he—and the political style he represents—would've been discredited for blowing a winnable election. The Republican moderates who'd counseled more outreach to black and Hispanic voters would've been strengthened.

The shock of Trump's unexpected win in 2016 overshadowed his underperformance. Early in the election, Vox took the leading political science models for forecasting presidential elections, weighted them by past accuracy, and, working with Jacob Montgomery of Washington University in St. Louis and Texas A&M's Florian Hollenbach, built a model that incorporated all of them. The result? Given the economy, Obama's approval rating, and other factors, the Republican should have been expected to win about 50.5 percent of the two-party vote.

Trump consistently polled far behind that prediction, and throughout the campaign, we tracked the difference between his polling and the model's prediction, calling it "The Trump Tax"—on Election Day, it was 3.8 points. "What we appear to be seeing is a remarkable example of a major political party blowing a totally winnable national election," we wrote, in one of many assessments shredded by Election Day.

Still, while Trump ultimately won through the electoral college's intervention, it's very likely that another Republican, like Marco Rubio or John Kasich, would've beat Hillary Clinton with a convincing popular vote majority (and hypothetical polling matchups consistently backed that up). If the election outcome had reflected the popular vote, Trump and his supporters, today, would be blamed for losing a race Republicans should've won, handing the Supreme Court to liberals for a generation.

And make no mistake, a different, more broadly competitive Republican Party is possible. As of the second quarter of 2019, the two most popular governors in the country—Massachusetts's Charlie Baker and Maryland's Larry Hogan—were Republicans in blue states.[21] There is absolutely a GOP message that can command true majorities. But freed from the need to appeal to the median voter, Republicans have hewed to a more conservative and confrontational path than the country would prefer. They have learned to win power by winning land, rather than by winning hearts and minds.

Republicans know that their coalition is endangered, buffeted by demographic headwinds and an aging base. And that has injected an almost manic urgency into their strategy. Behind the GOP's tactical extremism lurks an apocalyptic sense of political stakes. It feels to many that if they lose, they may never win again—and perhaps, with their current coalition, there's a kernel of truth in that. Still, there is nothing more dangerous than a group accustomed to wielding power that feels its control slipping. In their book *The Tea Party and the Remaking of Republican Conservatism*, Theda Skocpol and Vanessa Williamson report that it was this sense of desperation that powered the Tea Party's Obama-era rise:

> "I want my country back!" one Massachusetts man told us in 2010. "We need to take our country back," echoed a Virginia woman the following year. This plaintive call is perhaps the most characteristic and persistent theme in grassroots Tea Party activism. As Mark Lloyd of the Virginia Tea Party Patriots explains, people gravitate to the Tea Party when they anguish about "losing the nation they love, the country they planned to leave to their children and grandchildren." As a new president of diverse heritage promised to "transform America," perceived threats to the very nature of "our country" spurred many people, and particularly older people, to get involved with the Tea Party.[22]

In the run-up to the 2016 election, the conservative *Claremont Review of Books* published an anonymous, but influential, essay making the case for Trump. "2016 is the Flight 93 election," it said: "charge the cockpit or you die." The situation was dire, and there was no guarantee of success. "You may die anyway. You—or the leader of your party—may make it into the cockpit and not know how to fly or land the plane. There are no guarantees. Except one: if you don't try, death is certain." The piece went on to blast the conservatives who had spent decades warning of crisis but were sniffily dismissing Trump:

> Let's be very blunt here: if you genuinely think things can go on with no fundamental change needed, then you have implicitly admitted that *conservatism is wrong*. . . . This is the mark of a party, a society, a country, a people, a civilization that wants to die. Trump, alone among candidates for high office in this or

in the last seven (at least) cycles, has stood up to say: I want to live. I want my party to live. I want my country to live. I want my people to live. I want to end the insanity.[23]

The author of this apocalyptic bit of political analysis was later revealed as Michael Anton, and he took a job as a national security official in the Trump administration.

These dire rationalizations permeate the upper reaches of the Republican establishment. When William Barr joined the Trump administration as attorney general in February 2019, it was a puzzling decision. Barr had previously served as attorney general under George H. W. Bush, and had settled into a comfortable twilight as a respected member of the Republican legal establishment. The AG position in the Trump White House only opened after the president hounded Jeff Sessions out of office for being excessively ethical and insufficiently loyal. But Barr quickly proved himself all that Sessions wasn't, enthusiastically prosecuting the president's vendettas and flying around the world investigating his conspiracies. Why rewrite the end of a storied career this way? Why make this your legacy?

Speaking at Notre Dame in October 2019, Barr made his reasoning clear. He argued that the conflict of the twentieth century pitted democracy against fascism and communism—a struggle democracy won, and handily. "But in the twenty-first century, we face an entirely different kind of challenge," he warned. America, he said, was built atop the insight that "free government was only suitable and sustainable for a religious people." But "over the past fifty years religion has been under increasing attack," driven from the public square by "the growing ascendancy of secularism and the doctrine of moral relativism." This is a war Barr thinks progressives have been winning, and that conservatives fight in the face of long institutional odds. The left, he says, has "marshaled all the force of mass communications, popular culture, the entertainment industry, and academia in an unremitting assault on religion and traditional values. These instruments are used not only to affirmatively promote secular orthodoxy but also drown out and silence opposing voices, and to attack viciously and hold up to ridicule any dissenters."

In a subsequent speech to the Federalist Society, Barr expanded his analysis. "So-called progressives treat politics as their religion," he said. "Their holy mission is to use the coercive power of the state to remake man and society in their own image, according to an abstract ideal of perfection. Whatever means they use are therefore justified because, by definition, they are a virtuous people pursing a deific end. They are willing to use any means necessary to gain momentary advantage in achieving their end, regardless of collateral consequences and the systemic implications." In contrast, he continued, "conservatives tend to have more scruple over their political tactics and rarely feel that the ends justify the means. And this is as it should be, but there is no getting around the fact that this puts conservatives at a disadvantage when facing progressive holy war, especially when doing so under the weight of a hyper-partisan media."

Again, this was not a random conservative op-ed columnist, but the attorney general of the United States speaking.

In these speeches, Barr sounded like Liberty University President Jerry Falwell Jr., son of Christian right leader Jerry Falwell, who tweeted in September 2018, "Conservatives & Christians need to stop electing 'nice guys'. They might make great Christian leaders but the US needs street fighters like @realDonaldTrump at every level of government b/c the liberal fascists Dems are playing for keeps & many Repub leaders are a bunch of wimps!"

This is the context for much of the Republican establishment's ultimate embrace of Trump. Whatever Trump's moral failings, he's a ruthless street fighter suited for an era of political combat. Rightly or wrongly, many conservatives—and particularly Christian conservatives—believe that they've been held back by their sense of righteousness, grace, and gentility, and as a result, they are on the verge of being vanquished, and America forever lost. Trump is the enemy they believe the left deserves, and perhaps the only hope Christian conservatives have.

Democrats are often derided for playing identity politics, but that is not, in truth, a difference between the parties. Republicans have built their coalition on identity politics as well. The difference between the parties is that Democratic candidates are forced to appeal to many more identities, and more skeptical voters, than Republicans do. Successful national Democrats construct broad coalitions, and that's a practice that cuts against the incentives of pure polarization.

What national Republicans have learned to do is construct deep coalitions relying on more demographically and ideologically homogenous voters. Instead of winning power by winning the votes of most voters, they win power by winning the votes of most places. That's let them appeal to an electorate considerably to the right of the median voter, to get away with decisions and candidates that would've torched another party. But it's also forced them into dependence on an electorate that feels its power slipping away, and that demands a response proportionate to its fears.

This is the way in which the parties are not structurally symmetrical and thus why they have not responded to a polarizing era in the same ways: Democrats simply can't win running the kinds of campaigns and deploying the kinds of tactics that succeed for Republicans. They can move to the left—and they are—but they can't abandon the center or, given the geography of American politics, the center-right, and still hold power. And they know it.

In December 2018, well into the Trump era, Gallup asked

Democrats and Republicans whether they wanted to see their party become more liberal, more conservative, or more moderate. By a margin of 57–37, Republicans wanted their party to become more conservative; by a margin of 54–41, Democrats wanted their party to become more moderate.[24]

Chapter 10

Managing Polarization— and Ourselves

To call a politician polarizing is an epithet, to call a voter polarized is a dismissal. As such, books that explore polarization typically end with suggestions for tamping down our disagreements and rediscovering our common bonds as countrymen. It's stirring stuff.

I don't consider polarization, on its own, to be a problem. Just as often it's a solution. America's modern run of polarization has its roots in the civil rights era, in the Democratic Party choosing to embrace racial equality and the Republican Party providing a home to white backlash. Surely the polarization that followed that progress was preferable to the oppression that preceded it. In a multiparty system, polarization is sometimes required for our political disagreements to express themselves. The alternative to polarization often isn't consensus but suppression. We don't argue over the problems we don't discuss. But we don't solve them, either.

This is not to say American politics is untroubled. But we should be precise in our diagnosis. America's political system is distinct, and in the eras it has seemed to function best, it has relied on mixed parties. Because a less polarized country lies within living memory, the tendency is to imagine a return to an idealized past. This must be the aberration, and that the state of nature.

But, as I've tried to show in this book, the polarization we see around us is the logical outcome of a complex system of incentives, technologies, identities, and political institutions. It implicates capitalism and geography, politicians and political institutions, human psychology and America's changing demography. And for now, at least, it's here to stay. Absent an external unifying force like a war, the divisions—or worse—we see today will prove the norm, while the depolarized politics of mid-twentieth-century America will prove the exception. And if we can't reverse polarization, as I suspect, then the path forward is clear: we need to reform the political system so it can function amid polarization.

I should level with you. I don't like concluding chapters. Authors write whole books about devilishly complex social problems and then pretend they can be solved in a few bullet points. I have more confidence in my diagnosis than my prescription, and what I hope, above all, is that I've offered a framework here that others in politics will use to make sense of our problems and better the system.

What follows isn't a comprehensive policy agenda but a set of approaches. I have no illusions about "solving" social media's tilt toward outrage, the human brain's sensitivity to identity, or the dizzying escalation of political conflict. My intention here is more limited: what I want to do is offer principles that might help us build a political system that can function amid polarization— and that might help us craft our own political identities so we can engage in politics in a way that's better for the country and better for ourselves.

But let's start with the system. There are three categories of reform I think particularly worth exploring: bombproofing, democratizing, and balancing.

Bombproofing

We know that one result of our polarizing parties is that bipartisan agreement is becoming harder to achieve. We know that politicians are becoming more responsive to a media that amplifies conflict and a base that loathes weakness. We know that confrontation and paralysis have become divided government's natural state. Some of that political combat is necessary. Some of that gridlock simply reflects a divided country. But we should limit the damage it can do. We should, to the extent possible and consistent with political accountability, bombproof the government's operations against political disaster.

The most obvious candidate here is the debt ceiling. As discussed in chapter 8, the debt ceiling could take routine bickering in Congress and transform it into a full-blown global financial crisis. Even if you believe neither party truly wants to see a default, assume—and I think this is reasonable—that under current conditions, there's a 5 percent chance of miscalculation in any given debt ceiling confrontation such that it goes horribly wrong. If you believe that, then you believe, after a few decades, it's likelier than not that we will have defaulted at least once.

The debt ceiling is bizarre and unnecessary. It severs Congress's decision to spend money from its decision to pay its bills. We can and should get rid of it. There are plenty of other ways for members of Congress to express their views, gain some leverage, and grandstand before their constituents that don't threaten to tank the global economy and forever wound the world's faith in American Treasury bonds.

There are other possible candidates here, too. Congress's budgetary process has been broken for years. Instead of passing budgets, Congress typically debates, gridlocks, and often shuts down over the budget's pathetic cousin, "continuing resolutions," which carry the previous year's spending over to the next year, with some minor alterations. As a result, long-term fiscal planning is an impossibility throughout much of the federal government.

It is properly Congress's responsibility to manage spending, but it is also, in theory, Congress's responsibility to manage it well. Revamping the budget process to make budgeting more automatic, with predictable spending changes that trigger in the absence of a new budget, would be a more sensible way to finance the government and would permit Congress to fight at less cost to the American people and the services they depend on.

Similarly, a lesson of the Great Recession was that the relationship between polarization and extended economic suffering is dangerously dysfunctional. Moments of emergency, like the collapse of Lehman Brothers, might temporarily puncture the system's inertia, but as the crisis drags on, it becomes tempting for the minority party to cease cooperating and commence criticizing—the public anger that recessions generate is a potent electoral weapon. An expansion of automatic economic stabilizers offers a possible answer: as the unemployment rate rises, the federal government can automatically absorb more state Medicaid costs, boost unemployment and food stamp spending, and begin lowering payroll taxes or expanding Social Security checks.

Wonks could come up with hundreds of other ideas. But the governing principle is simple: where congressional inaction can do great damage, we should ask ourselves whether the upside of congressional deliberation truly outweighs the risk of unnecessary disaster. Representation is an honored value in our political system, but as I write these words in September 2019, Congress's approval rating in the RealClearPolitics average of polls is 16.6 percent, and its disapproval rating is 71.4 percent, so it's not clear to me that the American people feel all that well represented.

Which brings me to the next principle.

Democratizing

In the last chapter, I discussed the way exposure to democracy has proven something of an immune system for the Democratic Party, while the Republican Party has been warped by its ability to win elections without fashioning a majoritarian agenda. If we want politicians to adopt a broader and less polarizing approach to both politics and policy, we need to make them responsible for putting together broader, less polarized coalitions. A Republican Party that needed to put together popular vote majorities would be a healthier party, and that would make for a healthier politics.

Reinvigorating American democracy would take different forms at different levels. At the presidential level, it would simply mean doing away with the archaic electoral college. This is difficult to do through constitutional amendment but easy to do through legislative action: the National Interstate Popular Vote Compact is an agreement by states to throw their electoral votes to whichever presidential candidate wins the popular vote. It would take legal force the moment states representing a 270-vote majority in the electoral college sign it—and so far, the states that have joined represent 196 electoral votes, which is more than 70 percent of the way there.

At the House level, this could and should mean something like proportional representation. We're used to states carving themselves into gerrymandered congressional districts, but the Constitution doesn't demand that structure, and other countries don't use that structure. A smarter approach, as Lee Drutman, a senior fellow at the think tank New America, argues, would be to combine multimember districts with ranked-choice voting. Under this system, states would break into electoral zones represented by multiple members of Congress. Voters would list their favorite candidates in order. The least popular candidate would be eliminated, and her voters would see their second choice counted. In, say, a three-member zone, this process would continue until the top three candidates were discovered.

This has a few advantages. One is that voters can choose the candidate they like most, knowing their vote can still matter even if their favorite politician loses. Another is that voters would no longer have to live in the small fraction of swing districts for their votes to matter. Parties would have to compete for all voters, everywhere. But the third and most important advantage of a system like this is that it makes third parties viable, as unlike under our winner-take-all election rules, a party that gets 22 percent of the vote can get 22 percent of the seats, rather than nothing at all.

To see the difference this makes, imagine an election where Republicans have 40 percent support, Democrats have 45 percent support, and Libertarians have 15 percent support. In our current system, that leaves the Libertarians with nothing and their voters likely responsible for the Democrats' victory. That's why systems like ours create two-party duopolies. In a proportional representation system, conversely, that makes the Libertarians the crucial powerbroker. That's why proportional representation systems foster multiparty democracy.

There are some who see multiparty democracy as a cure for all that ails us. I don't. A quick survey of Europe, where multiparty democracy is common and plenty of countries are undergoing their own political crises, is enough to curb expectations. Still, one way of thinking about the midcentury American party system that I've described is that it was actually a four-party system: the Democrats, the Dixiecrats, the conservative Republicans, and the liberal Republicans, and it seems to have functioned more smoothly. Perhaps some form of proportional representation could nudge us back in that direction, albeit with less racism.

The Constitution makes the Senate harder to democratize than the House. As a Californian, I think the fact that my state gets exactly as much representation as Wyoming is insane. But given our founding design, we're not getting rid of the Senate, so I'll just have to simmer in my discontent. What we could do is twofold.

First, get rid of the filibuster, which takes an already undemocratic institution and adds an absurd supermajority requirement on top of it. The old hope that the filibuster would encourage compromise has failed. This is not a controversial point: we have more filibusters than ever and less compromise than ever.

But the filibuster's worst sin is that it drains the system of accountability. In theory, the way American politics works is that a party gets put in charge, that party governs, and then voters decide whether they like the results. In practice, the filibuster allows the Senate minority to hamstring the majority. This would be fine if voters were all congressional reporters, paid to watch the procedural maneuvering that drives the chamber. But they're not. What they know is that their roads aren't getting fixed, their jobs aren't coming back, and Washington doesn't seem to be doing anything to help them. So, reasonably, they blame the majority, even if it's not actually the majority's fault. A system where it's this hard to figure out why something didn't happen isn't a system where voters can act as an effective check on legislators. In an age where bipartisanship is irrational, making it impossible for partisan majorities to govern well simply ensures we'll be governed poorly.

Defenders of the filibuster—and they are rife in both parties—will cite all the horrible legislation that the other side might've passed if not for the rule. And true enough. But fundamentally, the question this raises is: Do you prefer the problems of governance or paralysis? I choose governance, in part because I trust the American people to ultimately look out for their own interests.

Democrats who worry that Obamacare would've been repealed in the absence of the filibuster give too little credit to a country that would've noticed health care being canceled for tens of millions of people. Either health care matters to people or it doesn't, but it can't both be central to their lives and irrelevant to their politics. Similarly, Republicans who believe the American people would rise up against unchecked liberalism should ask themselves why they're so afraid of permitting the country to see Democrats' true colors.

Second, it's long past time for Washington, DC, and Puerto Rico to have congressional representation. It's one thing for the Senate to represent states rather than people. It's another thing for so many Americans to be deprived of representation because the places they live have been denied statehood for political reasons. We live in a country built on the principle of representation. The fact that we deny it to so many of our citizens is indefensible. The fact that we particularly deny it to places with large African American and Hispanic populations compounds historical injustice and tilts the system toward white voters. If DC and Puerto

Rico have representation, that would be another push for the Republican Party to veer away from deepening racial polarization as an electoral strategy.

Of course, all of these reforms only work if people can actually vote. There's a broad range of ways to make voting easier—I like automatic voter registration and Oregon's vote-by-mail system myself—but more important than the details is the simple principle that voting should be easy, not hard. The harder you make it to vote, the surer it is that only the most polarized Americans end up at the polls.

It is disastrous that democracy has become a partisan issue, with Republicans viewing efforts to expand the franchise as conspiracies to weaken their party. It's possible that a more democratic America would be a more Democratic America, but it's also possible that a Republican Party that had to compete for more kinds of voters would reform itself to win that competition. As I noted before, the most popular governors in the country are moderate Republicans leading blue states, so there's no reason to believe the party lacks popular appeal when its incentives are properly aligned. There is no less dysfunctional politics without a less dysfunctional GOP, and the path to a less dysfunctional GOP is forcing the party to reach beyond the ethnonationalist coalition Trump rode to victory.

The alternative to democratizing America is scarier than mere polarization: it's a legitimacy crisis that could threaten the very foundation of our political system. By 2040, 70 percent of Americans will live in the fifteen largest states. That means 70 percent of America will be represented by only thirty senators, while the other 30 percent of America will be represented by seventy senators.[1] It is not difficult to imagine an America where Republicans consistently win the presidency despite rarely winning the popular vote, where they typically control both the House and the

Senate despite rarely winning more votes than the Democrats, where their dominance of the Supreme Court is unquestioned, and where all this power is used to buttress a system of partisan gerrymandering, pro-corporate campaign finance laws, strict voter ID requirements, and anti-union legislation that further weakens Democrats' electoral performance. That would not, in the long term, prove a stable system.

If this seems outlandish, well, it simply describes the world we live in now and assumes it continues forward. Look at Wisconsin, where state Republicans gerrymandered the seats to make Democratic control a near impossibility.[2] Look at *Citizens United*, which gave Republicans a 5 percentage point boost in elections for state legislators.[3] Look at the Trump administration's effort to add a citizenship question to the census that was designed to scare Latinos away from answering the form; its architect wrote that it would "be advantageous to Republicans and Non-Hispanic Whites."[4]

Too much of American politics is decided by efforts to restrict who votes or, as in gerrymandering, to manipulate the weight those votes hold. A more democratic system won't end polarization, but it will create a healthier form of competition.

Balancing

This is the principle that will feel strangest to people. It feels, to be honest, strange to me.

The threat to the United States of America has always been disunity. At the time of its founding, the strongest and most politically important identities were state identities, and the central tension was between those who feared the (white, male) voting public and those who trusted it, so we built a system meant to calm those divisions. We balanced big and small states in the Senate. We balanced democratic and elite rule by handing the House to the voters, the Senate to state legislatures (popular elections came to the US Senate only with the 1913 ratification of the Seventeenth Amendment), and the White House, through the peculiar institution of the electoral college, to both.

A central problem in any free political system is how to secure balanced competition. The problem in our system is that what we balanced for is no longer what's competing. Today, the strongest and most politically important identities are partisan identities. We don't talk about big states and small states but about red states and blue states. If there is a threat to American unity, it rests not in the specific concerns of Virginians or Alaskans but in the growing enmity between Democrats and Republicans. And here's the thing: the Founders did not think about how to balance parties, because they didn't think parties would exist.

"If the competing groups are states, you need a set of rules to make sure that competition is fair," says Lilliana Mason. "If the competing groups are parties, you need a set of rules to make sure the partisan competition is fair."

Those who trust in the Founders' wisdom need to take this more seriously: if they were wise to recognize that the most potent political units need to be represented in the system in a balanced, predictable way, then the path to honoring their insight lies in correcting their oversight. Perhaps there are places in the political system where, rather than unleashing the parties to fight to the death for every scrap of power, we should lower the stakes by guaranteeing them—or, in a multiparty system, any party that achieves support above a certain threshold—equal power.

One interesting proposal for this comes from law professors Daniel Epps and Ganesh Sitaraman.[5] They argue that the conflict swirling around the Supreme Court has reached dangerous levels, with McConnell's rejection of Garland kicking off an anything-goes era in the fight for control, with Democrats now seriously discussing a partisan court-packing as a last-ditch effort to negate McConnell's gambit. Epps and Sitaraman suggest rebuilding the Supreme Court so it has fifteen justices: each party gets to appoint five, and then the ten partisan justices must unanimously appoint the remaining five. Until all fifteen are agreed upon, the Court wouldn't be able to hear cases.

This system would have a few advantages. First, it could calm a conflict that is thoroughly politicizing an institution meant to keep at least some distance from politics. Second, it would create a path to serving on the Court that would reward candidates who aren't seen as intensely partisan and ideologically reliable, which basically disqualifies you now. In theory, both sides would feel and be equally represented on the Court, and the all-out warfare of recent years would ease. Am I sure this would work? No. But I'm sure that what we're doing now isn't working either, and so creative thinking is needed.

In Congress, rules could be rewritten to ensure participation and voice that don't rest on the veto power of the filibuster. It should be easier, for instance, for the minority party to bring full bills to the floor. In the House, the so-called Hastert Rule—wherein Republicans, and often Democrats, won't bring a bill to the floor unless it commands a majority among their own members—denies a vote to legislation that may pass atop unusual coalitions. You could also imagine a right to actual, ongoing debate that is not paired with a supermajority requirement.

The underlying principle in all this is that the two parties both represent huge swaths of Americans, and the fact that one has the majority does not mean the other should be deprived of a voice.

Depolarizing ourselves

A theme of this book has been that we, as individuals, aren't just responsible for changing the political system; we are also being changed by it. The primary way the system gets its hooks into us is by threatening or otherwise activating our political identities and using the catalytic energy to get us to contribute, vote, read, share, or just generally be pissed off. That's not always a bad thing, of course. Politics is a high-stakes enterprise, and there are plenty of times when we should contribute, vote, read, share, and, yes, be pissed off.

But there's a difference between polarization and manipulation. There's a difference between using politics for our purposes and being used for the political purposes of others. So I also want to discuss a few ways we can change our relationship to politics that can be both healthier for us and our country: identity mindfulness and rediscovering a politics of place.

Identity mindfulness

All politics is influenced by identity. That's not because all politics is literally identity politics. It's because all of human cognition is influenced by identity, and politics is part of human cognition. We cannot sever ourselves from our circumstances. We will never fully know how fully we've been shaped by our contexts. Who we are, where we grew up, whom we've learned to trust and fear, love and hate, respect and dismiss—it's deeper than conscious thought. The slate of mental processes built around the millisecond it takes an identity to activate isn't something we can simply slough off.

But if we can't turn off the power identity holds over us, we can harness it. Remember, our identities are manifold. "Republican" is an identity, as is "Democrat." But so is "fair-minded," or "Christian," or "curious," or "New Yorker." It can be as much an identity to see yourself as an advocate for the poor, for animals, or for children as to be a member of a political party. The thing about the organized identities promoted by political coalitions is that there is a massive apparatus for defining, policing, and activating them. If you want to get out of that superstructure, it takes work. But it is possible.

If the beginning of wisdom on identity politics is recognizing that all of us are engaging in it all the time, the path of wisdom on identity politics is to be mindful of which of our identities are being activated, so that we can become intentional about which identities we work to activate. Like a muscle or a neural pathway, the identities we use most grow strongest, the ones that lie fallow weaken. We can wield that to our advantage. Doing so starts with mindfulness.

Yeah, I know. Of course, the politics book by the liberal Californian vegan ends with a call to mindfulness. But slowly take ten breaths, making sure your mind doesn't wander, and hear me out. Our environments are designed to activate some identities and not others. American life is full of American flags, for instance. Political life is full of reminders of the red-blue divide and which side of it you're on. Religious life is meant to pull you in one direction, hipster consumerism drags you in another, and hey, how about that local sports team whose paraphernalia is literally everywhere? There are massive, well-funded efforts strengthening our identities everywhere we turn. It takes work to see this happening within us, in real time. But it's possible.

The practice of mindfulness is separable from the practice of meditation. Robert Wright, the eminent political journalist and

Buddhist scholar, writes, "The word 'mindful,' as used around the time of [its] translation, meant 'taking thought or care of; heedful of; keeping remembrance of.' In other words: a mindful person is an acutely aware person, a person who proceeds with careful attention to all relevant factors."[6]

In this case, the relevant factor I'm urging you to pay attention to is identity. What identity is that article invoking? What identity is making you defensive? What does it feel like when you get pushed back into an identity? Can you notice when it happens? If you log on to Twitter nine times a day, can you take a couple breaths at the end and ask yourself how differently you feel from before you logged on?

The idea here is to become more aware of the ways that politicians and media manipulate us. There are reams of research showing that our reaction to political commentary and information we don't like is physical. Our breathing speeds up, our pupils narrow, our hearts beat faster. Trying to be aware of how politics makes us feel, of what happens when our identities are activated, threatened, or otherwise inflamed, is a necessary first step to gaining some control of the process.

That is not to say we should become afraid of our identities being inflamed or strong emotions being forced forward. It's to say we should be mindful enough of what's happening to make decisions about whether we're pleased with the situation. Sometimes it's worth being angry. Sometimes it's not. If we don't take the time to know which is which, we lose control over our relationship with politics and become the unwitting instrument of others.

The point of this book is that we all inhabit a larger context that shapes our actions. Sometimes that context is difficult to change. But sometimes it is changeable. Our informational environments are one of those things. Once we recognize that we exist amid an omnipresent conspiracy to manipulate our identities, we can begin the hard work of fashioning our environment to shape and strengthen the identities we want to inhabit. And I have a suggestion of where to start.

Rediscovering a politics of place

In March 2018, the *New York Times* published an article I think about often. Entitled "The Man Who Knew Too Little," it tracked the bizarre world Erik Hagerman had constructed for himself after the election. Depressed by the results, he decided he didn't want to know a thing about Trump. Nothing. "It was draconian and complete," he said. "It's not like I wanted to just steer away from Trump or shift the conversation. It was like I was a vampire and any photon of Trump would turn me to dust."[7]

And so he set off building his bubble. A former Nike executive, he now lives alone on a pig farm in southeastern Ohio. He listens to white noise tapes at the coffee shop. He scolds friends who mention politics. He never looks at the news or social media. He goes to stores early to avoid overhearing talk of current events. When he visited his brother in San Francisco, "strict arrangements had to be made—the Sunday newspaper kept out of sight, the TV switched off, his teenage niece and nephew under special instructions."

So far, so nuts. But then, at the end, the story changed. Amid his withdrawal, he had focused his time on "a master project, one that he thinks about obsessively, that he believes can serve as his contribution to American society." He had purchased forty-five acres of land that used to sit atop a strip mine. The land became "his life's work." He is restoring it, protecting it, turning it into something his community can enjoy. Hagerman, it turns out, hadn't disengaged from civic life. He had simply disengaged from national politics to focus on local change. And he had constructed an informational ecosystem to support that choice. Perhaps he went too far in that project—way, way too far—but most of us are not going far enough.

I saw the article because the internet had erupted in outrage over it. "The *New York Times* managed to find the ultimate beacon of white privilege—and, arguably, the most insufferable person in the world," read a representative tweet.[8] Who did Hagerman think he was? This rich white guy who wasn't going to get deported, who wouldn't be jailed, who probably wouldn't suffer at all under the Trump administration. Who was he to tune out the news the second it made him feel sad?

But then, who did we think we were? Were those of us sending angry missives into the ether really doing more than this guy who was restoring land to gift back to his neighbors?

My point is not that we should all go informationally Galt. But I'll be blunt here in a way that cuts against my professional interests: we give too much attention to national politics, which we can do very little to change, and too little attention to state and local politics, where our voices can matter much more. The time spent spraying outrage over Trump's latest tweet—which is, to be clear, what he wants you to do; the point is to suck up all the media oxygen so he retains control of the conversation—is better spent checking in with what's happening in your own neighborhood.

"There are over five hundred thousand elected officials in the United States, only 537 of whom serve at the federal level," writes Daniel Hopkins in *The Increasingly United States*.[9] The 537 federal officials are the ones we have the least power to influence, if only because they have, on average, the most constituents. But we often don't know the names of the officials nearest to us, even though they'd be glad to meet for coffee.

This isn't because we're lazy, bad people. It's because media has nationalized, and there's been a particular reaping at the state and local level. I don't have an answer for that—revitalizing state and local journalism is a book unto itself—save to counsel effort. It's possible to make local and in-state news sources a bigger part of your media diet and thus make your local political identity more powerful. It's just a lift, particularly when those stories aren't being pushed at you by friends on social media or covered by the national publications you love.

But there's a real reward from rooting more of our political identities in the places we live. First, we tend to live among people more like us, so the politics is less polarized. Second, the questions are often more tangible and less symbolic, so the discussion is often more constructive and less hostile. Third, we can have a lot more impact on state and local politics than on national politics, and it feels empowering to make a difference. And fourth, even if your heart lies in national politics—I'm a journalist who covers national politics, I get it—being involved in state and local politics will make you much more effective, both because it's valuable experience and because local officials eventually become federal officials, and they keep in touch with the people they've known along the way. When the next presidential campaign rolls around, the people they're going to want most as volunteers are the folks who already know how to organize in their communities.

Again, I'm not counseling you to abandon national politics. But audit your informational diet and ask what percentage of political stories you read are national versus state or local. Watch yourself for a week and reflect on how much of your political emotion and energy attach to the national stories. If that mix is overwhelmingly tilted toward the national scene, consider tilting it back.

There are no solutions, only corrections

I'll be honest: even writing these suggestions for solutions makes me a little queasy. I began the book talking about midcentury political scientists desperate for more polarized parties. American politics is complex and unpredictable, and sometimes plans that are heralded as overdue solutions in one age become the defining problems of the next.

But then, that's the point, isn't it? There isn't an end state to American politics. The search for a static answer will always be folly. There is no one best way for the system to work. There is only the best we can do right now. And, if we do a good enough job at it, we will see today's successes ossify into tomorrow's frustrations. What works in one era fails in the next. That's okay. The point is to get to that next era with the most progress and the least violence.

I get asked often whether I'm optimistic or pessimistic about American politics. I think I'm an optimist, but that's because I try to hold to realism about our past. For all our problems, we have been a worse and uglier country at almost every other point in our history.

You do not need to go back to the country's early years—when new arrivals from Europe drove out and murdered indigenous peoples, brought over millions of enslaved Africans, and wrote laws making women second-class citizens—to see it. Just a few decades ago, political assassinations were routine. In 1963, President John F. Kennedy was murdered on the streets of Dallas. In 1965, Malcolm X was shot to death in a crowded New York City ballroom. In 1968, Martin Luther King Jr. was killed, as was Robert F. Kennedy. In 1975, Lynette "Squeaky" Fromme, standing about arm's length from President Gerald Ford, aimed her gun and fired; the bullet failed to discharge. Harvey Milk, the pioneering gay San Francisco city supervisor, was killed in 1978.

President Ronald Reagan was shot in 1981; the bullet shattered a rib and punctured a lung.

For much of the twentieth century, the right to vote was, for African Americans, no right at all. Lynchings were common. Freedom Riders were brutally beaten across the American South. Police had to escort young African American children into schools as jeering crowds shouted racial epithets and threatened to attack.

Violence broke out at the 1968 Democratic National Convention. Urban riots ripped across the country. Crime was rising. The United States launched an illegal, secret bombing campaign in Cambodia. National Guard members fired on and killed student protesters at Kent State. Richard Nixon rode a backlash to the civil rights movement into the White House, launched an espionage campaign against his political opponents, provoked a constitutional crisis, and became the first American president driven to resign from office by impeachment proceedings.

This is not a counterintuitive take on American history, by the way. Among experts, it is closer to the consensus. The Varieties of Democracy Project, which has been surveying experts on the state of global democracies since 1900, gave the US political system a 48 on a 1 to 100 scale in 1945 and a 59 in 1965. It was only after the civil rights movement that America began scoring in the '70s and '80s, marking it as a largely successful democracy.[10]

The era that we often hold up as the golden age of American democracy was far less democratic, far less liberal, far less decent, than today. Trump's most intemperate outbursts, his most offensive musings, pale before opinions that were mainstream in recent history. And the institutions of American politics today are a vast improvement on the regimes that ruled well within living memory. If we can do a bit better tomorrow, we will be doing much, much better than we have ever done before.

Afterword

I began this book with a statement of intent. "What I am trying to develop here isn't so much an answer for the problems of American politics as a framework for understanding them. If I've done my job well, this book will offer a model that helps make sense of an era in American politics that can seem senseless."

Why We're Polarized came out in January of 2020. Then history accelerated. The novel coronavirus turned into a pandemic weeks later, and, as I write these words, has killed more than 500,000 Americans and millions more globally. Then came Joe Biden's victory in the Democratic primary, followed by his victory in the election. Then there was the Capitol insurrection, on January 6, followed by the second impeachment of President Donald Trump and the first months of Joe Biden's presidency. I'm exhausted just writing all that out. But it was plenty of tragedy and tumult with which to test the framework of this book. So on the eve of the paperback publication, I want to look back on the major political events of the past year and assess how the model fared.

Coronavirus

If you'd told me, the day I published this book, that a virus would soon rip across the country, killing hundreds of thousands of people while the president picked fights with blue state governors, refused to wear a mask, promoted unproven miracle drugs, and mused about injecting Americans with bleach, I'd have thought would be the kind of political shock that could overwhelm the logic of polarization. It's one thing to let partisan identity drive when the issues are complex and abstract, it's another to try and wave away the deaths of friends and family. I don't know what I would've predicted Donald Trump's exact approval rating would be in the aftermath of such horror. But I would have predicted either a real rise from a rally-around-the-leader effect or a sharp fall in the case of incompetence—either way, a clear change.

In this case, I made a mistake—but the mistake was not believing in the book's thesis enough. On August 27, 2019, Trump's approval was 41.3 percent, and his disapproval was 54.2 percent, according to the website FiveThirtyEight's poll tracker. Exactly one year later—a year that carried not just the coronavirus pandemic but Trump's first impeachment, unemployment rising from 3.7 percent to 10.2 percent, and the protests following George Floyd's murder—as Trump prepared to give his speech at the Republican National Convention, FiveThirtyEight had Trump at 42.2 percent approval and 54.3 percent disapproval. Everything had happened, and politically nothing had mattered. Opinions about Trump had barely budged.

I had written in this book's introduction, "We are so locked into our political identities that there is virtually no candidate, no information, no condition, that can force us to change our minds.

We will justify almost anything or anyone so long as it helps our side, and the result is a politics devoid of guardrails, standards, persuasion, or accountability." I realize now that I believed that statement to come with more caveats than I'd offered. I meant that to apply to normal eras in American politics—fights over tax policy and health care and campaign finance scandals. I didn't think it'd apply to a body count well into the six digits. But here we are.

Joe Biden

When I finished writing this book, one of the big, unanswerable questions for me was which path the Democratic Party would take. I'd written at length about the way Republicans had radicalized further and faster than the Democrats. I'd argued that both parties were subject to many of the same polarizing forces, but that different coalitional structures led to different outcomes. In particular, Democratic candidates for president had to win over a more racially, religiously, and ideologically diverse coalition— white liberals and conservative African Americans, Catholics in Boston and witches in Marin. On top of that, Democrats knew they couldn't win the presidency while losing the popular vote, or even just winning a bare majority of the popular vote. Because of their geographic disadvantage in the electoral college, they had to win a majority and then some, which meant winning voters who were definitionally right-of-center.

But two theories split Democrats here. There was the traditional theory, in which you run a more ideologically, temperamentally, and—though I dislike much that this implies—stylistically moderate candidate, in a bid to reassure voters disappointed by Trump but skeptical of Democrats. But there was also the choice-not-an-echo theory, which was that Democrats could reshape the electorate by running a democratic socialist like Bernie Sanders, turning out nonvoters and inspiring those who wanted the kind of populism Trump had promised but failed to deliver. Put more simply, Democrats faced a choice between moving to the center and moving to the left.

In the end, Democrats chose Joe Biden, and they did so because of the coalitional dynamics I'd written about. It was more moderate, conservative, and religious Black voters in South Carolina, and then nationwide, who saved and then propelled Biden's candidacy. And it was the long-running "electability" argument—the idea that an older, moderate, Catholic, white guy from Scranton, Pennsylvania, would seem a safer choice to white, Trump-curious voters in the Midwest—that powered his victory. Many in the Democratic Party wanted a candidate who would be an ideological or demographic first, both a symbol and an agent of a changing America, but enough Democrats feared losing again in 2020 that they went with Biden as the safe choice.

You also saw the relative strength of the institutional Democratic Party in Biden's victory: the slew of endorsements, first by South Carolina Congressman James Clyburn and then, on the eve of Super Tuesday, by Amy Klobuchar and Pete Buttigieg, were crucial in Biden's victory. Earlier in the book, I'd argued that even as the Democratic Party "has moved ideologically left, [it] has remained tethered to traditional institutions and behaviors." House Democrats, for instance, continue to be led by the same three members as in 2006, while House Republicans have cycled through multiple speakers and majority leaders. It's a striking difference, and a rejection of the old saw that "Democrats fall in love, Republicans fall in line."

I'll admit I don't have a full theory for why the Democratic establishment maintains a level of influence and power that the Republican establishment has clearly lost. I suspect some of the difference lies in the media ecosystems, where Democrats still trust a mix of mainstream and liberal sources and Republicans cluster inside a conservative ecosystem that's become increasingly antiestablishment as the different outlets vie for audience. I also think that Democratic leaders represent their voters better than establishment Republican leaders do. Congressional Democrats mostly agree with their base about the general direction of policy, even if there are arguments over how far and how fast to go. But much of the GOP's congressional agenda—tax cuts tilted for the rich, opposition to a higher minimum wage, corporate deregulation, Medicaid cuts—is unpopular even among Republicans, and that difference in goals has turned corrosive to the party.

The 2020 election

It's tricky to analyze the 2020 election in detail, because the voting disruptions caused by the pandemic left exit polls even messier and less trustworthy than usual. Still, a few trends stood out.

First, it's worth admitting the unnerving closeness of the result. In 2016, Trump won because of 40,000 voters in Pennsylvania, Wisconsin, and Michigan. In 2020, he lost because of 22,000 voters in Wisconsin, Georgia, and Arizona—if those votes had flipped, the electoral college would've been tied, and the election would've been decided by state congressional delegations, which Republicans control.

One might object, of course, that Trump lost the popular vote by a huge margin—about 7 million votes, more than twice the margin by which he lost the 2016 popular vote. But the popular vote doesn't matter for who wins the presidency, only the electoral college does. And in 2020, the electoral college's divergence from the popular vote increased from 2016, tilting the election even further in the GOP's favor. Democrats won, but they needed a popular vote landslide to avoid an electoral college loss. It is hard to imagine the politics of the country if Democrats had won by 7 million only to watch congressional Republicans declare Trump the victor, but we were inches from that outcome.

A similar story holds in Congress. Take the Senate. Democrats' dual victories in the Georgia Senate runoffs gave the party a 50-50 split in the Senate and handed Vice President Kamala Harris the tie-breaking vote. But that 50-50 split makes American politics look far more evenly divided than it actually is. As Vox's Ian Milhiser calculated, the 50 Senate Democrats represent 41 million more Americans than the 50 Senate Republicans.

A key argument of this book is that polarization isn't the problem, it's the interaction between polarization and our political institutions that's the problem. That's on particular display in the 2016 and 2020 elections: If Republicans had lost proportionally to their popular vote deficits, they would've lost in landslides, and the party would've either reformed itself so it could win more votes in a changing country or shrunk into near-irrelevance. But our strange electoral institutions protect Republicans from the true consequences of the political path they've chosen, which has allowed the Republican Party to radicalize in ways that a more straightforward democracy would've punished. In another system, polarization might even be disciplining, because the more you fear the other side winning, the more you're willing to make the strategic decisions and ideological compromises necessary to beat them. But Republicans have a sufficiently clear minoritarian path to power that they need not make the difficult choices necessary to rediscover a majoritarian path to power.

That said, the 2020 election highlighted something I'd missed in this book. Political systems can polarize across many dimensions, and the dimensions I'd emphasized were party, ideology, geography, and race. But race, in particular, depolarized a bit in the 2020 election—Trump saw significant gains with Hispanic voters—probably on the order of 8 to 9 points—and smaller but still real gains with Black and Asian voters. Democrats, meanwhile, won more white voters—the Democratic data analyst David Shor estimates they gained .5 percentage points among non-college whites and 7 percentage points among college-educated whites.

I didn't talk much about educational polarization in the book, but it's a growing part of the story. What's a little unclear is what education is doing here. Education might be, at least in part, a handmaiden of ideology: college-educated voters tend to be more ideological, and in particular, they tend to be more ideologically liberal, so educational polarization might be a close relative of ideological polarization. It also might be a corollary of certain kinds of political trust: one reason that pollsters keep underestimating Donald Trump's support in states with lots of non-college white voters is that those voters don't trust pollsters and are less likely to answer their questions. There's also a connection between education and white voters' views on race. And in an economy in which diplomas are increasingly demanded for middle-class jobs, and cultural power is increasingly aimed at more urban and educated consumers, voters without an education are going to be angrier at both economic and cultural institutions they feel locked out of and more receptive to populist candidates who promise to fight for them against elites.

I won't be able to untangle how education is changing the

electorate in this afterword. But it's a reminder that societies can polarize in many ways, and particularly in a country with as weird an electoral system as ours, the particular traits across which we polarize can have outsized consequences. The GOP's growing advantage in the electoral college reflects educational polarization among white voters, who are overrepresented in electorally important states. If Democrats want to reduce their geographic handicap, they need to run candidates, and emphasize issues, who reduce educational and geographic polarization.

The insurrection, and the Big Lie

Trump's refusal to admit he lost the election, and his incitement of a mob that stormed the Capitol—some of them with the intention of murdering Nancy Pelosi and hanging Mike Pence—was shocking but not surprising. Trump had telegraphed all of it in advance. He had been clear that he would declare any election that he lost rigged or stolen—just as he had done, though few remember it, when Ted Cruz beat him in the 2016 Iowa caucus. But Trump was just one of many Republicans running for president then. In January of 2020, he was the president, and his bond with his most fervent supporters was unshakeable. Is it any surprise they believed him when he told them the election was ripped from them? Is it any surprise they erupted in violence in an effort to stop a crime of that magnitude?

There is little to say about the events of January 6 that has not already been said. That two-thirds of Republicans tell pollsters they believe Trump rightfully won the election is a crisis, and one fed by craven and cowardly Republican elites, who've refused to frontally challenge Trump's lies. Most House Republicans voted against certifying the results of the election, and many, like House Republican Leader Kevin McCarthy, joined a lawsuit to overturn those results. They've lit a match in a country soaked in gasoline, and they should be ashamed. Not everything in American politics can be blamed on polarization. There is, in any age, a place for leadership, and danger beckons when leaders fail. Republican leaders have failed, and the Republican Party now believes the problem is not that it is losing votes but that it is the victim of an ongoing political conspiracy.

A party that keeps losing voters has two choices. It can change itself—its agenda, its standard-bearers, its temperament—to win over new voters. Or it can turn against democracy, using the power it still holds to disenfranchise or weaken the voters who threaten it. The Republican Party, for now, has chosen the second path and chosen it decisively. Republicans control far more state legislatures than Democrats, which will give them control over the next redistricting. They are using their power in state legislatures to pass new laws making it harder to vote. The Brennan Center for Justice, which focuses on voting rights issues, calculated in mid-February of 2021 that the number of bills introduced to restrict the right to vote so far that year was seven times the number that were introduced by the same point in 2020. House Republicans in Georgia just passed a thick bill of voting restrictions that include outlawing offering food or water to anyone standing in line to vote. The rest of the bill was designed to make those voting lines longer for the voters Georgia Republicans lose. The assault on the Capitol failed, but the assault on democracy in the states is, in many cases, succeeding.

Democrats, however, have the power to secure democracy, if they choose to use it. They hold the White House, the Senate, and the House. They are considering HR1, the For The People Act, and

HR4, the John Lewis Voting Rights Act, which together would be the largest expansion and protection of voting rights since the 1960s. These bills would get rid of partisan gerrymandering, match small-donor donations 6 to 1, rebuild the Voting Rights Act after the Supreme Court gutted it in 2013, ensure automatic voter registration and vote-by-mail options across the country, and far more. Democrats could also make DC a state and offer Puerto Rico statehood, extending the franchise to millions of American citizens currently denied equal representation. These bills would pass easily, if not for the filibuster and the super-majority it demands. And so the defining question of this next period in American politics is not whether we will be polarized. We already are. It is whether we will be democratized.

March 2021

Acknowledgments

This book is all about how individuals reflect the people, communities, and systems that surround them. So, in any proper accounting, the acknowledgments should be far longer than the rest of the text. Since I'm reliably informed that's frowned upon in the publishing world, I apologize in advance to all those left out. And I apologize, too, to all those included: nothing I say here can possibly do justice to the role you played in shaping this project, and in shaping me.

Thank you, first, to Ben Loehnen at Simon & Schuster, who believed in the book I pitched him, and then also believed in the very different book I wrote for him, six years later. This book would not exist without Ben's faith, patience, editing, and encouragement. My agent, Andrew Wylie, struck a lovely balance between reminding me I needed to get this done without scaring me with how much there was left to do. I hope the wait was worth it. Parts of this book appeared first as articles in Vox and the *New Yorker*, and I'm indebted to both the editors who helped shape them and the publications for letting me build on that work here. Ben Kalin fact-checked the book with remarkable rigor and cheer. John Sides, Lilliana Mason, and Yuval Levin provided crucial comments on an early draft, and John, in particular, has been an invaluable sherpa to the world of political science, and a dear friend. All of them made this book better, and its remaining mistakes and shortcomings are mine alone.

My first job in journalism was at the *American Prospect*, where Mike Tomasky took a chance on me, despite my total lack of actual journalism experience, and then took the time to teach me how to be a journalist. "Pick up the damn phone"—or PUTDP, as I came to think of it—rings in my head years later.

My community of friends in DC welcomed me into the first social world where I ever truly felt at home. It meant more to me than they'll ever know. In particular, my roommates at the Hobart House—Ben Adler, Brian Beutler, and Ben Miller—deserve particular note, as do Kate Steadman and Ethan Pollack.

I was an unorthodox hire for the *Washington Post*, and I am forever grateful to Steve Pearlstein for convincing them to make it, and for the mentorship, argument, friendship, lessons, and dinners that followed. Thank you to Kelly Johnson for being such a wonderful editor, friend, and confidante; to Marcus Brauchli, Raju Narisetti, Greg Schneider, Marty Baron, and Donald Graham for modeling so much decency, curiosity, integrity, and kindness.

But above all, thank you to the *Washington Post* for believing in Wonkblog. The years of partnership with Lydia DePillis, Neil Irwin, Suzy Khimm, Sarah Kliff, Tim Lee, Dylan Matthews, and Brad Plumer mean more to me than I can ever express. The truest measure of our work is the people who work alongside us, and the fact that I got to work alongside Sarah and Brad for so long, and that I continue to work alongside Dylan, makes me certain I'm doing something right.

Building Vox has been the most amazing, challenging, and meaningful experience of my career. I am terrified to even attempt to name names here, but thank you to Jim Bankoff and Trei Brundrett for creating an amazing company; to Lauren Williams, Allison Rockey, and Joe Posner for their leadership, brilliance, focus, and generosity; to Laura McGann for her many late-night edits and keen insights; and to our whole remarkable staff for believing in the vision and working so incredibly hard and creatively every day to make it reality. As the endnotes to this book prove, I have learned an enormous amount from their efforts. Clear eyes, full hearts, explain the news.

I founded Vox alongside Matt Yglesias and Melissa Bell. Matt's college blog was the inspiration for my blog, his encouragement kept me going, his recommendation got me hired at the *American Prospect*, he welcomed me into his community in DC, and he makes me smarter every day. There is no acknowledgment that could pay back the role he has played in my life.

I met Melissa at the *Washington Post*, where she was in every digital meeting despite no one being able to explain to me what, exactly, her role was. Eventually, I figured it out: If you want to get big things done, you do them with Melissa. It is a lesson I have lived by ever since. I cannot imagine the past decade without her partnership, but even more, I cannot imagine it without her friendship, even if we disagree on when exactly that friendship began.

During the course of this book, I moved out to the Bay Area— the land of Milk and Honey—and I'm grateful for the wonderful community that welcomed me here. And though it feels like I've known him longer, Bilal Siddiqi and I became friends amidst this project, and he's been a crucial source of encouragement and whiskey.

I met Tristan Reed when I was twelve, and Grant Gordon a few years later. They have been my best friends since. I have no idea who I would be without them. Grant had the particular misfortune of moving near me just as I began working on the book in earnest, and he has cheerfully absorbed its weight, buoyed me through its challenges, and bought me drinks when they were most needed, as he has done for so much else in my life. Thank you.

I do not know how to even begin thanking my family. I get my love of politics from my brother, Gideon Kracov, who took me to marches, to meetings, and on one particularly memorable day, to ride across Los Angeles with the late, great, Paul Wellstone. I am forever trying to live up to his example. My mother, Jacqueline Klein, and father, Abel Klein, modeled unconditional love even at times when I tested the concept, and they have supported, watched, and cheered for me every day of my life. My sister, Liliana Klein, is one of my best friends and first calls. Linda Levine and Sara Weissman entered my life later, but every day has been richer for their presence.

I have the great fortune to be married to the most interesting person I have ever met. Getting to experience the world along-side Annie Lowrey is one of the great gifts of my life, and I am a better man in every way for her partnership. She is the editor, coconspirator, and thinker I trust most, and I cannot imagine this journey without her love, care, and brilliance.

Finally, Thomas Moses Lowrey-Klein was born during the writing of this book. Being his father is the identity I cherish most deeply. The worst part of this project, by far, were the hours it took me away from him. I hope it contributes, in some small way, to building a world as good as he is.

Notes

Introduction—What Didn't Happen

1 Hillary Rodham Clinton, *What Happened* (New York: Simon & Schuster, 2017).
2 Emily Guskin and Scott Clement, "Clinton Leads by Five Points Nationally as Trump Personality Concerns Persist, Post-ABC Tracking Poll Finds," *Washington Post*, November 6, 2016, washingtonpost .com/news/the-fix/wp/2016/11/06/clinton-leads-by-five-points -nationally-with-large-advantages-on-temperament-and-qualifi cations-post-abc-tracking-poll-finds/?utm_term=.c56d2927cb83.
3 Adam Gopnik, "Did the Oscars Just Prove That We Are Living in a Computer Simulation?," *New Yorker*, February 27, 2017, newyorker .com/culture/cultural-comment/did-the-oscars-just-prove-that-we -are-living-in-a-computer-simulation.
4 "Against Trump," editorial, *National Review*, January 22, 2016, national review.com/2016/01/donald-trump-conservative-movement -menace.
5 Andrew Gelman and Pierre-Antione Kremp, "The Electoral College Magnifies the Power of White Voters," Vox, December 17, 2016, vox .com/the-big-idea/2016/11/22/13713148/electoral-college-democracy -race-white-voters.
6 Sidney Dekker, *Drift into Failure: From Hunting Broken Components*

to Understanding Complex Systems (Farnham, UK; Burlington, VT: Ashgate, 2011).

7 Keeanga-Yamahtta Taylor, *How We Get Free: Black Feminism and the Combahee River Collective* (Chicago: Haymarket Books, 2017).

Chapter 1—How Democrats Became Liberals and Republicans Became Conservatives

1 Joanne B. Freeman, *The Field of Blood: Violence in Congress and the Road to Civil War* (New York: Farrar, Straus and Giroux, 2018).

2 *Towards a More Responsible Two-Party System: A Report of the Committee on Political Parties* (Washington, DC: American Political Science Association, 1950).

3 The APSA report: jstor.org/stable/1950999.

4 Thomas E. Dewey, "The Two-Party System" (1950), in *Politics in the United States: Readings in Political Parties and Pressure Groups*, ed. Henry Turner (New York: McGraw Hill, 1955), archive.org/stream/politicsinunitedooturn/politicsinunitedooturn_djvu.txt.

5 Qtd. in ibid.

6 Qtd. in ibid.

7 Qtd. in ibid.

8 Qtd. in Geoffrey Kabaservice, *Rule and Ruin: The Downfall of Moderation and the Destruction of the Republican Party, from Eisenhower to the Tea Party*, Studies in Postwar American Political Development (New York: Oxford University Press, 2012).

9 Clinton Rossiter, *Parties and Politics in America* (Ithaca, NY: Cornell University Press, 1960).

10 Morris P. Fiorina, *Party Sorting and Democratic Politics*, series no. 4, Hoover Institution, Stanford University, hoover.org/sites/default/files/research/docs/fiorina_party_sorting_and_democratic_politics_4.pdf.

11 Alan Abramowitz and Steven Webster, "All Politics Is National: The Rise of Negative Partisanship and the Nationalization of U.S. House and Senate Elections in the 21st Century," Annual Meeting of the Midwest Political Science Association, Chicago, IL, April 16–19, 2015.

Available at stevenwwebster.com/research/all_politics_is_national
.pdf. The 2018 numbers from Abramowitz email to the author.

12 Abramowitz and Webster, "All Politics Is National." Extension to 2016
from Webster email to author.

13 Corwin Smidt, "Polarization and the Decline of the American Floating
Voter," *American Journal of Political Science* 61, no. 2 (Apr. 2017):
365–81, doi.org/10.1111/ajps.12218.

14 "Partisanship and Political Animosity in 2016," Pew Research Center,
June 2016, people-press.org/2016/06/22/partisanship-and-political
-animosity-in-2016.

15 Sean Wilentz, "The Mirage," *New Republic*, October 25, 2011, new
republic.com/article/96706/post-partisan-obama-progressives
-washington.

16 Yanna Krupnikov and Samara Klar, "Why People Call Themselves
'Independent' Even When They Aren't," *Washington Post*, January 10, 2014, washingtonpost.com/news/monkey-cage/wp/2014
/01/10/why-people-call-themselves-independent-even-when-they
-arent/?noredirect=on&utm_term=.f99ff7b6c2f2.

17 Carroll Doherty, "Key Takeaways on Americans' Growing Partisan
Divide over Political Values," *Fact Tank* (blog), Pew Research Center, October 5, 2017, pewresearch.org/fact-tank/2017/10/05/take
aways-on-americans-growing-partisan-divide-over-political-values.

18 "The Partisan Divide on Political Values Grows Even Wider," Pew
Research Center, October 2017, people-press.org/2017/10/05/the
-partisan-divide-on-political-values-grows-even-wider.

19 npr.org/templates/story/story.php?storyId=128303672.

20 Anna North, "How Abortion Became a Partisan Issue in America," Vox, April 10, 2019, vox.com/2019/4/10/18295513/abortion
-2020-roe-joe-biden-democrats-republicans.

21 "1976 Republican Platform: Equal Rights and Ending Discrimination,"
Gerald R. Ford Library, fordlibrarymuseum.gov/library/document
/platform/rights.htm.

22 Bill Barrow and Elana Schor, "Biden: Congress Should Protect Abortion Rights, if Necessary," Associated Press, May 22, 2019, apnews
.com/37bcf15a80a54014bd37fa4298d5d5c1.

23 Smidt, "Polarization."
24 "Partisanship and Political Animosity in 2016," Pew Research Center, June 22, 2016, people-press.org/2016/06/22/partisanship-and-political-animosity-in-2016/.

Chapter 2—The Dixiecrat Dilemma

1 Joseph Crespino, *Strom Thurmond's America* (New York: Hill & Wang, 2012).
2 David A. Bateman, Ira Katznelson, and John Lapinski, "*Southern Politics* Revisited: On V. O. Key's 'South in the House,'" *Studies in American Political Development* 29, no. 2 (Oct. 2015): 154–84, doi.org/10.1017/S0898588X1500005X.
3 Robert Mickey, *Paths Out of Dixie: The Democratization of Authoritarian Enclaves in America's Deep South, 1944–1972* (Princeton, NJ: Princeton University Press, 2015).
4 Ezra Klein, "American Democracy Has Faced Worse Threats Than Donald Trump," Vox, May 10, 2018, vox.com/2018/5/10/17147338/donald-trump-illiberal-undemocratic-elections-politics.
5 Ira Katznelson, *Fear Itself: The New Deal and the Origins of Our Time* (New York: Liveright, 2013), 61.
6 Ibid., 63.
7 Mickey, *Paths Out of Dixie*, 38.
8 Carol Anderson, *White Rage: The Unspoken Truth of Our Racial Divide* (New York: Bloomsbury, 2016).
9 Mickey, *Paths Out of Dixie*.
10 Brenda Wineapple, *The Impeachers: The Trial of Andrew Johnson and the Dream of a Just Nation* (New York: Random House, 2019).
11 Mickey, *Paths Out of Dixie*.
12 Ira Katznelson, *Fear Itself*.
13 Qtd. in ibid.
14 Kabaservice, *Rule and Ruin*.
15 Michael Oreskes, "Civil Rights Act Leaves Deep Mark on the American Political Landscape," *New York Times*, July 2, 1989, nytimes.com

/1989/07/02/us/civil-rights-act-leaves-deep-mark-on-the-ameri
can-political-landscape.html.

16 mischiefsoffaction.com/2014/06/polarization-is-about-more-than
-just.html.

17 Ezra Klein, "No One's Less Moderate Than Moderates," Vox, February
26, 2015, vox.com/2014/7/8/5878293/lets-stop-using-the-word
-moderate.

18 Lilliana Mason, *Uncivil Agreement: How Politics Became Our Identity*
(Chicago; London: University of Chicago Press, 2018).

19 Steven Levitsky and Daniel Ziblatt, *How Democracies Die* (New York:
Crown, 2018).

20 "Religious 'Nones' Now Largest Single Religious Group among Democrats," Pew Research Center, October 23, 2015, pewforum.org/2015
/11/03/u-s-public-becoming-less-religious/pf_15-10-27_secondrls
_overview_nonesdems640px.

21 Pew Research Center, "Partisan Divide."

22 Alan Abramowitz, *The Great Alignment: Race, Party Transformation,
and the Rise of Donald Trump* (New Haven, CT: Yale University
Press, 2018).

23 Author correspondence with Wilkinson, vice president of research
at the Niskanen Institute.

24 Ronald Brownstein, "How the Election Revealed the Divide between
City and Country," *Atlantic*, November 17, 2016, theatlantic.com
/politics/archive/2016/11/clinton-trump-city-country-divide/507902.

25 David Choi, "Hillary Clinton: "I Won the Places That Are 'Dynamic,
Moving Forward,' while Trump's Campaign 'Was Looking Back-
wards,'" *Business Insider*, March 13, 2018, businessinsider.com
/hillary-clinton-says-trump-won-backwards-states-in-2016-2018-3.

26 Mark Muro and Sifan Liu, "Another Clinton-Trump Divide: High-Out-
put America vs. Low-Output America," *Avenue* (blog), Brookings
Institution, November 29, 2016, brookings.edu/blog/the-avenue
/2016/11/29/another-clinton-trump-divide-high-output-america
-vs-low-output-america.

27 Bill Bishop, *The Big Sort: Why the Clustering of Like-Minded America
Is Tearing Us Apart* (Boston: Houghton Mifflin, 2008).

28 twitter.com/Redistrict/status/1071968383837618176.

29 Jonathan Mummolo and Clayton Nall, "Why Partisans Do Not Sort: The Constraints on Political Segregation," *Journal of Politics* 79, no. 1 (Oct. 2016): doi.org/10.1086/687569.

30 Pew Research Center, "Partisan Divide."

31 Christopher D. Johnston, Howard G. Lavine, and Christopher M. Federico, *Open versus Closed: Personality, Identity, and the Politics of Redistribution* (Cambridge and New York: Cambridge University Press, 2017).

32 Marc J. Hetherington and Jonathan Weiler, *Prius or Pickup? How the Answers to Four Simple Questions Explain America's Great Divide* (Boston; New York: Houghton Mifflin Harcourt, 2018).

33 John R. Hibbing, Kevin B. Smith, and John R. Alford, *Predisposed: Liberals, Conservatives, and the Biology of Political Differences* (New York: Routledge, 2013).

34 Interview with author.

35 William F. Buckley Jr., "Our Mission Statement," *National Review*, November 19, 1955, nationalreview.com/1955/11/our-mission-state ment-william-f-buckley-jr/.

36 Hetherington and Weiler, *Prius or Pickup?*

37 Johnston, Lavine, and Federico, *Open versus Closed.*

Chapter 3—Your Brain on Groups

1 Henri Tajfel, "Experiments in Intergroup Discrimination," *Scientific American* 223, no. 5 (Nov. 1970): 96–103, jstor.org/stable/24927662.

2 W. Peter Robinson, *Social Groups and Identities: Developing the Legacy of Henri Tajfel* (Oxford: Butterworth Heinemann, 1996).

3 Ibid.

4 Ibid.

5 Tajfel, "Experiments in Intergroup Discrimination."

6 Ibid.

7 Henri Tajfel et al., "Social Categorization and Intergroup Behaviour," *European Journal of Social Psychology* 1, no. 2 (Apr./June 1971): 149–78, doi.org/10.1002/ejsp.2420010202.

8 Carl Bialik, "The Latest Kentucky Riot Is Part of a Long, Destructive Sports Tradition," FiveThirtyEight, April 6, 2015, fivethirtyeight.com /features/the-latest-kentucky-riot-is-part-of-a-long-destructive -sports-tradition.

9 Will Blythe, *To Hate Like This Is to Be Happy Forever: A Thoroughly Obsessive, Intermittently Uplifting, and Occasionally Unbiased Account of the Duke–North Carolina Basketball Rivalry* (New York: HarperCollins, 2006).

10 Murthy, Vivek. "Work and the Loneliness Epidemic." *Harvard Business Review*, September, 2017, hbr.org/cover-story/2017/09 /work-and-the-loneliness-epidemic.

11 Johann Hari, *Lost Connections: Uncovering the Real Causes of Depression—and the Unexpected Solutions* (New York: Bloomsbury USA, 2018).

12 Joseph Heath, *Enlightenment 2.0: Restoring Sanity to Our Politics, Our Economy, and Our Lives* (Toronto: HarperCollins, 2014).

13 Patrick R. Miller and Pamela Johnston Conover, "Red and Blue States of Mind: Partisan Hostility and Voting in the United States," *Political Research Quarterly* 68, no. 2 (June 2015): 225–39, doi.org /10.1177/1065912915577208.

14 Ezra Klein, "The Single Most Important Fact About American Poli- tics," Vox, April 28, 2016, vox.com/2014/6/13/5803768/pew-most-im portant-fact-american-politics.

15 Christopher D. Johnston, Howard G. Lavine, and Christopher M. Federico, *Open versus Closed: Personality, Identity, and the Politics of Redistribution* (Cambridge and New York: Cambridge University Press, 2017).

16 Barack Obama, "Obama: The Vox Conversation," interview by Ezra Klein, Vox, January 23, 2015, vox.com/a/barack-obama-inter view-vox-conversation/obama-domestic-policy-transcript.

17 Lessley Anderson, "Fanboys," *Verge*, January 21, 2014, theverge.com /2014/1/21/5307992/inside-the-mind-of-a-fanboy.

18 Obama, "Obama: The Vox Conversation."

19 Mason, *Uncivil Agreement*.

20 "Conservatives Launch TV Attack Ad on Dean," *Washington Times*,

January 5, 2004, washingtontimes.com/news/2004/jan/5/20040105
-103754-1355r.

21 Donald J. Trump (@realDonaldTrump), "Just like the NFL, whose
ratings [. . .]," Twitter, September 5, 2018, 6:39 a.m., twitter.com
/realdonaldtrump/status/1037334510159966214?lang=en.

22 Marilynn Brewer and Sonia Roccas, "Social Identity Complexity,"
Personality and Social Psychology Review, Vol. 6, Issue 2, (May 1,
2002).

23 Qtd. in Mason, *Uncivil Agreement.*

24 Joshua R. Gubler and Joel Sawat Selway, "Horizontal Inequality,
Crosscutting Cleavages, and Civil War," *Journal of Conflict Resolution*
56, no. 2 (Apr. 2012): 206–32, doi.org/10.1177/0022002711431416.

25 Mason, *Uncivil Agreement.*

26 Shanto Iyengar and Sean J. Westwood, "Fear and Loathing across
Party Lines: New Evidence of Group Polarization," *American Journal
of Political Science* 59, no. 3 (July 2015): 690–707.

27 Ezra Klein and Alvin Chang, "'Political Identity Is Fair Game for
Hatred': How Republicans and Democrats Discriminate," Vox,
December 7, 2015, vox.com/2015/12/7/9790764/partisan-discrim
ination.

28 Ibid.

29 Klein and Chang, "'Political Identity Is Fair Game.'"

30 Tajfel, "Experiments in Intergroup Discrimination."

31 Julián Castro, "Julián Castro's Quiet Moral Radicalism," interview by
Ezra Klein, Vox, September 12, 2019, vox.com/policy-and-politics/2019
/9/12/20860452/julian-castro-2020-immigration-animals-policy
-trump-climate-homeless.

Chapter 4—The Press Secretary in Your Mind

1 Stuart M. Butler, "Assuring Affordable Health Care for All Americans,"
Heritage Foundation, 1989, thf_media.s3.amazonaws.com/1989
/pdf/hl218.pdf.

2 Milton Friedman, "Gammon's Law Points to Health-Care Solution,"
Wall Street Journal, November 12, 1991.

3 Mark Pauly, "An Interview with Mark Pauly, Father of the Individual Mandate," by Ezra Klein, *Washington Post*, February 1, 2011, voices .washingtonpost.com/ezra-klein/2011/02/an_interview_with_mark _pauly_t.html.

4 Interview with author.

5 Qtd. in Haynes Johnson and David Broder, *The System: The American Way of Politics at the Breaking Point* (Boston: Little, Brown, 1996).

6 Ezra Klein, "Unpopular Mandate," *New Yorker*, June 18, 2012, new yorker.com/magazine/2012/06/25/unpopular-mandate.

7 Ibid.

8 Ibid.

9 Chuck Grassley, "Fox News Sunday," interview by Chris Wallace, June, 14, 2009. realclearpolitics.com/articles/2009/06/14/senators _grassley_and_dodd_on_fox_news_sunday_96993.html.

10 Ibid.

11 Andrew Prokop, "The Change in Republican Voters' Views of Putin Since Trump's Rise Is Remarkable," Vox, December 14, 2016, vox .com/2016/9/9/12865678/trump-putin-polls-republican.

12 Heath, *Enlightenment 2.0.*

13 Solomon E. Asch, "Opinions and Social Pressure," *Scientific American*, November 1955, lucs.lu.se/wp-content/uploads/2015/02/Asch-1955 -Opinions-and-Social-Pressure.pdf.

14 Geoffrey L. Cohen, "Party over Policy: The Dominating Impact of Group Influence on Political Beliefs," *Journal of Personality and Social Psychology* 85, no. 5 (2003): 808–22, pdfs.semanticscholar .org/4ecc/34af1b002340a02ed830d296819f64e1172f.pdf.

15 Jason Brennan, *Against Democracy* (Princeton, NJ: Princeton University Press, 2016).

16 Jason Brennan, "Epistocracy: A Political Theorist's Case for Letting Only the Informed Vote," interview by Sean Illing, Vox, November 9, 2018, vox.com/2018/7/23/17581394/against-democracy-book-ep istocracy-jason-brennan.

17 Dan M. Kahan et al., "Motivated Numeracy and Enlightened Self-Government," *Behavioural Public Policy* 1, no. 1 (May 2017): 54–86, doi.org/10.1017/bpp.2016.2.

18 D. N. Perkins, Michael Farady, and Barbara Bushey, "Everyday Reasoning and the Roots of Intelligence," in *Informal Reasoning and Education*, edited by James F. Voss, David N. Perkins, and Judith W. Segal (Hillsdale, NJ: Lawrence Erlbaum, 1991), 83–105.

19 Dan M.Kahan, Ellen Peters, Maggie Wittlin, Paul Slovic, Lisa Larrimore Ouellette, Donald Braman, and Mandel, Gregory, "The Polarizing Impact of Science Literacy and Numeracy on Perceived Climate Change Risks" (December 23, 2012), *Nature Climate Change* 2, pp. 732–35 (2012); Temple University Legal Studies Research Paper No. 2013-04; Yale Law & Economics Research Paper No. 464; Yale Law School, Public Law Working Paper No. 278, available at SSRN: ssrn.com/abstract=2193133.

20 Dan M. Kahan, Hank Jenkins-Smith, and Donald Braman, "Cultural Cognition of Scientific Consensus" (February 7, 2010), *Journal of Risk Research* 14, pp. 147–74 (2011); Yale Law School, Public Law Working Paper No. 205, available at SSRN: ssrn.com/abstract= 1549444.

21 Christopher Achen and Larry Bartels, "It Feels Like We're Thinking: The Rationalizing Voter and Electoral Democracy," Annual Meeting of the American Political Science Association, Philadelphia, PA, 2006.

22 Larry Bartels, "The Irrational Electorate," *The Wilson Quarterly* (Fall 2008), https://www.wilsonquarterly.com/quarterly/fall-2008-the -glory-and-the-folly/the-irrational-electorate/

23 Christopher Achen and Larry Bartels, *Democracy for Realists: Why Elections Do Not Produce Responsive Government* (Princeton, NJ: Princeton University Press, 2016).

24 Dan M. Kahan, "Making Climate-Science Communication Evidence-Based—All the Way Down" (February 13, 2013), *Culture, Politics and Climate Change*, ed. M. Boykoff and D. Crow (Milton Park, Abingdon, UK: Routledge Press, 2014), available at SSRN: ssrn .com/abstract=2216469 or http://dx.doi.org/10.2139/ssrn.2216469.

25 "The Disillusionment of David Brooks," *The Ezra Klein Show* (podcast), May 2, 2019, listennotes.com/podcasts/the-ezra-klein-show /the-disillusionment-of-david-OnVcTGXr46D.

26 Qtd. in Klein, "Unpopular Mandate."

27 Marc A. Thiessen, "Why Are Republicans So Awful at Picking Supreme Court Justices?," *Washington Post*, July 2, 2012, washingtonpost .com/opinions/marc-a-thiessen-why-are-republicans-so-awful-at -picking-supreme-court-justices/2012/07/02/gJQAHFJAIW_story .html?utm_term=.bd04998cedaf.

28 Qtd. in Klein, "Unpopular Mandate."

29 Ibid.

30 Paul Bloom, "The War on Reason," *Atlantic*, March 2014, theatlantic .com/magazine/archive/2014/03/the-war-on-reason/357561.

Chapter 5—Demographic Threat

1 D'Vera Cohn, "It's Official: Minority Babies Are the Majority among the Nation's Infants, but Only Just," *Fact Tank* (blog), Pew Research Center, June 23, 2016, pewresearch.org/fact-tank/2016/06/23 /its-official-minority-babies-are-the-majority-among-the-nations -infants-but-only-just.

2 Jonathan Vespa, David M. Armstrong, and Lauren Medina, *Demographic Turning Points for the United States: Population Projections for 2020 to 2060*, Current Population Reports, U.S. Department of Commerce, Economics and Statistics Administration, U.S. Census Bureau, 2018.

3 Ezra Klein, "White Threat in a Browning America," Vox, July 30, 2018, vox.com/policy-and-politics/2018/7/30/17505406/trump -obama-race-politics-immigration.

4 Jed Kolko (@JedKolko), "Most common age in U.S. [. . .]," Twitter, June 21, 2018, 5:09 a.m., twitter.com/JedKolko/status/1009 770292418306054.

5 Rogelio Sáenz and Kenneth M. Johnson, "White Deaths Exceed Births in a Majority of U.S. States," Applied Population Lab, June 2018, apl.wisc.edu/data-briefs/natural-decrease-18.

6 "Table 303.70. Total undergraduate fall enrollment in degree-granting postsecondary institutions, by attendance status, sex of student, and control and level of institution: Selected years, 1970 through

2026," *Digest of Education Statistics*, National Center for Education Statistics, nces.ed.gov/programs/digest/d16/tables/dt16_303.70.asp.

7 "Women More Likely Than Men to Have Earned a Bachelor's Degree by Age 29," *TED: The Economics Daily*, Bureau of Labor Statistics, April 13, 2016, bls.gov/opub/ted/2016/women-more-likely-than -men-to-have-earned-a-bachelors-degree-by-age-29.htm.

8 Neil Monahan and Saeed Ahmed, "There Are Now as Many Americans Who Claim No Religion as There Are Evangelicals and Catholics, a Survey Finds," CNN, April 26, 2019, cnn.com/2019/04/13/us /no-religion-largest-group-first-time-usa-trnd/index.html.

9 Robert P. Jones, *The End of White Christian America* (New York: Simon & Schuster, 2016).

10 "Behind the Panic in White, Christian America," *The Ezra Klein Show* (podcast), July 1, 2019, listennotes.com/podcasts/the-ezra-klein -show/behind-the-panic-in-white-YxmLpl2Ofsz.

11 James Baldwin, *The Devil Finds Work* (New York: Dial Press, 1976).

12 Maureen A. Craig and Jennifer A. Richeson, "On the Precipice of a 'Majority-Minority' America: Perceived Status Threat from the Racial Demographic Shift Affects White Americans' Political Ideology," *Psychological Science* 25, no. 6 (2014): 1189–97, spcl.yale.edu/sites /default/files/files/Craig_RichesonPS_updated%20version(1).pdf.

13 Maureen A. Craig and Jennifer A. Richeson, "More Diverse yet Less Tolerant? How the Increasingly Diverse Racial Landscape Affects White Americans' Racial Attitudes," *Personality and Social Psychology Bulletin* 40, no. 6 (June 2014): 750–61, groups.psych.northwest ern.edu/spcl/documents/Craig%20&%20Richeson%202014%20 PSPB.pdf. Alexander Kuo, Neil Malhotra, and Cecilia Hyunjung Mo, "Social Exclusion and Political Identity: The Case of Asian American Partisanship," *Journal of Politics* 79, no. 1 (January 2017), journals.uchicago.edu/doi/abs/10.1086/687570.

14 Ryan D. Enos, "How Segregation Leads to Racist Voting by Whites," Vox, November 28, 2017, https://www.vox.com/the-big-idea/2017/11 /28/16707438/social-geography-trump-rise-segregation-psychology -racism.

15 Michael Tesler, *Post-Racial or Most-Racial? Race and Politics in the*

Obama Era (Chicago and London: University of Chicago Press, 2016).

16 P. R. Lockhart, "How Russia Exploited Racial Tensions in America During the 2016 Elections: New Reports Detail How Russian Internet Trolls Manipulated Outrage over Racial Injustice in America," Vox, December 17, 2018, vox.com/identities/2018/12/17/18145075 /russia-facebook-twitter-internet-research-agency-race.

17 Amy Chua, *Political Tribes: Group Instinct and the Fate of Nations* (New York: Penguin, 2018).

18 Alexandra Bruell, "P&G Challenges Men to Shave Their 'Toxic Masculinity' in Gillette Ad," *Wall Street Journal*, January 14, 2019, wsj .com/articles/p-g-challenges-men-to-shave-their-toxic-masculinity -in-gillette-ad-11547467200.

19 Klein, "White Threat."

20 Ronald Kessler, "Donald Trump: Mean-Spirited GOP Won't Win Elections," Newsmax, November 26, 2012, newsmax.com/Newsfront /Donald-Trump-Ronald-Kessler/2012/11/26/id/465363/.

21 Qtd. in Klein, "White Threat."

22 Qtd. in ibid.

23 Betsy Cooper et al., "How Immigration and Concerns About Cultural Change Are Shaping the 2016 Election: PRRI/Brookings Survey," Public Religion Research Institute, June 2016, prri.org/research /prri-brookings-poll-immigration-economy-trade-terrorism-pres idential-race.

24 Sean Trende, "The Case of the Missing White Voters," RealClearPolitics, November 8, 2012, realclearpolitics.com/articles/2012/11 /08/the_case_of_the_missing_white_voters_116106-2.html.

25 Ashley Jardina, *White Identity Politics* (Cambridge and New York: Cambridge University Press, 2019).

26 "When You're Accustomed to Privilege, Equality Feels Like Oppression," Quote Investigator, October 24, 2016, quoteinvestigator.com /2016/10/24/privilege/.

27 John Sides, Michael Tesler, and Lynn Vavreck, *Identity Crisis: The 2016 Presidential Campaign and the Battle for the Meaning of America* (Princeton, NJ: Princeton University Press, 2018).

28 Zack Beauchamp, "White Riot," Vox, January 20, 2017, vox.com/2016 /9/19/12933072/far-right-white-riot-trump-brexit.

29 Eric Kaufmann, *Whiteshift: Populism, Immigration, and the Future of White Majorities* (New York: Abrams, 2019).

30 Klein, "White Threat."

31 Ibid.

32 Ibid.

33 Bret Stephens (@BretStephensNYT), "The right to offend is [. . .]," Twitter, January 7, 2015, 1:16 p.m. [account deleted].

34 Bret Stephens, "Dear Millennials: The Feeling Is Mutual," *New York Times*, May 17, 2019, nytimes.com/2019/05/17/opinion /biden-2020-millennials.html.

35 Dave Karpf (@davekarpf), "The bedbugs are a metaphor [. . .]," Twitter, August 26, 2019, 2:07 p.m., twitter.com/davekarpf/status /1166094950024515584.

36 Emma Pettit, "This Professor Compared a Columnist to a Bedbug. Then the Columnist Contacted the Provost," *Chronicle of Higher Education*, August 27, 2019, chronicle.com/article/this-professor -compared-a/247013.

37 Stephens, "Dear Millennials."

38 mediaite.com/news/bret-stephens-backs-out-of-public-debate-with -bedbug-professor-because-public-event-wouldn't-be-closed-to-the -public/.

39 Klein, "White Threat."

40 Matthew Yglesias, "The Great Awokening," Vox, April 1, 2019, vox .com/2019/3/22/18259865/great-awokening-white-liberals-race -polling-trump-2020.

41 Klein, "White Threat."

42 Ibid.

43 Ibid.

44 Aaron Zitner, Dante Chinni, and Brian McGill, "How Clinton Won," *Wall Street Journal*, June 8, 2016, graphics.wsj.com/elections/2016 /how-clinton-won.

45 "Issues: Racial Justice," Bernie 2020, berniesanders.com/issues /racial-justice.

46 Bernie Sanders. Interview by Ezra Klein, Vox, July 28, 2015, vox.com /2015/7/28/9014491/bernie-sanders-vox-conversation.

Chapter 6—The Media Divide beyond Left-Right

1 Markus Prior, "News vs. Entertainment: How Increasing Media Choice Widens Gaps in Political Knowledge and Turnout," *American Journal of Political Science* 49, no. 3 (July 2005): 577–92.

2 James Hamilton, *All the News That's Fit to Sell: How the Market Transforms Information into News* (Princeton, NJ: Princeton University Press, 2004).

3 Ibid.

4 Douglas J. Ahler and Gaurav Sood, "The Parties in Our Head: Misperceptions About Party Composition and Their Consequences," *Journal of Politics* 80, no. 3 (July 2018): 964–81, doi.org/10.1086/697253.

5 Krista Tippett, "How to Oppose Trump without Becoming More Like Him," interview by Ezra Klein, *The Ezra Klein Show*, January, 22, 2018, podcasts.apple.com/gd/podcast/how-to-oppose-trump -without-becoming-more-like-him/id1081584611?i=1000400418072.

6 Chris Hayes, "Antisocial Media with Andrew Marantz," *Why Is This Happening?* September 29, 2019, podcasts.apple.com/us/podcast/anti social-media-with-andrew-marantz/id1382983397?i=1000450994455.

7 Zeynep Tufekci, "YouTube, the Great Radicalizer," *New York Times*, May 10, 2018, nytimes.com/2018/03/10/opinion/sunday/you tube-politics-radical.html.

8 Jia Tolentino, *Trick Mirror: Reflections on Self-Delusion* (New York: Random House, 2019).

9 Obama, "Obama: The Vox Conversation."

10 Christopher A. Bail et al., "Exposure to Opposing Views on Social Media Can Increase Political Polarization," *PNAS* 115, no. 37 (Sept. 2018): 9216–21, doi.org/10.1073/pnas.1804840115.

11 Ezra Klein, "When Twitter Users Hear Out the Other Side, They Become More Polarized," Vox, October 18, 2018, vox.com/policy-and -politics/2018/10/18/17989856/twitter-polarization-echo-chambers -social-media.

12 Kevin Arceneaux and Martin Johnson, "Does Media Fragmentation Produce Mass Polarization? Selective Exposure and a New Era of Minimal Effects," APSA 2010 Annual Meeting Paper, 2010, papers .ssrn.com/sol3/papers.cfm?abstract_id=1642723.

13 pubs.aeaweb.org/doi/pdfplus/10.1257/aer.20160812.

14 Jane Mayer, "The Invention of the Conspiracy Theory on Biden-Ukraine," *New Yorker*, October, 4, 2019, newyorker.com/news /news-desk/the-invention-of-the-conspiracy-theory-on-biden-and -ukraine.

15 Sides, Tesler, and Vavreck, *Identity Crisis*.

16 John Sides and Kalev Leetaru, "A Deep Dive into the News Media's Role in the Rise of Donald J. Trump," *Washington Post*, June 24, 2017, washingtonpost.com/news/monkey-cage/wp/2016/06/24 /a-deep-dive-into-the-news-medias-role-in-the-rise-of-donald-j -trump.

17 Sides, Tesler, and Vavreck, *Identity Crisis*.

18 Jay Rosen, "Is the Media Making American Politics Worse?" interview by Ezra Klein, Vox, October 22, 2018, vox.com/ezra-klein-show -podcast/2018/10/22/17991170/press-media-trump-polarization -jay-rosen-avenatti.

19 Donald J. Trump (@realDonaldTrump), "Nick Sandmann and the students [. . .]," Twitter, January 22, 2019, 4:32 a.m., twitter.com /realDonaldTrump/status/1087689415814795264.

20 Zack Beauchamp, "The Real Politics behind the Covington Catholic Controversy, Explained," Vox, January 23, 2019, vox.com /policy-and-politics/2019/1/23/18192831/covington-catholic-maga -hat-native-american-nathan-phillips.

Chapter 7—Post-Persuasion Elections

1 Matthew Dowd interview in "Karl Rove—The Architect," *Frontline*, PBS, 2005, pbs.org/wgbh/pages/frontline/shows/architect/rove /2004.html.

2 Mark McKinnon interview in ibid.

3 Costas Panagopoulos, "All About That Base: Changing Campaign

Strategies in U.S. Presidential Elections," *Party Politics* 22, no. 2 (Mar. 2016): 179–90, doi.org/10.1177/1354068815605676.

4 Julia Azari, "Weak Parties and Strong Partisanship Are a Bad Combination," Vox, November 3, 2016, vox.com/mischiefs-of-faction/2016 /11/3/13512362/weak-parties-strong-partisanship-bad-combination.

5 Dan Senor (@DanSenor), "It's disorienting to have had commiserated w/someone re: Trump—about how he was unacceptable, & then to see that someone become Trump's VP," Twitter, July 15, 2016, 9:49 a.m., twitter.com/dansenor/status/753994913830703104

6 Helsel, Phil, "Paul Ryan: Trump Is Not Perfect, But He's Better Than Clinton," NBCNews.com, July 13, 2016, nbcnews.com /politics/2016-election/paul-ryan-trump-not-perfect-better-hillary -n608336.

7 Levitsky and Ziblatt, *How Democracies Die*.

8 Robert Boatright, *Getting Primaried: The Changing Politics of Congressional Primary Challenges* (Ann Arbor: University of Michigan Press, 2013).

9 James Rosen, "Joe Wilson's Obama 'You Lie' Shout Having a Big Payoff," McClatchy, October 4, 2009, mcclatchydc.com/news/politics -government/article24557848.html.

10 Ibid.

11 Raymond La Raja and Brian Schaffner, *Campaign Finance and Political Polarization: When Purists Prevail* (Ann Arbor: University of Michigan Press, 2015).

12 Hans J. G. Hassell, "Principled Moderation: Understanding Parties' Support of Moderate Candidates," myweb.fsu.edu/hanhassell 4/HassellPartiesasModerators.pdf.

13 Joe Trippi, *The Revolution Will Not Be Televised: Democracy, the Internet, and the Overthrow of Everything* (New York: ReganBooks, 2004).

14 "Small Donations to Presidential Primaries Are on Rise, Study Finds," Phys.org, October 4, 2018, phys.org/news/2018-10-small-donations -presidential-primaries.html.

15 Shane Goldmacher, "Trump Shatters GOP Records with Small Donors," *Politico*, September 19, 2016, politico.com/story/2016/09 /trump-shatters-gop-records-with-small-donors-228338.

16 Michael J. Barber, "Ideological Donors, Contribution Limits, and the Polarization of American Legislatures," *Journal of Politics* 78, no. 1 (Jan. 2016): 296–310, doi.org/10.1086/683453.

17 Glenn Thrush and Alex Isenstadt, "Welcome to the GOP Civil War," Politico, March 3, 2016, politico.com/story/2016/03/gop-civil-war-2016-republicans-220209.

18 Stephen M. Utych, "Man Bites Blue Dog: Are Moderates Really More Electable Than Ideologues?" *Journal of Politics* (forthcoming 2019): researchgate.net/publication/330565898_Man_Bites_Blue_Dog_Are_Moderates_Really_More_Electable_than_Ideologues

19 "Against Trump," *National Review*, January 22, 2016, nationalreview.com/2016/01/donald-trump-conservative-movement-menace/.

20 Sean Illing, "Can American Nationalism Be Saved? A Debate with *National Review* Editor Rich Lowry," Vox, November 22, 2019, vox.com/policy-and-politics/2019/11/22/20952353/trump-nationalism-america-first-rich-lowry.

Chapter 8—When Bipartisanship Becomes Irrational

1 "Constitution a 'Dead, Dead, Dead' Document, Scalia Tells SMU Audience," *Dallas Morning News*, January 28, 2013, dallasnews.com/news/highland-park/2013/01/28/constitution-a-dead-dead-dead-document-scalia-tells-smu-audience.

2 Scalia was often criticized for abandoning originalism when politically convenient. Cass Sunstein, "Antonin Scalia, Living Constitutionalist," Harvard Public Law Working Paper No. 16-15, *Harvard Law Review*, dx.doi.org/10.2139/ssrn.2759938.

3 Antonin Scalia, "In Conversation: Antonin Scalia," interview by Jennifer Senior, *New York*, October 4, 2013, nymag.com/news/features/antonin-scalia-2013-10.

4 Thomas Ferraro, "Republican Would Back Garland for Supreme Court," Reuters, May 6, 2010, reuters.com/article/us-usa-court-hatch/republican-would-back-garland-for-supreme-court-idUSTRE6456QY20100506.

5 Robin Bradley Kar and Jason Mazzone, "The Garland Affair: What

History and the Constitution Really Say About President Obama's
Powers to Appoint a Replacement for Justice Scalia," *NYU Law
Review* 91 (2016): nyulawreview.org/online-features/the-garland
-affair-what-history-and-the-constitution-really-say-about-presi
dent-obamas-powers-to-appoint-a-replacement-for-justice-scalia.

6 Mike DeBonis, "Will Hillary Clinton Stick with Merrick Garland If
She Wins the White House?" *Washington Post*, August 16, 2016,
washingtonpost.com/news/powerpost/wp/2016/08/16/the-forgotten
-nominee-merrick-garlands-fate-rests-on-forces-beyond-his-control/.

7 Jennifer Bendery, "Democrats, Still Bitter over How Their SCOTUS
Pick Was Treated, Now Weigh Trump's," *Huffpost*, January 31, 2017,
huffpost.com/entry/democrats-merrick-garland-supreme-court_n
_58911e44e4b02772c4ea1f68.

8 Ted Barrett, "In Reversal from 2016, McConnell Says He Would Fill a
Potential Supreme Court Vacancy in 2020," CNN, May 20, 2019, cnn
.com/2019/05/28/politics/mitch-mcconnell-supreme-court-2020
/index.html.

9 Juan Linz, "The Perils of Presidentialism," *Journal of Democracy* 1, no. 1
(Winter 1990): 51–69, scholar.harvard.edu/levitsky/files/1.1linz.pdf.

10 Ibid.

11 Matthew Yglesias, "American Democracy Is Doomed," Vox, October
8, 2015, vox.com/2015/3/2/8120063/american-democracy-doomed.

12 Linz, "Perils of Presidentialism."

13 Lee Epstein and Eric A. Posner, "If the Supreme Court Is Nakedly
Political, Can It Be Just," *New York Times*, July 9, 2018, nytimes.com
/2018/07/09/opinion/supreme-court-nominee-trump.html.

14 Abby Rogers, "Justice Scalia Flipped Out Last Night When People
Asked Why the Court Was So Political," *Business Insider*, September
18, 2012, businessinsider.com/scalia-speaks-out-about-politicized
-court-2012-9.

15 Daniel J. Hopkins, *The Increasingly United States: How and Why
American Political Behavior Nationalized* (Chicago: University of
Chicago Press, 2018).

16 Jonathan Allen, "The Case for Earmarks," Vox, June 30, 2015, vox
.com/2015/6/30/8864869/earmarks-pork-congress.

17 Manu Raju, "Neb. Gov. to Nelson: Keep the Money," *Politico*, December 23, 2009, politico.com/story/2009/12/neb-gov-to-nelson-keep -the-money-030947.

18 Robert Pear and Michael Cooper, "Reluctance in Some States over Medicaid Expansion," *New York Times*, June 29, 2012, nytimes .com/2012/06/30/us/politics/some-states-reluctant-over-medicaid -expansion.html.

19 Frances E. Lee, *Insecure Majorities: Congress and the Perpetual Campaign* (London; Chicago: University of Chicago Press, 2016).

20 Qtd. in ibid.

21 Qtd. in ibid.

22 Qtd. in ibid.

23 Ezra Klein, "How the Filibuster Was Invented," *Washington Post*, March 8, 2010, voices.washingtonpost.com/ezra-klein/2010/03 /how_the_filibuster_was_invente.html.

24 Gregory Koger, *Filibustering: A Political History of Obstruction in the House and Senate*, Chicago Studies in American Politics (Chicago: University of Chicago Press, 2010).

25 Ezra Klein, "How a Letter from 1964 Shows What's Wrong with the Senate Today," *Washington Post*, November 25, 2009, voices.washing tonpost.com/ezra-klein/2009/11/how_a_letter_from_1964_shows _w.html.

26 Tom Harkin, "End the Filibuster! An Interview with Sen. Tom Harkin," by Ezra Klein, *Washington Post*, December 26, 2009, voices .washingtonpost.com/ezra-klein/2009/12/end_the_filibuster_an _intervie.html.

27 Interview with author.

Chapter 9—The Difference between Democrats and Republicans

1 Thomas E. Mann and Norman J. Ornstein, *It's Even Worst Than It Looks: How the American Constitutional System Collided with the New Politics of Extremism* (New York: Basic Books, 2012).

2 Norm Ornstein, "Maybe This Time Really Is Different," *Atlantic*,

August 21, 2015, theatlantic.com/politics/archive/2015/08/maybe
-this-time-really-is-different/401900.

3 Errin Haines Whack, "2020 Democratic Hopefuls Embrace New
Meaning of Reparations," Associated Press, February 25, 2019,
apnews.com/afdefe3ec65e488baa1917101a9a7f0b.

4 Hetherington and Weiler, *Prius or Pickup?*

5 Lydia Saad, "U.S. Still Leans Conservative, but Liberals Keep Recent
Gains," Gallup, January 8, 2019, news.gallup.com/poll/245813
/leans-conservative-liberals-keep-recent-gains.aspx.

6 Matt Grossmann and David Hopkins, *Asymmetric Politics: Ideological Republicans and Group Interest Democrats* (New York: Oxford
University Press, 2016).

7 Jeffrey M. Jones, "Subgroup Differences in Trump Approval
Mostly Party-Based," Gallup, March 29, 2019, news.gallup.com
/poll/248135/subgroup-differences-trump-approval-mostly-party
-based.aspx.

8 Michael Barber and Jeremy C. Pope, "Does Party Trump Ideology?
Disentangling Party and Ideology in America," *American Politi-
cal Science Review* 113, no. 1 (Feb. 2019): 38–54, doi.org/10.1017
/S0003055418000795.

9 Justin Amash, "Justin Amash on Trump, Impeachment, and the
Death of the Tea Party," interview by Jane Coaston, Vox, July 3,
2019, vox.com/policy-and-politics/2019/7/3/18759659/justin
-amash-trump-impeachment-gop-tea-party-republicans.

10 Jeffrey Gottfried, Michael Barthel, and Amy Mitchell, "Trump,
Clinton Voters Divided in Their Main Source for Election News,"
Pew Research Center, January 18, 2017, journalism.org/2017/01/18
/trump-clinton-voters-divided-in-their-main-source-for-election
-news.

11 Rob Faris et al., "Partisanship, Propaganda, and Disinformation:
Online Media and the 2016 U.S. Presidential Election," Berkman
Klein Center, Harvard University, August 16, 2017, cyber.harvard
.edu/publications/2017/08/mediacloud.

12 Rush Limbaugh, "Climategate Hoax: The Universe of Lies versus the
Universe of Reality," *Rush Limbaugh Show*, November 24, 2009,

rushlimbaugh.com/daily/2009/11/24/climategate_hoax_the_uni
verse_of_lies_versus_the_universe_of_reality/.

13 Matt Grossmann and David A. Hopkins, "How Information Became Ideological," Inside Higher Ed, October 11, 2016, insidehighered.com/views/2016/10/11/how-conservative-movement-has-under mined-trust-academe-essay.

14 David Roberts, "Donald Trump and the Rise of Tribal Epistemology: Journalism Cannot Be Neutral Toward a Threat to the Conditions That Make It Possible," Vox, May 19, 2017, vox.com/policy-and-pol itics/2017/3/22/14762030/donald-trump-tribal-epistemology.

15 David Roberts, "Donald Trump Is the Sole Reliable Source of Truth, Says Chair of House Science Committee: 'Better to Get Your News Directly from the President,' said Rep. Lamar Smith of Texas," Vox, January 27, 2017, vox.com/science-and-health/2017/1/27/14395978 /donald-trump-lamar-smith.

16 David Hookstead, "This Sexy Model Is Blowing Up the Internet [SLIDESHOW]," Daily Caller, December 16, 2016, dailycaller.com/2016/12/16/this-sexy-model-is-blowing-up-the-internet-slide show/; David Hookstead, "This UFC Octagon Girl's Instagram Account Is Sizzling Hot [SLIDESHOW]," Daily Caller, December 24, 2016, dailycaller.com/2016/12/24/this-ufc-octagon-girls-insta gram-account-is-sizzling-hot-slideshow/; Kaitlan Collins, "13 Syr ian Refugees We'd Take Immediately [PHOTOS]," Dailey Caller, November 18, 2015, dailycaller.com/2015/11/18/13-syrian-refugees -wed-take-immediately-photos/.

17 Jonathan A. Rodden, *Why Cities Lose: The Deep Roots of the Urban-Rural Political Divide* (New York: Basic Books, 2019).

18 Ezra Klein, "What Nate Silver's Learned Abouty Forecasting Elec tions," *Vox*, October 23, 2018, vox.com/ezra-klein-show-podcast /2018/10/23/18014156/nate-silver-538-forecasting-2018-2020-ezra -klein-podcast.

19 Osita Nwanevu, "How Much Do Democrats Need to Win By?" *Slate*, March 27, 2018, slate.com/news-and-politics/2018/03/how-much -do-democrats-need-to-win-by.html.

20 Michael Geruso, Dean Spears, and Ishaana Talesara, "Inversions in US

Presidential Elections: 1836–2016," *National Bureau of Economics Research*, Working Paper No. 26247 (September 2019), nber.org /papers/w26247.

21 "Morning Consult's Governor Approval Rankings," *Morning Consult*, Q2 2019, morningconsult.com/governor-rankings-q2-19/.

22 Theda Skocpol and Vanessa Williamson, *The Tea Party and the Remaking of Republican Conservatism* (New York: Oxford University Press, 2012).

23 Publius Decius Mus [Michael Anton], "The Flight 93 Election," *Claremont Review of Books*, September 5, 2016, claremont.org/crb /basicpage/the-flight-93-election.

24 Megan Brenan, "Democrats Favor More Moderate Party; GOP, More Conservative," Gallup, December 12, 2018, news.gallup.com /poll/245462/democrats-favor-moderate-party-gop-conservative .aspx.

Chapter 10—Managing Polarization—and Ourselves

1 Adam Wisnieski, "Next 100 Days: In the Era of Trump, NYS Is Out of Step and in the Crosshairs," *City Limits*, June 30, 2017, citylimits .org/2017/06/30/next-100-days-in-the-era-of-trump-nys-is-out-of -step-and-in-the-crosshairs.

2 Nicholas Stephanopoulos, "The Research That Convinced SCOTUS to Take the Wisconsin Gerrymandering Case, Explained," Vox, July 11, 2017, vox.com/the-big-idea/2017/7/11/15949750/research-gerry mandering-wisconsin-supreme-court-partisanship.

3 Nour Abdul-Razzak, Carlo Prato, and Stéphane Wolton, "How *Citizens United* Gave Republicans a Bonanza of Seats in U.S. State Legislatures," *Washington Post*, February 24, 2017, washingtonpost.com /news/monkey-cage/wp/2017/02/24/how-citizens-united-gave-re publicans-a-bonanza-of-seats-in-u-s-state-legislatures/?noredirect =on&utm_term=.9bcda4584bd6.

4 Tara Bahrampour and Robert Barnes, "Despite Trump Administration Denials, New Evidence Suggests Census Citizenship Question Was Crafted to Benefit White Republicans," *Washington Post*, May 30,

2019, washingtonpost.com/local/social-issues/despite-trump-ad
ministration-denials-new-evidence-suggests-census-citizenship
-question-was-crafted-to-benefit-white-republicans/2019/05/30
/ca188dea-82eb-11e9-933d-7501070ee669_story.html.

5 Daniel Epps and Ganesh Sitaraman, "How to Save the Supreme Court,"
   Vox, October 10, 2018, vox.com/the-big-idea/2018/9/6/17827786
   /kavanaugh-vote-supreme-court-packing.

6 Robert Wright, "'Mindful Resistance' Is the Key to Defeating Trump,"
   Vox, October 9, 2017, vox.com/the-big-idea/2017/10/2/16394320
   /mindful-resistance-key-defeating-trump-mindfulness.

7 Sam Dolnick, "The Man Who Knew Too Little," New York Times,
   March 10, 2018, nytimes.com/2018/03/10/style/the-man-who-knew
   -too-little.html.

8 Shadi Hamid (@shadihamid), "The New York Times Managed to Find
   [. . .]," Twitter, March 14, 2018, 11:06 a.m., twitter.com/shadihamid
   /status/973983762135515137.

9 Hopkins, Increasingly United States.

10 Klein, "American Democracy Has Faced Worse Threats."

Index

Page numbers in *italics* refer to charts.